Anselm of Canterbury

The Beauty of Theology

DAVID S. HOGG
Southeastern Baptist
Theological Seminary, USA

ASHGATE

© David S. Hogg, 2004

David S. Hogg has asserted his moral right under the Copyright, Designs and Patents Act, 1988, to be identified as the author of this work.

Published by
Ashgate Publishing Limited
Gower House
Croft Road
Aldershot
Hants GU11 3HR
England

Ashgate Publishing Company
Suite 420
101 Cherry Street
Burlington, VT, 05401– 4405 USA

Ashgate website: http://www.ashgate.com

British Library Cataloguing in Publication Data
Hogg, David S.
 Anselm of Canterbury: The Beauty of Theology. – (Great Theologians Series)
 1. Anselm, Saint, Archbishop of Canterbury, 1033–1109. I. Title
 270'.092

Library of Congress Cataloging in Publication Data
Hogg, David S.
 Anselm of Canterbury: The Beauty of Theology. / David S. Hogg.
  p. cm. (Great Theologians Series)
 Includes bibliographical references and index.
 1. Anselm, Saint, Archbishop of Canterbury, 1033–1109. I. Title. II. Series.
 B765.A84H64 2004
 230'.2'092–dc22

                                                                    2004006146

ISBN 0 7546 3218 0 (hbk)
ISBN 0 7546 3232 6 (pbk)

Typeset in Times Roman by N^2productions
Printed and bound in Great Britain by T.J. International, Padstow.

ANSELM OF CANTERBURY
THE BEAUTY OF THEOLOGY

Anselm is a major figure in theological, philosophical and historical studies. This book provides a fresh approach to the study of this great figure; one which provides critical interaction with current critical thinking whilst arguing in favour of the idea of theological unity in Anselm's corpus. Exploring the *Proslogion* but also more 'minor' works, David Hogg interacts with the theological content of Anselm's writings: showing how Anselm's ontological argument fits into the wider context of his theology; comparing the holistic approach of Anselm's thought with that of other medieval personages and fitting him into the wider medieval context; and revealing how Anselm's theology integrates the atonement and questions of predestination, the fall of the Devil, free will, and other issues.

The book concludes with an assessment of the impact of Anselm's theology during his own time and the continuing effect his thinking has had on succeeding centuries of theological development.

Great Theologians Series

Series Editors:
Revd Professor John Webster, University of Aberdeen, UK
Professor Trevor Hart, St Mary's College, University of St Andrews, UK
Professor Douglas B. Farrow, McGill University, Canada

The Ashgate series, *Great Theologians*, presents a cluster of high profile titles focusing on individual theologians from the ancients through to the contemporary. The series includes a balance between important new perspectives on major figures who have already received much research attention in the past, and lesser-known theologians or those on whom there has been little published to date. Offering a fresh approach to in-depth theological studies, each book presents an accessible, stimulating new study and comprehensive overview of the theologian and their writing, whilst providing a detailed survey of the historic and contemporary international research already undertaken from a range of different perspectives, and analysing important trends of interpretation and research. This series is intended to provide an invaluable and lasting resource at the upper level of study and academic research.

Other titles in the series:

Thomas Aquinas
Theologian of the Christian Life
Nicholas M. Healy

Karl Barth
Theologian of Christian Witness
Joseph L. Mangina

Contents

Preface

When studying the works of a medieval theologian one must decide whether or not to provide a translation of the Latin. On the one hand, it may seem more scholarly to leave Anselm's words in their original language and assume that the readers are sufficiently acquainted with Latin that a translation would be tantamount to an insult. On the other hand, constantly inserting a different language into the text can disturb the flow for the reader. There is, of course, the median position wherein the English translation is provided in the main body of the work and the Latin is provided in a footnote, but so often the English translation sufficiently conveys the meaning of the Latin that such a practice becomes cumbersome.

The solution I have alighted upon after no small consideration is to provide an English translation in all cases except where the point being made warrants the inclusion of the original. To this end, I have used accepted translations of Anselm's works except where I found that I disagreed (in which case I have provided my own translation). The translations of Anselm's major works are, unless otherwise noted, taken from Brian Davies' and G.R. Evans' edited edition of Anselm's major works; whereas the translations of Anselm's *Prayers and Meditations* are, unless otherwise noted, taken from Benedicta Ward's edition of the Penguin Classics Series. In all cases, however, I have provided the notation for Schmitt's critical edition (marked by S.#.#.#) so that the reader may more easily refer to the original. Apart from Anselm's own works, when I have referred to a passage in the Bible I have used the New International Version.

Acknowledgments

There are a number of people who have guided and encouraged me through what I can only describe as an enjoyable and enlightening experience. My former supervisor, Professor Trevor Hart, deserves many thanks for his insightful comments and helpful discussions. It can be true that familiarity breeds contempt, but in this case familiarity has bred respect. Professor Hart's learning and knowledge have been as a well from which I have drawn on more than one occasion.

I would also like to thank Dr Steven R. Guthrie. I fear I alone will ever fully appreciate how helpful he has been, and how patient with my constant interruptions.

Closer to home, my wife deserves a lion's share of gratitude and appreciation. Sarah has endured more than anyone I know the trials of sustaining me. The jobs, the travel, the uncertainty cannot have been easy to shoulder, but she has done so, and with strength to spare. Sarah has set the bar of faithfulness at no mean standard; I only hope that, with God's help, I too can prove myself faithful to support and sustain.

I do not know if it is customary to end by thanking one's parents, but in my case I know of no others who have poured so much of themselves into what at times (always?) might appear to be an altogether overly porous vessel. A little more than thirty years and a few more than thirty (metaphorical) grey hairs later their efforts to raise this child up in the way he should go have culminated, partially, in this book. In some respects I hope that these hundred thousand words or so are enough to prove that the prayers of righteous parents do indeed availeth much.

At the risk of sounding pious or simple-minded I cannot help but rejoice with Anselm that God has granted me access into his inner chamber where he has permitted me a taste of the beatific glory to come, the beauty yet untapped, and the joy to be fully known at the end of the age. Herein lies my initial attempt to record that panoply of proportioned beauty as experienced in the polyphony of divine harmony and the concord of creation in the light of the incarnate Christ.

To my father and mother

Chapter 1

Introduction

The student of Anselm is bound to be apprehensive when writing yet another commentary on his works. The sheer volume of material produced on the influence and persuasiveness of the ontological argument is enough to warrant caution to any potential pupil. Work on Anselm's doctrine of the atonement is no less daunting since it too has yielded a prodigious amount of scholarship in the nine hundred years since its formulation. As for the amount of work that has been done on his monastic context, not to mention the political or social context, here too the reader discovers an embarrassment of riches. What reason, then, could anyone have for turning up what already appears to be well-tilled soil?

Perhaps the best way to answer this question, and to extend the metaphor, is to look at the whole landscape. It is indeed true that the fields of Anselm's inquiry concerning the existence of God and the atonement have been well worked, but if we were to raise our eyes to the surrounding fields I would venture to argue that they have been left largely untouched. The advantage of this is that there is a richness in the terrain of these texts which has perennated due to the abeyance of activity surrounding them. The disadvantage is that without the wider landscape of Anselm's thinking in view, we run the risk of failing to appreciate the tenor of his writing and the essence of his thinking. The attending consequences run the gamut from interpretations which are anachronistic to those which, while representing Anselm's thought well, present an asymmetric view because of their lack of breadth.

Anselm's theory of the atonement, for instance, might be slighted for not taking adequate account of the Trinity. His *Proslogion* is notoriously refuted on the basis of presuppositions deemed out of date and out-moded. As apparently legitimate as these sorts of criticisms may appear, one wonders to what degree those making such claims have tried to enter Anselm's context and ask their questions in the light of an agenda that stretches over a lifetime. Should we, for example, understand the *Cur Deus Homo* as an occasional work or one whose fullness can best be appreciated when it is set beside the *Monologion* (Chapter 39 and following, in particular)? And is our understanding of the Trinity as it relates to the incarnation which expedited the atonement enhanced by our reading of the *Proslogion* wherein we discover not the mere existence of God, but the nature of the God in whom all things live and move and have their being?[1]

Clearly, the minutiae of Anselm's arguments need to come under scrutiny but can we expect just adjudication apart from a comprehensive perscrutation?

Gillian Evans' echo of J. McIntyre's lament of more than forty years ago is still true. There has been a proliferation of interest in Anselm's doctrine of the atonement and the philosophy that lies behind the *Proslogion* 'almost to the exclusion of his views on the Trinity, the attributes of God, the procession of the Holy Spirit, free will and predestination'.[2] Granted, any given work in Anselm's corpus has a certain autonomy, but is it not also the case that the more the reader is aware of his wider literary output, the better he or she will be at understanding and interpreting his thought?

As we shall see, the literary context in which Anselm was writing was so thoroughly infused with a particular model of reality and a way of interpreting sensible data in the light of revealed truth that we cannot afford to neglect it. This is, of course, not a popular position to espouse, as the range of articles and monographs that have been written on, for instance, the *Proslogion* testify. Occasionally, references are made to chapters fourteen and fifteen, and every now and again a few comments are made about the genre of prayer throughout the text, but, on the whole, the interest has been keenly focused on chapters two, three and four. Now it could be argued that that is where the emphasis rightly belongs since it is on the basis of the logic in those introductory chapters that the rest of the work seems to flow, but what if the reverse is true? What if the argument (or arguments, depending on who is doing the interpreting) in chapters two through four is not constituent for the rest of the work, but it is, in fact, the revelation outlined in chapter one and expanded in chapters five through twenty-six that provide the groundwork for the kind of argument forwarded in chapters two through four? In other words, is it possible that those who neglect to take the time to study the model of reality evident in the larger body of Anselm's writings (as well as those of contemporary and earlier scholars) will ultimately supply unsuccessful expositions which not only distort a part, but also misrepresent the whole?

The answer to this question will be based on the merits of each source as it is introduced into the discussion, but on the whole it is true that our modern context has coloured our understanding of medieval concepts. It is, after all, characteristic of our mindset to prefer logical progression to proceed sequentially from one proposition to the next. The question is, did the medieval mind work in the same fashion? The best answer is probably yes and no. Yes, it is true that medieval theologians and philosophers[3] framed their arguments in logical sequences of propositions; but no, this was not always the exclusive nor even the most desirable means of expressing an argument or idea.

What other way is there, then, of presenting an argument? One character-istically medieval way of communicating truth and expressing ideas is found in the repeated appeal to an undergirding aesthetic ideal. It is the presupposition of beauty and fittingness as displayed in the proportion and harmony between the creator and creation that, to the medieval mind, provides the only basis on which any proposition or series of propositions can be made. Consider, for instance, Boethius' *Consolation of Philosophy*. In that work Boethius allows his mind to range over a number of perplexing problems associated with his unfortunate circumstances. He discusses the apparently hapless nature of fortune and fate and questions the extent of divine intervention and manipulation in human affairs. He addresses the problematical relationship between the foreknowledge of God and human freedom. His musings with Lady Philosophy are remarkably succinct yet detailed, but undergirding everything Boethius says is his continual appeal to order, goodness, beauty, symmetry and balance.

In his investigation into what constitutes false happiness, Boethius contrasts the eternal beauty and order of the 'vault of heaven' with the fleeting beauty of that found in humanity.[4] The preceding arguments in favour of happiness as the world so often defines it all crumble before the immutable rule of order and beauty that transcends the mutable, fickle, transitory equivalent that we see within and around us. It is necessary, Boethius claims, that in order to make sense out of the multifaceted nature of reality, with all its complexities and conundrums, there must be something, indeed, someone, who holds it all together:

> Nature's fixed order could not proceed on its path and the various kinds of change could not exhibit motions so orderly in place, time, effect, distance from one another, and nature, unless there was one unmoving and stable power to regulate them. For this power, whatever it is, through which creation remains in existence and in motion, I use the word which all people use, namely God.[5]

A little further on, Boethius asserts that

> ... since we are right in thinking that God controls all things by the helm of goodness, and all things, as I have said, have a natural inclination towards the good, it can hardly be doubted, can it, that they are willingly governed and willingly obey the desires of him who controls them, as things that are in harmony and accord with their helmsman.[6]

Harmony and accord, order and beauty: these are the pillars on which Boethius built his philosophy for, ultimately, 'a thing exists when it keeps its proper place and preserves its own nature. Anything which departs from this ceases to exist, because its existence depends on the preservation of its nature.'[7] How does one exist? How, as Boethius asked earlier on, do we attain perfection? How do we achieve true happiness? Where can meaning be found in a chaotic world? These are the questions which, to Boethius' way of thinking, cannot be answered by well-ordered and proven propositions. This is because in the medieval mind logic does not provide the basis upon which we order the world, but order, as guaranteed by the nature of God who created in his own image and sustains by his own power, is the necessary prerequisite for logic.

Inverting our thinking in this way is necessary if we are to grasp the purport of medieval theological writing. As Evans points out in her book on theology

and philosophy in the Middle Ages, Boethius' *Consolation* is representative
of a pattern wherein the world is viewed as chaotic in its sin, and thus needs to
be restored to order, balance and due proportion. That was what Boethius was
trying to accomplish in his work; that is part of what Bede was doing when
he wrote his *History*,[8] and that is what Pseudo-Dionysius was doing when he
wrote:

> This – the One, the Good, the Beautiful – is in its uniqueness the Cause of the
> multitudes of the good and the beautiful. From it derives the existence of every-
> thing as beings, what they have in common and what differentiates them, their
> identicalness and differences, their similarities and dissimilarities, their sharing of
> opposites, the way in which their ingredients maintain identity, the providence
> of the higher ranks of beings, the interrelationship of those of the same rank, the
> return upward by those of lower status, the protecting and unchanged remaining
> and foundations of all things amid themselves. Hence, the interrelationship of
> all things in accordance with capacity. Hence, the harmony and the love which
> are formed between them but which do not obliterate identity. Hence, the innate
> togetherness of everything. Hence, too, the intermingling of everything, the
> persistence of things, the unceasing emergence of things. Hence, all rest and hence,
> the stirrings of mind and spirit and body. There is rest for everything and
> movement for everything, and these come from that which, transcending rest and
> movement, establishes each being according to an appropriate principle and gives
> each the movement suitable to it.[9]

Any goodness, beauty or order that we see around us is due to God's
sustaining presence, and any deviation, ugliness or disorder is due to sin, but
can be remedied through a new creation effected by God. This, as we will
see, is part of Anselm's agenda in writing the *Cur Deus Homo*. He is not
merely interested in outlining an objective view of the atonement, nor simply
engaged in explaining the necessity for penal substitution or vicarious
suffering. The overarching impression Anselm leaves on the reader of the *Cur
Deus Homo* is that God is a God of order, harmony and beauty, and he must
and will act in accordance with those aspects of his nature. Thus, the different
words and expressions Anselm uses to describe fittingness, order or beauty
become central to any study of that work.

Evans evinces her inclination in this direction in a footnote when she
comments that the use of *convenientia* and *decentia* 'occur often enough in
the *Cur Deus Homo* for it to seem likely that "fittingness" was an important
consideration in Anselm's mind throughout the writing of the work'.[10] She
later expands on this when she claims that the arguments Anselm offers
in the first few books of the *Cur Deus Homo* 'are meant to appeal to the
spiritual "aesthetic sense"' and that, throughout the remainder of the treatise,
he departs 'no further than he must from arguments which have this kind of
direct appeal to every man's sense of "rightness"'.[11]

Unfortunately, while Evans recognizes the presence of aesthetic categories
in Anselm, she denies that such categories apply equally to all aspects of the

Cur Deus Homo. She contends, for example, that Boso's question about the redeemed making up the number of the fallen angels is not integral to the main argument, but a digression justified by friendship.[12] Frank Brown, on the other hand, does admit that aesthetics plays a deeper role in the *Cur Deus Homo*, even to the point where the discussion on the relation between the number of the fallen angels and the number of the redeemed (though still essentially deemed a digression) is a demonstration of 'Anselm's belief that the God who redeems is intent on perfection in the created order, down to the most minor detail'.[13]

Hans Urs von Balthasar also discerns beauty in Anselm's writings and, like Evans and Brown, spends most of his time noting the presence of aesthetic concerns in the *Cur Deus Homo*. He does, however, have some appreciation for aesthetics as a wider category in Anselm's writing,[14] but his lack of detailed interaction with the texts leaves the reader wanting for more concrete and specific indications of just how aesthetics infuses Anselm's theology. He readily borrows from the *Monologion* and the *Cur Deus Homo*, but what about Anselm's other works? If it is genuinely true that Anselm imbibed a model of reality which informs the very structure of his thought such that the aesthetic dimension is a fully integrated part of creator and creation, should we not be able to identify it in more than a few obvious examples from two works? Let me be clear here: I do not intend to intimate that Evans, Brown or von Balthasar have offered facile accounts. It is my contention, however, that these scholars, while noting the beauty of Anselm's prose and reasoning, and the indications of his interest in an aesthetic dimension, have not fully acknowledged the pervasiveness of an aesthetic ideal in Anselm's thinking.

From Logic to Longing: Anselm's Prayers

Apart from Anselm's more obvious references to beauty and order in the *Monologion* and the *Cur Deus Homo*, the student of his works will undoubtedly also gravitate towards the *Prayers and Meditations*. Here even the *illiterati* in Latin can see the beauty in both form and content. The metre, the rhythm, the assonance and resonance peek through even in translation. But it is remarkable in this context that Southern, a writer so familiar with the life and work of Anselm, should still only see in these prayers and meditations an example of monastic piety and religious devotion. Granted, the aesthetic structure of the prose is not lost on Southern, but he is willing only to say that the prayers bear a similarity to the *Monologion* and the *Proslogion* in their 'theme and method: they are all about the mental and spiritual awakening which is the origin of love. They all have the same fanciful, yet precise, word-play, which expresses Anselm's feeling for the subtle links between words and reality.'[15]

For Southern, the question of beauty in Anselm's prayers is 'fanciful' or 'too elaborate and artificial for our taste'.[16] In fact, Southern goes so far as to argue in his biography of Anselm that beauty 'is a new word in Anselm's theological vocabulary, which first comes into prominence in the *Cur Deus Homo*'.[17] Quite how this can be true is uncertain. Beauty as a category in the *Monologion* has already been noted, and it is no less present in the *Proslogion*. Moreover, the prayers in particular are not only examples of beautiful writing, but beyond that they are also a witness to the beauty and order inherent in Anselm's perception of reality. What makes Southern's comment all the more strange is that he does not appear to undervalue the import of Anselm's spiritual context. Knowing Anselm's ardent avocation in meditation on the Psalms and his abundant alacrity for the experience of intimacy with God, not to mention his emphasis on reforging the relationship between creator and creation through the restitution accomplished in redemption, one would think that the concomitant preponderance of aesthetic categories as an inherent aspect of epistemic development would be a more prominent feature in Southern's assessment. Instead, it is noted as little more than a characteristic of his writing style and an innovation in his late thinking.

In her translation and introduction to the *Prayers and Meditations*, Benedicta Ward is somewhat more sensitive to beauty in Anselm's work but really only with respect to the piety it engenders in a liturgical context. For Ward, Anselm's great achievement appears to be the refinement of personal devotion in both a public and private context. In a number of different places she outlines the various stages pertinent to monastic prayer; often adding that Anselm's prayers bear the marks of an existential outpouring of his soul which he hopes will involve the reader in the reality of the reconciliation achieved by Jesus on the cross.[18] It seems to me, though, that this very theological aspect of the prayers is also precisely where we discover Anselm's aesthetic dimension.

What is it, we must ask ourselves, that drives Anselm's theological agenda? It is in part the desire to teach those around him the elements of the Christian faith. He is also partially interested in exploring the deeper questions of the faith to satisfy his own curiosity and enjoyment, for, as he makes so clear in the *De Incarnatione Verbi*, the one who searches the hidden treasures of revelation is the one who, despite the relative success or failure of his endeavours, will find himself rejoicing in the opportunity to experience the depth and mystery of God. This, it seems to me, brings us to the point of Anselm's life and work: an experience of the divine. That is what Anselm seeks so eagerly in the *Monologion* and so diligently in the *Proslogion*. That is what Anselm wishes for everyone who hears about the atoning sacrifice of Christ. That is what drives the *Prayers and Meditations* and gives them their profound gravity. It is, as Fröhlich has noted in his article, 'Anselm's *Weltbild* as Conveyed in His Letters', the very *raison d'être* of the church that humanity should hear about the possibility of reconciliation through re-creation 'in order to enable [each person] to regain the beatific vision'.[19]

Yes, there is artistry in his prayers. Yes, there is beauty in his style. Yes, there is order and fittingness in his doctrine of the atonement. Yes, there is harmony in the Godhead. But why should we stop at simply observing it in a few places? Anselm did not believe his prayers were beautiful because he was adept at playing with words, nor did he believe that his theology was worth reading because it discerned order; rather, by constantly straining towards recapturing what was lost at the Fall[20] and continually striving for that which is ahead, forgetting what is behind, he pressed on 'to win back the lost celestial heritage' and to share not just 'in the company of the angels' but, more than that, to participate in the very being of God.[21] The call of God to be holy as he is holy resounds through the corridors of Anselm's mind and is most often expressed in terms of appropriating all that God offers, for 'heaven and the kingdom of God were no distant and strange reality for Anselm. Heaven will be perfect union and complete concordance of the wills of all the citizens with the will of God.'[22] There is, in the meantime, the responsibility to search out and the opportunity to experience as much of that beatific vision as possible.

Aesthetics: Bringing Together Particularity and Diversity

It is not uncommon to hold that there is no central theme in Anselm's writings precisely because they are occasional. Students, fellow monks, even the pope on one occasion, approached Anselm with their questions and problems.[23] On account of this information any attempt to demonstrate a unity in the diversity of topics covered appears futile. That is why I propose that we not try to search for a unity in the topics Anselm chose, but to discern the *weltbild* that informed the manner of his responses, for in this we will discover the foundation which, in a far deeper sense, unifies all Anselm wrote.

Let me be clear here. I do not intend to give an exhaustive account of Anselm's model of reality and to demonstrate its presence on every page of every treatise he wrote. What I am proposing is that we study Anselm's works to see if they reveal comparable patterns of expression. The framework within which Anselm operated can tell us much about why he said the things he did in the way he did. In this way we can transcend the particularity of each treatise and begin to perceive the unity that underlies them all because all of them, regardless of their subject matter, will be related to and within a certain understanding of reality.

The most pervasive constituent of Anselm's *weltbild*, and the one which I will concentrate on, is aesthetics. That is, an understanding of reality that is based on the conviction that the harmony and unity, the beauty and fittingness that is part of God's being have been imprinted on his creation. Such a view of the relationship between creator and creation dominated the literature Anselm read and the milieu of which he was a part. Reading psalms which dwell extensively on the beauty of creation, the glory of God and the harmony of God's purposes would not have gone unnoticed by Anselm and his colleagues. Meditating on the final chapters in Job where God describes his attention to detail during creation, how could Anselm have remained unaffected by the obvious implications for proportion, symmetry and fittingness?[24] Reading the record of John's apocryphal vision in Revelation, a foretaste of beatific eschatological realities described through analogies with the present age would have whetted Anselm's appetite to admonish his contemporaries to secure for themselves the glory of what will inevitably occur.

This is the environment Anselm inhabited; such was the taxonomy of Anselm's expression. In what follows we will explore the extent and impact of such thinking in Anselm's theology. We will begin by examining the *Prayers and Meditations* which were written throughout Anselm's life and so provide a good place to start since they evince an aesthetic model of reality throughout his writing career. Although there are only nineteen prayers and three meditations, there is still more contained in this collection than can possibly be covered in one chapter. Nevertheless, even the bounds of one chapter will be sufficient to demonstrate the extent of the impact Anselm's aesthetic *weltbild* had on his devotional literature. In contrast to the beauty of Anselm's *Prayers*, we will move on to consider the arid and, perhaps for that reason, parsimoniously studied *De Grammatico*. There I believe we will find the seeds of aesthetic thinking which germinate in succeeding treatises. In the course of the chapter, connections will be drawn with the *Monologion*. This will lead us most naturally into a discussion of the *Proslogion* to see if there is more there than the profusion of current scholarship generally allows. Following that we will turn our attention to the three dialogues (*De Veritate*, *De Libertate Arbitrii*, *De Casu Diaboli*). Here we will see just how suffusive aesthetic categories are in Anselm's years as Abbot of the monastery at Bec. Finally, the *Cur Deus Homo* will be assessed as one of the chief examples of how deeply Anselm's model of reality was rooted in an aesthetic ideal. Within this structure references to Anselm's other works will be made as befits the overall flow of our investigation.

Anachronism: The Frustration of Future Contingency

It will not have missed the reader's attention that the term 'aesthetic' was distinctly absent from the medieval period. In fact, the word itself was not coined for another 650 years after Anselm's time. How, then, can I so cavalierly use this term as if it were as much a part of medieval life as feudalism and kingship?

While it is certainly true that concepts of beauty, symmetry, harmony and order were part of medieval culture, their aggregation under the rubric of aesthetics was unknown. It was, as I mentioned, not until the eighteenth century that Baumgarten coined the word,[25] and even then it was neoterized to denote the sensible as a particular aspect of epistemological inquiry. Now, while it is true that Baumgarten's definition of aesthetics was challenged by Kant in his *Critique of Judgement*, delineating the parameters of their differences and recapitulating the ensuing discussions on the matter lies well beyond the scope of our present interest. It is notable, however, that with Kant and Baumgarten a distinctly new direction was taken with respect to the place of the aesthetic within the study of epistemology.[26]

On a philosophical level, then, it might seem that applying the term 'aesthetics' to a body of medieval literature is inappropriate and blatantly anachronistic. The case is made all the stronger when we consider that, as Eco informs us, Baumgarten described aesthetics 'by means of such expressions as the science of sense knowledge, the theory of the liberal arts, the epistemology of the lower level of knowledge, the rules of thinking aesthetically, the rules of reasoning by analogy'.[27] In spite of this, I would agree with Eco that such definitions of aesthetics, whether taken from Baumgarten or Kant, are not the definitive word on the matter. Surely, aesthetics can be broadened to refer 'to a whole range of issues connected with beauty'.[28] Granted, the intended connotation of the term when it was first coined had mainly to do with things perceptible by the senses as opposed to those things which are particular to the mind, but why should aesthetics be denied a place in the noetic or even in the ontic categories of Christian theology?

Medieval Aesthetics: Extending the Paradigm

By making this suggestion I am aware that I am exposing myself to all manner of criticism because I am trying to extend or even redefine 'aesthetics'; I do not, however, perceive such a proposal as exceptionally subversive. The reason for this is that while it is patently obvious that medieval theologians did not undertake the study of aesthetics in the way Baumgarten described or in the way that Kant developed it, medievals did incorporate ideas into their theology and models of reality that one would have a difficult time categorizing as anything but aesthetic. But just what are the ideas that medieval theologians used? What words did they use to indicate their awareness of aesthetic categories? Eco suggests *pulchritudo*, *suavitas*, *proportio* and *harmonia*[29] as examples and contends that

> Even a short and cursory examination of the everyday aesthetic sensibility of medieval people will show that their aesthetic terminology did in fact relate to their experience. Whether they felt pleasure in looking at things or in engaging in activities, whether they spoke of philosophical entities such as 'form' or theological realities such as 'beauty', medieval thinkers employed the same concepts that we do today, with all their connotations and implications.[30]

This is, in some respects, a bold statement on Eco's part; yet it is, in another sense, a most perspicuous proposition. It is, in the first place, evident because, as Eco comments, even a cursory examination of medieval literature will reveal the depth to which aesthetic ideals permeated the medieval mind and, indeed, the minds of their theological predecessors. From Irenaeus we read about the plan of redemption that

> … the Lord then was manifestly coming to His own things, and was sustaining them by means of that creation which is supported by Himself, and was making a recapitulation of that disobedience which had occurred in connection with a tree, through the obedience which was [exhibited by Himself when He hung] upon a tree, [the effects] also of that deception being done away with, by which that virgin Eve, who was already espoused to a man, was unhappily misled, was happily announced, through means of the truth [spoken] by the angel to the Virgin Mary, who was [also espoused] to a man. For just as the former was led astray by the word of an angel, so that she fled from God when she had transgressed His word; so did the latter, by an angelic communication, receive the glad tidings that she should sustain (*portaret*) God, being obedient to His word. And if the former did disobey God, yet the latter was persuaded to be obedient to God, in order that the Virgin Mary might become the patroness (*advocata*) of the virgin Eve. And thus, as the human race fell into bondage to death by means of a virgin, so is it rescued by a virgin; virginal disobedience having been balanced in the opposite scale by virginal obedience. For in the same way the sin of the first created man (*protoplasti*) receives amendment by the correction of the First-begotten, and the coming of the serpent is conquered by the harmlessness of the dove, those bonds being unloosed by which we had been fast bound to death.[31]

At first glance one might wonder what weight Irenaeus should be given in our investigation. He is, after all, a very early figure in the history of Christian thought. Furthermore, it is debatable to what extent medieval scholars had access to his work. For our purposes this criticism is significant because, despite not knowing exactly what Anselm wrote, affinities drawn between Irenaeus and Anselm are rarely made, if at all. Initially, a connection between Irenaeus and Anselm would certainly seem inapposite, but further reflection on this excerpt in conjunction with Anselm's *Cur Deus Homo* leaves one wondering. In *Cur Deus Homo* 1.3 Anselm writes, 'how fitting it is that the restoration of mankind has been brought about in this way', and how 'appropriate [it is] that, just as death entered the human race through man's disobedience, so life should be restored through a man's obedience' and that 'just as the sin which was the cause of our damnation originated from a woman, similarly the originator of our justification and salvation should be born of a woman.' Anselm goes on to marvel at how fitting it is that 'the devil, who defeated the man whom he beguiled through the taste of a tree, should himself similarly be defeated by a man through tree-induced suffering which he, the devil, inflicted.'

To make the case that Anselm was drawing on Irenaeus directly would be hard to prove. Simple resonance between the two passages does not warrant a claim for dependence. Unfortunately, exactly what Anselm read, and just how wide and deep his knowledge was of the Church Fathers at large will never likely be known.[32] There have, of course, been attempts to reconstruct the library at Bec during the eleventh and twelfth centuries,[33] but such estimations, as good as we deem them to be, still leave the historian and theologian with many questions. In light of this, perhaps the most fruitful avenue of inquiry is not to investigate the probability of direct borrowing or even to attempt to reconstruct the library or possible gamut of material Anselm knew. While it is true that our understanding of context needs, as much as possible, to be grounded in the particulars surrounding Anselm's life, we must remain open to the possibility that general themes which run through the works of the early Fathers and apologists also have their place in Anselm's overall context.

What these themes are, and how we are able to discern between the peripheral and the pertinent certainly raises potentially vexed questions; but surely the identification of recurrent motifs in different authors conveys a model of reality which was not merely espoused by scholars and the learned, but was an integral aspect of the cultures they inhabited. Naturally, one may wonder to what degree the varying cultures in which early and medieval scholars lived were similar, but considering the almost universal agreement that medieval theologians depended heavily on classical authors and the early Church Fathers,[34] it should come as no surprise that such a rigorous dependence would lead to similar thought patterns. As C.S. Lewis has so shrewdly pointed out, medieval commentaries on Plato, for example, transformed or Christianized his thoughts and arguments such that his Ideas became the ideas in the mind of God. Plato was no longer 'the logician, nor the philosopher of love, nor the author of the *Republic*. He was, next to Moses, the great monotheistic cosmogonist, the philosopher of creation; hence, paradoxically, the philosopher of that Nature which the real Plato so often disparaged.'[35] It is not so much the original intent of the authors of antiquity and the early church that matters, but the history of interpretation that surrounds them; for it is the history of their interpretation which, though extended and expanded by each succeeding generation, informs the thinking and development of those generations.

Equipped with this understanding, the question of Anselm's specific sources fades into the background (though, we must stress, never out of sight) if we begin to think more broadly about those themes and patterns that pervaded the church in the early and successive centuries of its life. By viewing the heritage of Anselm's context in this way we may lose something of the specificity we in the modern period so dearly cherish, but we gain a more ancient perspective. That is to say, the context out of which Anselm wrote was formed by more than the sum total of what books he read or who taught him. Beyond the particulars of Anselm's education lie the universals of a common human understanding of the nature of reality.

For Irenaeus, God worked in a most fitting way, balancing his justice and his grace in due proportion to the necessary degree. How could it be otherwise? Should not the God who created and ordered the world in perfect harmony not also sustain it in that same manner?[36] There is, in Irenaeus, a strong sense that creation and, perhaps more importantly, re-creation, have and will be ordered in a way that reflects the nature of the divine – a nature in which humanity is invited to participate and so take part in the unity that is being wrought between the creator and the creation.[37] So too in Anselm we see the same pattern. God is the creator and sustainer of all things,[38] and he has created us to participate, as much as possible, in his nature,[39] so that our wills may be one with his such that we experience and know his love and power both now (though partially) and at the arrival of the eschaton when the kingdom of God is fully established and we reign with him in harmony and order.[40]

Enumerating all the relevant texts up to the eleventh century which evince this trend would take up more space than we have, but the combination of some of the references just given in conjunction with the above discussion on Boethius' *Consolation of Philosophy* and the following brief excursus of a few of the more salient passages from Augustine will, it is hoped, suffice to demonstrate the lineage of which Anselm is so firmly a part.[41]

Sampling Symmetry: Tracing the Trail

Although we could linger further in the writings of the early Church Fathers,[42] it seems most prudent to turn our attention to St Augustine for a moment as Anselm himself more than once professed his preference for and partisanship in favour of this theologian.[43] What it was that Anselm found particularly intriguing about Augustine is left to our imagination, but it is interesting to note that of all the Church Fathers available to him Anselm chose the one who seems to evince the greatest appreciation for aesthetic categories. Augustine's *De Ordine* and *De Musica* are his most explicit examples of aesthetic appreciation, but, as Carol Harrison has aptly shown, aesthetic categories and appreciation abound throughout Augustine's writings.

In the *Confessions*, for example, Augustine asks,

> 'Do we love anything but the beautiful? What, then, is the beautiful? And what is beauty? What is it that allures and unites us to the things we love; for unless there were a grace and beauty in them, they could by no means attract us to them?' And I marked and perceived that in bodies themselves there was a beauty from their forming a kind of whole, and another from mutual fitness, as one part of the body with its whole, or a shoe with a foot, and so on.[44]

He is not, of course, wondering here about beautiful things; rather, he is concerned with beauty as a transcendental category. From where or what, he is inquiring, do beautiful things and beauty more widely conceived receive their beauty? Interestingly enough, when considering this question,

Augustine adds that beauty can be seen not only in certain objects themselves, but also in their relationships to other objects and the world around them. Augustine's concept of beauty stretches beyond fine art to incorporate relatedness and proportion. True, at this point in his life Augustine was unable to resolve his questions satisfactorily (in part, no doubt, because at this point in the *Confessions* Augustine is not yet converted, and therefore does not fully comprehend the nature of reality and truth set before him), but there is much in his post-conversion works which attests to his ongoing fascination with the concerns here raised in embryonic form.

Carol Harrison points out that Augustine eventually came to the point where he believed that beauty is intrinsic to all creation, but because of our fallenness we are not always able to appreciate that beauty.[45] Nevertheless, due consideration of the aesthetic in creation, whether it be in form or function, particularity or relatedness, will lead us 'to God, its creator and orderer'.[46] From this, and in conjunction with a myriad of other evidence from Augustine, Harrison argues that 'temporal manifestations of divine Beauty in Creation are therefore given a positive role to play, in revealing and leading men back to their source, when it is remembered that their very existence and beauty (or 'form') is received from the Divine.'[47]

Again, as with Irenaeus' work, we can identify remarkable resonances between Anselm and Augustine. A more substantial comparison of how similar these two theologians are is given in the following chapters, but for now let us note that in the *De Grammatico*, the *Monologion* and the *Proslogion* Anselm relies heavily on the notion that there is a correspondence between the creator and creation.

What Anselm conveys in his correspondence between creator and creation becomes clear once we realize that when he refers to creation he means anything and everything that can be considered created. Thus, when Anselm thinks about creation, it is not merely a matter of thinking about plants and animals, but of language and thought. There is a very strong belief in Anselm that creation is derivative; it bears the imprint of God's communicable attributes. In the *De Grammatico*, for instance, Anselm contends that words have a dual character. On one level, they signify something that is real and true because we have ordered them in a way which communicates the desired connotation. But more than that, words are able to signify something because they participate in that which they are signifying. Words partake of, or have invested in them, that which is beyond them. Anselm believes all reality operates in a similar way. He makes it clear in the *Proslogion*, for instance, that humanity reaches the apogee of fulfilment when we partake of or, more accurately, participate in, those aspects of the divine which fulfil who and what we were created to be and do.[48]

As Anselm makes abundantly clear in the *Proslogion*, for instance, one of the driving factors behind so much of his work is the desire to attain to and enjoy as much of the beatific vision as possible in this life. It is a shame that so little work has been done on Anselm's eschatological context because, as we shall have cause to see in later chapters, there is a tension in his work between the necessity of inhabiting this world and attending to the tasks granted him by the covenant community or imposed on him by the state, and the ambition to leave this world so as to enter fully into the final glory and beauty of the eschaton. He says in a letter to Queen Matilda, for example, that those who act in a manner worthy of Christ are beautiful in the way the woman in the Song of Solomon is described.[49] He is clear, though, that the beauty to which Matilda ought to aspire is not the sort of beauty that she can create; instead, it is a beauty that is shared by the church at large as the bride of Christ – apart from whom she could not hope to be beautiful. This must necessarily be the case because all that the Christian has of worth comes from God.

Anselm admits this when, in contrast to his explication of the transcendence of God, he alludes to Acts 17:28 and claims that 'in you I move and in you I have my being.'[50] All that Christians are and do is bound up in their participation in the divine nature. Certainly, it is a mystery how a transcendent God can also be immanent and how a finite, mortal creature can, indeed must, have contact with an infinite God; but tensions such as these breathe life into Anselm's understanding of reality. Without the present promise of realized salvation and the future hope of beatific glory the accomplishment of redemption could either never be experienced in this life or never be improved upon in the next. Without the paradox of the transcendence and immanence of God his existence would either be unknown and unknowable or contingent and inadequate. Without contact between the creator and the creation, the infinite and the finite, believers could never hope to transcend their own situations and so rise above the chaos of this world and move into the irenic concord of the next.

Maintaining these contrasts and comparisons is what provides Anselm's model of reality with order and harmony, symmetry and proportion, unity and beauty, fittingness and propriety. Like Augustine, Anselm's concept of beauty extends far beyond fine art and beauty as a description of the physical appeal of an object. For Anselm, as for Augustine (and as for Aquinas after them), beauty, aesthetic appeal and appreciation had to do with the judgements of the mind, for 'looking at an object aesthetically means looking at its structure, physical and metaphysical, as exhaustively as possible, in all its meanings and implications, and in its proportionate relations to its own nature and to its accidental circumstances. It means, that is, a kind of *reasoning about* the object, scrutinising it in detail and in depth.'[51] At first glance this approach to aesthetics may appear overly cerebral, and thus Kantian, but the act of identifying aesthetic elements in creation takes into account the very nature of reality and its givenness in God. It is, therefore, not an exercise in subjective appraisal nor even an endeavour towards objective determination, but a thorough attempt to assimilate and appropriate the distinctives of the divine perspective. Such an exercise is not only possible, but desirable because, as Augustine so ardently stressed, God is present in his creation and can therefore be seen and known through it. Thus, Anselm's aesthetic sensibilities are supremely displayed in those works which concentrate on the incarnation (recall the preponderant use of the *Cur Deus Homo* in Evans, Brown, von Balthasar and Southern) because in Christ dwells the fullness of creation and creator, the immanent and transcendent, the finite and infinite, and, paradoxically, beauty and ugliness.

How strange that he who is supreme beauty[52] and who communicates that beauty to all creation should become buffeted and scourged, pierced and punctured, made to drink bitter tears and endure scoffing from those who never wept;[53] yet how glorious that although Christ was handed over to die he became the power to overcome death, and that through the loss of his life others may gain theirs. In the last analysis, then, what appears to be Christ's defeat in disproportionate suffering and discordant mocking is actually the very means by which 'the world is renewed and made beautiful by truth.'[54] Even the moment of supreme disfigurement is, from a divine perspective, transformed into an act effecting unparalleled beauty.

Anselm's application of aesthetics does not, however, begin and end with the incarnation and redemption. Anselm extended his thoughts on harmony and beauty to include a discussion on will. It is, we have noted, only in so far as an individual's will is in harmony with God's will that there is any hope of achieving the beatific state both now and in the future. But the prevalence of these ideas extends further back in Anselm's thinking to the very nature of freedom itself. What is freedom of choice? How do we know we are free? These are the types of questions Anselm's interlocutor posed in the *De Libertate Arbitrii*.

The student opens the interrogation with the assumption that freedom should be defined as a function of possible choices. The more choice one has, the more free one is. Anselm denies this position outright, in spite of its wide acceptance, and stipulates that freedom is defined by the degree to which our wills are in accord with the divine will. He holds to this position because, as he explains, if freedom is defined by the number of possible choices available to someone, then the greatest number of possible choices would include those which are sinful, and choosing a sinful option cannot be free since, according to biblical exegesis, sin is binding. Furthermore, Anselm believes that whatever one says about freedom should apply to creation as well as the creator. This is not to suggest that creation and creator are on a par, but to steadfastly maintain that since God made the world with all its concomitant parts and characteristics, he did so in a way that reflected his nature. Thus, the way in which God is free must be the supreme example and template for our freedom. Consequently, even in the one area of life where we might expect to find deviation from pattern and order, Anselm reveals an undiminished emphasis on the unity of humanity and divinity through participation in God's nature. Proportion and harmony remain integral aspects of an overall aesthetic which, as in the case of Augustine, is a cardinal component of theology since it leads us ineluctably toward the source of our being.

We could, of course, protract this discussion on the medieval penchant for order, praise for proportion and predilection for beauty almost indefinitely, but the point has been sufficiently made: the medieval mind, drawing as it did from the writings and traditions of the early church, appreciated the aesthetic nature of reality in a way that few present models of reality or interpretations appear to comprehend. For this reason, our reading and understanding of medieval texts is often tainted by our neglect to take heed of their *weltbild*. Instead of appreciating the fittingness of an argument, we risk rejecting it because it does not conform to our modern proclivity for formal logic.

Colin Gunton bemoans this short-sightedness when he relates how, on this side of the Enlightenment, 'the realms of science, ethics and art are understood in radically different ways and ... the very possibility of a universe of meaning, a world and experience making overall unified sense, is lost to view.'[55] This is the sort of milieu in which aesthetics, as a technical concept, was born, and this remains the context in which so many continue to examine it. Beauty altogether too often tends to be confined to the physical, denuded of any connection to the metaphysical, and is thereby robbed of its multifaceted expression. Gunton is right to conclude that 'it is important for the health of a culture ... that we should be able to hold in some positive relation, yet without reducing one to another, the three central dimensions of human being: its formation by truth, goodness and beauty. Without a measure of integration of our knowledge, ethics and experience of beauty we are not fully what we might be.'[56] This sort of integration is present in the medieval western tradition, and it is an essential element of Anselm's work which must be integrated into our perlustration of his life and writings if we are properly to appreciate his contribution to theological thinking.

Notes

1   Cf. *Proslogion*, 5ff (S.1.104.11ff).
2   Cf. G.R. Evans (1977), 'The *Cur Deus Homo*: The Nature of Anselm's appeal to Reason', *Studia Theologia* 31:33–50, p. 33. cf. also John McIntyre (1954), *St Anselm and his Critics: A Re-interpretation of the* Cur Deus Homo, Edinburgh: Oliver and Boyd, p. 2.
3   There is no clear distinction between these two categories of thinkers until later in the Middle Ages: cf. the discussion in G.R. Evans (1993), *Philosophy and Theology in the Middle Ages*, London: Routledge.
4   Boethius (1969), *The Consolation of Philosophy*, trans. V.E. Watts, London: Penguin Books, sect. 3.8.
5   Boethius, 3.12.
6   Boethius, 3.12.
7   Boethius, 4.2.
8   Evans, *Philosophy and Theology*, p. 5.
9   Pseudo-Dionysius (1987), *The Divine Names* in *The Complete Works*, trans. Luibheid, London: SPCK, sect. 4.7.
10   Evans, '*Cur Deus Homo*: appeal to reason', p. 33, n. 4.
11   Evans, p. 41; cf. also G.R. Evans (1989), *Anselm*, London: Geoffrey Chapman, p. 106.
12   Evans, '*Cur Deus Homo*: appeal to reason', p. 47ff.

13 Frank Burch Brown (1993), 'The Beauty of Hell: Anselm on God's Eternal Design', *Journal of Religion*, 73:329–56, p. 336.

14 Cf., for example, Hans Urs von Balthasar (1982), *The Glory of the Lord: A Theological Aesthetics*, vol. 2, trans. Andrew Louth, Edinburgh: T&T Clark, p. 211.

15 Benedicta Ward (1973), *The Prayers and Meditations of St Anselm*, London: Penguin Books, p. 14.

16 Ward, *Prayers*, p. 10.

17 R.W. Southern (1995), *Saint Anselm: A Portrait in a Landscape*, Cambridge: Cambridge University Press, p. 212.

18 Benedicta Ward (1986), 'Anselm of Canterbury and his Influence', in *Christian Spirituality: Origins to the Twelfth Century*, Bernard McGinn & John Meyendorff (eds), London: Routledge & Kegan Publishers, p. 198.

19 Walter Fröhlich (1988), 'Anselm's *Weltbild* as Conveyed in His Letters', *Anselm Studies: An Occasional Journal*, vol. 2, J.C. Schnaubelt, T.A. Losconcy, F. Van Fleteren and Jill A. Frederick (eds), New York: Kraus International Publications, p. 517.

20 Cf. *Proslogion*, 1 (S.1.98.16–1.99.7).

21 Fröhlich, p. 505; cf. also Epp. 2, 8, 35, 37, 56, 62, 66, 67, 78, 79, 80, 81, 95, 99, 101, 112, 114, 120, 121, 131, 133, 134, 143, 168, 169, 335, for references to sharing in and with the angels.

22 Fröhlich, p. 506.

23 Cf. the *Monologion*, *Proslogion*, *De Processione Spiritus Sancti*, and the many dialogues which indicate a similar situation.

24 cf. Job 38:4–7: [4]Where were you when I laid the earth's foundation? Tell me, if you understand. [5]Who marked off its dimensions? Surely you know! Who stretched a measuring line across it? [6]On what were its footings set, or who laid its cornerstone – [7]while the morning stars sang together and all the angels shouted for joy? (NIV).

25 Although any number of sources could be cited here, the simplest is the entry for aesthetics in the OED.

26 Kant's *Critique of Judgement* (trans. James Creed Meredith, Oxford: Clarendon Press, 1978 [1790]) is the obvious place to go for further discussion on this topic, but Anne Shepherd's book, *Aesthetics: An introduction to the philosophy of Art* (Oxford: Oxford University Press, 1987) also provides some helpful insights.

27 Umberto Eco (1997), *The Aesthetics of Thomas Aquinas*, trans. Hugh Bredin, Cambridge: Harvard University Press, p. 2.

28 Eco, p. 2.

29 Eco, p. 3.

30 Eco, p. 4.

31 Cf. Irenaeus, *Against Heresies* 5.19 in *Ante-Nicene Fathers*, vol. 1.

32 According to Anselm's cover letter for the *Cur Deus Homo* (S.2.39.2–2.40.9), it would appear that he believed he had a fairly representative collection of the Fathers' writings; though just how representative and by what standard remains a mystery.

33 Cf. for example, Geneviève Nortier (1971), *Les Bibliothèques Médiévales des Abbayes Benedictines de Normandie*, Paris: P. Lethiesseux in the series, *Bibliothèque d'Histoire et d'Archéologie Chrétiennes*, esp. pp. 34–60.

34 Cf. Henri de Lubac (1998), *Medieval Exegesis*, vol. 1, trans. Mark Sebanc, Edinburgh: T&T Clark, and Anselm's Ep. 77.

35 C.S. Lewis (1964), *The Discarded Image*, Cambridge: Cambridge University Press, p. 52.

36 Cf. Irenaeus, *Against Heresies*, 2.1.1–2; 2.2.1–5; 3.9.1; 3.25.1.

37 Cf. Irenaeus, *Against Heresies*, 3.23.1–2; 5.3.1–3; 5.32.1.

38 Cf. 'Prayer to Christ' (S.3.6.4ff) and 'Prayer before receiving the Body and Blood of Christ' (S.3.10.3).

39 *Proslogion*, 1 (S.1.100.8–11).

40 Cf. Ep. 112, and the discussions on the *De Libertate Arbitrii*, and the *De Veritate* in Chapter 2.

41   For a fuller treatment of the history of aesthetics prior to and after Anselm see James
     Alfred Martin, Jr (1990), *Beauty and Holiness: The Dialogue between Aesthetics and
     Religion*, Princeton: Princeton University Press.
42   We could, for instance, pause to consider Origen's *De Principiis*, section 2.11.4 in
     particular, and its effect on contemporary and subsequent authors.
43   Cf. for example, Ep. 77.
44   Augustine, *Confessions*, 4.13.20 in *Nicene and Post-Nicene Fathers*, series 1, vol. 1.
45   Carol Harrison (1992), *Beauty and Revelation in the Thought of Saint Augustine*, Oxford:
     Carendon Press, p. 41.
46   Augustine, *De Ordine*, 1.27 as cited in Harrison, p. 23.
47   Harrison, p. 42.
48   Cf. *Proslogion*, 1 and 17 (S.1.97.4ff and S.1.113.8–15).
49   Ep. 243.
50   *Proslogion*, 16 – 'In te moveor et in te sum' (S.1.113.3).
51   Eco, *Aesthetics of Thomas Aquinas*, p. 196.
52   *Monologion*, 16 (S.1.31.5).
53   Cf. 'Prayer to Christ' (S.3.6.4).
54   Cf. 'Prayer to the Holy Cross' (S.3.11.3).
55   Colin Gunton (1993), *The One, the Three and the Many*, Cambridge: Cambridge
     University Press, p. 115.
56   Gunton, p. 117.

Chapter 2

The Beatific Vision:
The Ecstasy of Thought and Prayer[1]

One of the great joys of studying the life and work of Anselm is that we have a wealth of information. In addition to the contemporary witness from which we have drawn and the letters we have now explored, there exist a number of relatively brief treatises and a small but rich treasury of prayers and meditations. In fact, making such a division is not without its problems, for much of what Anselm wrote is couched in the language of prayer and an expression of a life steeped in meditation. What is most remarkable about all of Anselm's works, however, is that he did not write any theological or devotional literature for public consumption until he was about thirty-seven.[2] The only work that appears to break this period of literary silence is the *De Grammatico*, but it is a work which is set apart as much by its early date (*c.* 1060) as by its content.[3] We will have cause to examine its form and arguments later, but for now it will suffice to note that its most celebrated and recognizable concern is with language. The thrust of the *De Grammatico* is to demonstrate the care a theologian must take when using words since they are not merely a string of syllables, but a reflection and approximation of ultimate realities.

I do not think it is coincidental that the *De Grammatico* was written first, and possibly simultaneously to the *Prayers and Meditations*, *Monologion* and *Proslogion*.[4] Anselm's interest in words is directed towards his desire to forge a language which can not only communicate with God, but can also communicate the truth of the nature of God. What sin has clouded, the redeemed must attempt to make clear.[5] This is Anselm's aim whenever he applies pen to paper. Where others saw increasing levels of difficulty and confusion, Anselm perceived ever-widening vistas of clarity and harmony.[6] And yet there can be no question that Anselm was a grammarian most learned who took great care in constructing his works. In the case of the *Prayers and Meditations* this longing for linguistic perfection gives, in some cases, the impression that they are contrived.[7] And yet, Anselm's elegance and polished prose are never for the sake of words or appearances, but part of his *excita mentum* towards God.[8] Consequently, the play on words which we will see over and over again is not simply a game, but, 'as for the whole monastic school of "grammatica", an expression of inner coherence', for the order and balance of words are 'vital to his meaning'.[9] Order and balance are profoundly vital to his meaning because it is through the lens of aesthetic appreciation that Anselm seems particularly able to interpret and express the reality he sees before him. To be sure, logical propositions, the application of reason, and the sequential progression of arguments are present in Anselm's works, but at no time do they transcend the aesthetic – that which is fitting and therefore beautiful. It is anachronistic to understand reason as the prerequisite for fittingness and beauty. This is the mistake that has led so many away from the heart of Anselm's theology. We must pay close attention to the form and content, the flow and tenor of Anselm's writings lest we miss the beauty that motivated, sustained and gave hope to his theological enterprise.

Indeed, the *Prayers and Meditations* exhibit the convergence of carefully selected words producing pleasing prose with the insertion of scriptural allusions. Add this to the statement and development of orthodox doctrine and the reader is immediately alerted to the fact that form and emotion can no more be separated from each other than they can from prayer and meditation. Like the Fathers before him, Anselm's theology is 'a hymn, a prayer, the point where knowledge and love become praise'.[10] A mere glance at the works of many of the Fathers will suffice to evince how often their theological arguments, whether against heresy or for the enlightenment of the faithful, break out into spontaneous praise and prayer.[11] In the *Prayers and Meditations* we observe expressions of piety borne out of a liturgical context which touch on and augment the weighty matters of theological inquiry.

There is, however, more to the *De Grammatico* which affects Anselm's *Prayers and Meditations*. Many scholars have, for example, commented on the similarity between Aristotle's *Categoriae* (and Boethius' commentary on them) and Anselm's focus in the *De Grammatico*.[12] Others have noted that Anselm's treatise on language follows a more Platonic pattern (although undoubtedly influenced by Augustine). While the fact that such divergent philosophical traditions have been identified is itself interesting, what is more pertinent to our present concern is how many of Anselm's readers have noted his penchant to relate distinct aspects of reality to one another in a coherent whole. That is to say, Anselm sought to apply all his faculties to those questions and interests which pertained to the intersection of the spiritual and the sense-perceptible world. Even on his death-bed Anselm is reported to have said, 'if [God] would prefer me to remain among you, at least until I can settle the question about the origin of the soul, which I am turning over in my mind, I should welcome this with gratitude, for I do not know whether anyone will solve it when I am dead.'[13] Before his death Anselm had written on the free will of humanity and divine predestination, the imputation of original sin and God's plan for atonement, Mary's virgin conception and the incarnation of the second person of the Trinity, the fall of the Devil and the way to overcome him. Anselm was constantly relating the spiritual, invisible world with the physical, visible one. He was demonstrating the necessity of God's being and activity and how all creation is related to or participates in that being and doing. What Thomas Aquinas was later to call due proportion,

Anselm was outlining and explaining as part of his *modus operandi* because it was part of his model of reality.

In order to fully appreciate and comprehend this directing impulse, we must return once more to the *De Grammatico* for there the undergirding schema helps us to discern more acutely the building blocks of Anselm's thought. In that work Anselm makes it clear that he agrees with Aristotle that any given object is made up of accident and substance. The substance of the object is its true nature, that which can be properly predicated about it. The accidents, however, are what we perceive with our senses and are that part of the object which partakes of or reflects 'a quality and a having'.[14] What Anselm seems to be getting at may be put into grammatical terms. Accidents are, essentially, equivalent to adjectives; whereas substance is, essentially, equivalent to nouns. When Anselm is presented with a table, for example, his five senses permit him access only to those parts which can be described. The table is brown. The table is hard. What Anselm's sensible contact with the physical table cannot reveal, is the brownness, hardness and, ultimately, the tableness in which the table is participating. In other words, the brown table is only a particular of the universal.

Now it will be immediately obvious that this analogy is not entirely adequate. After all, Anselm is able to look at the table and say that it is a table (a noun). However, we must remember that while the object is identified with a noun, that noun carries, in some sense, the connotation of an adjective since it, like an adjective, is not equal to the actual quality it is describing. Consequently, to look at an object and declare that it is a table is to say something about its accident or its particularity, but not to identify that object as *the* universal. I mention this somewhat esoteric bit of medieval philosophy because it helps to point out what lies behind Anselm's statements in, for example, the *Proslogion* where he says that 'harmony, fragrance, sweetness, softness, and beauty are in God according to His own ineffable manner.'[15]

When talking about these aspects of God's being Anselm comments that he looks around him but does not see God's beauty; he listens, but cannot hear God's harmony; he smells, but is unable to sense God's fragrance; he tastes, but misses the savour; he feels, but fails to notice the softness. All of Anselm's senses are engaged in seeking God, but they fail because, in the end, he is only using his senses. Although God infused his creation with those qualities which are ineffably his, they are not the reality itself. Anselm can only perceive the accidental with his corporeal capacities. Only after Anselm has realized that he must use his spiritual discernment, as it has developed through careful meditation on revelation, will he comprehend the universal within the particular; that is to say, the divine within the mundane. Given this understanding, harmony in music neither witnesses to itself nor to the musician, but to the God who inspired and gifted the musician to order a sequence of notes, themselves a creation of God, in such a way that they partake of and reflect the harmony of their ultimate source. Similarly, the beauty of a rose or any other object does not witness to beauty itself, but to the one who is beauty and thereby supplies that rose with the quality of beauty.

The examples could be multiplied, but enough has been said to illustrate that Anselm was utterly absorbed in discovering and disclosing the multifaceted nature of the relatedness and relationships that exist between God and humanity through language. The chief end of all of this was, naturally, a clearer understanding of God and his revelation, but, more than that, it was the attainment of the knowledge and experience of the presence of the triune God.[16] Thus, whether we are reading his devotional, theological or academic works, we are reading the words of a man whose every thought, whose every desire, was to marshal all his learning for the purpose of narrowing the gap between God and humanity. Anselm was not seeking answers so much as he was seeking an audience with God. It is absolutely paramount that we take this into account. Apart from achieving entry into the presence of God the theological task could neither begin nor end. The nature of reality, that is, our relation as the creation to the creator, was not, for Anselm, bound up in the pure application of logic and reason to any given question, but in the communication of God's character to his creation and the reciprocal participation of the creation in the being of God. The restlessness of human souls about which Augustine wrote could not be satisfied in any way until those souls rest in God. To put it simply, Anselm's theology does not revolve around 'what', but 'who'. This is why he begins his greatest and best-known work, the *Proslogion*, as he does:

> Come now insignificant soul, leave aside your daily distractions, escape for a time from your disquieting deliberations. Abandon your weighty worries, and postpone your perplexing occupations. Free yourself awhile for God, and rest awhile in him. Enter into the inner chamber of your being; exclude everything except God, and what you require for seeking him; and, when the door is shut, seek him, invite him, implore him with your whole heart saying, 'I seek your face, Lord; your face do I seek.'[17]

It is a wonder that so many scholars with profound exegetical acumen, incisive discernment and keen intellect should so often pass over what Anselm must have considered foundational for what followed. Perhaps it is the content of the treatise or its acclaimed apodictic argument that causes many readers to forget that this is a work which is framed and infused with the intimate language of prayer – a language which is made all the more penetrating and personal because it is expressed in words which at once come from the Word of God and belong to his faithful followers.

Prayer as More than Pious Pedantry

It may be said that prayer in the theological and philosophical disciplines has rarely been deemed worthy of consideration. Take, for example, the life of Jean de Fécamp. Here was an older contemporary of Anselm who wrote many prayers and influenced many of his contemporaries, probably including Anselm, but is excluded from the *Patrologia Latina* and does not even appear in *The Oxford Dictionary of the Christian Church.* For such writers as these, who never wrote theological treatises or histories or biographies or hagiographies, their fate lies in being assigned to that interminable category: mystic. To be sure, some of the greatest theologians the church has produced are included in this category. Gregory of Nyssa, Augustine, Pseudo-Dionysius and others have, among their better-known works, produced some rather esoteric pieces we would rather relegate to the mystical dimension of religious experience. And yet, strangely enough, every now and then these writers make it abundantly clear that, to their way of thinking, the so-called mystical is so real and integral to their overall understanding that it cannot be neglected. St Augustine's *Confessions* is, perhaps, the supreme example of this. It is a work which, though autobiographical in nature, touches not only on prayer, and the immediate interaction between the divine and the human (aspects predicated of mysticism), but also addresses the weightier theological matters of hamartiology and soteriology to name only two.

When we turn to Anselm and consider that he spent at least ten years of his mature life meditating on the works of, chiefly, Augustine, should we not expect that he would produce works which will mirror an approach in which neither the devotional nor the didactic, neither form nor content, overshadow each other? Apparently, if we look at the literature surrounding Anselm's life and work, the answer is no. The character of Anselmian studies has been piecemeal and taxonomic. The *De Grammatico* is relegated to the trivium. The *Monologion* and *Proslogion* are adaptations of various aspects of Platonic and Aristotelian philosophy. The *Cur Deus Homo* fits in with atonement theory; the *De Veritate*, *De Libertate Arbitrii* and *De Casu Diaboli* are examples of early dialectic, and the work on the incarnation and the procession of the Holy Spirit are simply responses to current conflicts. At times, the antiseptic, distant character of Anselmian studies leaves one with the impression that Anselm practised a benign form of Christianity. Was the suffusion of Anselm's works with prayer ineffectual? Are Anselm's presuppositions misleading in the search for truth because they lack the insight of a post-Enlightenment acumen? Does the possession of faith negate the rigour of reason? Is the possession of religious conviction counter-intuitive to the search for God? It is easy to assume that a faith placed in what is culturally acceptable is superior to one placed in the ancient or the outmoded. What we must seek, if we want to guard against such anachronism, is the model of reality to which Anselm subscribed. In so doing we must remember that if we discover a model of reality that is different from our own it is not necessarily wrong, for 'no model is a catalogue of ultimate realities, and none is a mere fantasy.'[18]

Our appreciation of Anselm's context must, then, begin with the Bible. In the *Proslogion* as in the *Monologion*, in the *De Incarnatione Verbi* as in his *Prayers and Meditations*, in the *Cur Deus Homo* as in so much of what he wrote, the emphasis continually falls on the necessity of contemplation as the key to right understanding. Still, it is not contemplation for its own sake that Anselm requires of his readers, but contemplation on the Bible. What Anselm implies in some of his works, he outlines explicitly in the first section of the *De Incarnatione Verbi*.

He quotes, for example, Psalm 119:99 to say that it is on the testimony given to us in the Bible that we ought to set our affections.[19] Indeed, apart from inculcating the Word, claims to theological awareness are little more than mendacious proclamations devoid of substance.[20] Such people are, says Anselm, 'so wrapped up in material fancies that they cannot extricate themselves from [these] fancies' nor are they able to 'distinguish from the very fancies the things that, themselves alone and pure, they ought to contemplate'.[21] One cannot ascend the heights of theological inquiry until the ladder of faith has first been obtained.[22] For when the discipline of contemplating the Word of God is combined with faith, then can the mountains of questions and knowledge be traversed.

Transcending Logic

Now it is all well and good to admit that Anselm's was a world in which meditation played an important role, and it is certainly important to keep that in perspective, but how do we guard against the danger of offering little more than lip service to that context? By recognizing that Anselm's world was a place where order and pattern were pre-eminent and that such aspects were so prevalent in his life and culture that we should expect them in his writings. He was a monk whose day was carefully divided and monitored. He followed a rule which prescribed his activities for him and guarded against the errors of individual judgement. He lived a coenobitic life and enjoyed the benefits of mutual exhortation and stimulation it offered. There was a coherence, a harmony, a structure, a continuity to Anselm's situation and circumstance. Wherever he looked he saw symmetry, balance and proportion. When he read the Psalms he was wracked by compunction, but relieved by confession; moved by undulations of praise, but perplexed by his unworthy personhood; humbled to the place of prayer, but exalted to the presence of God. The metaphysical became the manifest, the invisible could be touched through the visible. There was a connection between the creator and the created such that those qualities which are often considered abstract became, for Anselm, concrete as they participated in God's perfect being.

This outlook was most lucidly mediated to Anselm through his meditations on the Psalms. In a monastery the Psalms were read or listened to in their entirety during the course of a week,[23] so we can be sure that they played a pre-eminent role in informing Anselm's thoughts. In the first place, the Psalms are public expressions of private thoughts and emotions. The writers of the Psalms repeatedly used the first-person personal pronoun. The effect this has is simultaneously to communicate their inner feelings and to invite the reader to share in them. Second, the Psalms are addressed to God. Here we witness intimate communication between the human and the divine, a communication that invites the reader to join the writer and together to approach the ineffable. In an age when the bounds of reality incorporated the physical as much as the spiritual, the living as well as the dead, the sense of the community of God's people throughout history would not have been lost. These two observations move us, thirdly, to better appreciate the reason why the Psalms were such an integral part of the liturgy of the medieval church. Whatever the form of a liturgy, its purpose is to direct the attention of an assembly towards the divine, and to channel the gamut of emotions and thoughts to a particular end. In as far as one reads the Psalmist's words, feels the compunction of emotion, and utters the words of confession, that individual is joining with the church triumphant, expectant and militant in worshipping God. Whether the Psalms are sung, read, recited or heard, the monastic community was in continual interchange with God: God speaking to them primarily through the Bible, but also in those orthodox Fathers through whom he has provided further illumination and explanation.[24]

Another characteristic of the Psalms is that they are poetic. They are terse; they use imagery, metaphors and similes; they indulge in assonance, symmetry and anaphora. Above all the Psalms are a template *par excellence* for a monk's own praise and prayer. In both their content and their form they reflect the beauty and perfection of the one to whom they are directed. It is in this treasury of knowledge that Anselm sought to savour the sustenance of truth, for, as Arnoul of Boheriss wrote, 'the Holy Scripture is the well of Jacob from which the waters are drawn which will be poured out later in prayer. Thus there will be no need to go to the oratory to begin to pray; but in reading itself, means will be found for prayer and contemplation.'[25]

Here we see how tightly medieval Christians bound the activity of reading to prayer and contemplation. Reading a given text did not merely lead into prayer or contemplation; rather, the way in which one read a text engendered a prayerful and contemplative disposition: 'Reading was an action of the whole person.'[26] Jean Leclercq has noted in connection with this that

> for the ancients, to meditate is to read a text and to learn it 'by heart' in the fullest sense of this expression, that is, with one's whole being: with the body, since the mouth pronounced it, with the memory which fixes it, with the intelligence which understands its meaning and with the will which desires to put it into practice.[27]

In this way it might be argued that instead of the Middle Ages being a period of gross illiteracy and intellectual torpor, it was a time when the book was truly significant and reading was supremely important.[28]

It is in this milieu that Anselm wrote his *Prayers and Meditations* to which we will now turn more specifically. He was writing at a time when reading mattered; when one pored over the pages; when one sought to be transformed by internalizing the external. This is why Anselm prefaced his prayers by instructing the reader that 'they are not to be read in turmoil, but quietly, not skimmed or hurried through, but taken a little at a time, with deep and thoughtful meditation.' Moreover, the reader is encouraged to 'begin and leave off wherever he chooses' for 'in this way he will not get bored with too much material but will be able to ponder more deeply those things that make him want to pray.'[29] Mary Carruthers has suggested that the paragraph divisions Anselm introduced were also intended to aid the memory. As good as one's memory may be, taking in by small portions is always best.[30] Such an estimation comports well with Leclercq's description of reading, as it does with Anselm's 'Prayer to God'.

Where Heaven and Earth Meet

Anselm begins this prayer by raising the mind of the reader to the 'Almighty God, merciful father, and good Lord'.[31] To a monk or one well versed in Scripture, this line alone provides enough material on which to dwell for some time. But what is more interesting than speculating on what early readers of this prayer might have thought, is the juxtaposition of the second line against the first. Anselm goes on to say, 'be merciful to me a sinner.'[32] After raising his sights to the heights of the divine Anselm immediately lowers his sights to the baseness of his sinful nature. What Anselm has done is to set the stage for the rest of this prayer, as well as for the following prayers. In each one, even in his prayers to saints, God is always supreme and unsurpassed and Anselm, along with the saints and the community of believers, stands before this God as a sinner seeking salvation.

These opening two lines are also intriguing because they mirror Psalm 123. There the eyes of the writer are lifted to the heights of heaven where God is enthroned in splendour, but they are just as easily directed back down again to the contemptuous hearts of sinners who cry out for grace. It is also notable that the second line of Anselm's prayer echoes the words of the tax collector in Jesus' parable in Luke 18. There the tax collector, standing at a distance from the Pharisee, recognizes his lowly condition in the presence of an almighty and holy God and pleads for mercy. It is, however, true that our estimations of which texts may have been in the mind of Anselm at the time of writing can never be certain, but such ambiguity was intentional because it enriches the text and gives our minds all the more scope to range over the compass of Scripture and contemplate each possibility in light of our position before God.

It is no wonder Anselm suggested that the reader take his or her time over these prayers.

In fact, our consideration of these first two lines, as indeed to the whole of the prayer, could extend to grammar. When asking for mercy Anselm uses a somewhat curious construction: the imperfect passive subjunctive. The subjunctive is certainly an appropriate and popular mood to use in this situation, as is the passive voice, but why use the imperfect? In this context it sounds like a plea or a request, but the present is normally used in those cases. Could it be that Anselm used the imperfect to indicate the continuing application of mercy which was inaugurated in the past? If we combine this understanding of the imperfect with the subjunctive it appears that Anselm is seeking the assurance of a present condition based on a past action.

Such a grammatical evaluation may seem highly improbable, if not forced, but let us not forget that Anselm was an especially exacting grammarian who believed a thorough grounding in the trivium was essential for further study in theology. Recall, moreover, the earlier comments about the *De Grammatico*. Two significant lessons we gleaned from that work were the importance of the meaning and relation of words, and the role language plays in describing and reflecting that which is beyond us. In the *De Grammatico*, this discussion took on a more abstract and, according to Anselm, accessible form, but in the *Prayers and Meditations* these two lessons coalesce as the desire to attain a vision and experience of the presence of God was pursued through the careful and painstaking application of language to that end. But as we have already seen, the language which is used is not simply contrived in the mind of a monk, but flows out of and uses material from the Bible. The apophatic approach of earlier centuries gives way in Anselm to a positive programme where the aesthetic dimension of the divine as revealed in the Word is paradigmatic for theological discourse. Whether in the closet of one's private worship, the cloister of collegial scholarship or the choir of corporate praise, the beauty of God's truth and being presented itself continually to Anselm's mind, and infused all he thought and wrote.

Medieval Liturgy: The Conduit Between Human and Divine

To the biblical and monastic contexts we should also add the pre-eminent influence of liturgy. The exact form of the liturgy Anselm would have practised at various times throughout his life is difficult to assess. Certainly, St Benedict's *Rule* gives us a good idea of the more popular readings and the general order of the day, but the *Rule* is a remarkably flexible document. Whilst it is true that Benedict was eager to set down certain rules and limitations beyond which a monk could not trespass, it is also the case that he did not desire to administer every possible aspect of daily affairs. To have done so would have run counter to his purpose of setting down 'nothing harsh, nothing burdensome'.[33]

In addition to the freedom of the *Rule* with respect to liturgy, Benedict also allowed time and opportunity for reading more widely.[34] Indeed, part of the work many monks performed was copying texts. Were it not for monasteries we would be much less informed than we are about ancient and medieval life and literature. Now what it was that monks were copying is not an easy question to answer.[35] The difficulty is all the more compounded when we narrow the investigation to find out what liturgical texts were of interest. The search is exacerbated all the more when we consider that sacramentaries, the books used by both clergy and monks in worship, differed from church to church, and from monastery to monastery.[36]

As formidable and potentially unfruitful as efforts to discover the precise liturgy Anselm used are, it does seem sure that he was at least influenced by the style of early liturgies. Benedicta Ward, among others, has noted that Anselm's earliest prayer, 'To God', is 'in the style of the Carolingian prayers'.[37] What marks this prayer as such is its series of brief petitions and short sections.[38] This prayer, though by no means underdeveloped, does not share the use of rhetorical devices and elaborate language that is characteristic of so many of Anselm's other prayers and meditations. We have already noticed its use of Psalm 123 and Luke 18, but we should also note that, at its most obvious and basic level, it mimics the Lord's Prayer found in Matthew 6. In broad terms, the prayer begins with a hallowing of God's name, asks for forgiveness of sins, seeks action in accord with the divine will, and expresses a longing to be delivered from evil. It is a simple prayer modelled on Scripture and the Carolingian pattern.

Beyond these outward similarities with Carolingian liturgy it is instructive to compare Anselm's collection with earlier collections of prayers. Although a thoroughgoing examination of this kind would take us away from our immediate concern, a brief comparison with the *Book of Cerne* will, arguably, provide us with some remarkable insight.[39]

The first thing that strikes us about the *Book of Cerne* is that it is a collection of prayers intended for 'private devotion and meditation'.[40] As early as the eighth and ninth centuries there is evidence of a movement towards individual piety outside of monastic life. Consequently, it should come as no surprise when we discover that Anselm wrote his collection of private prayers for devotion and meditation at the request and for the needs of lay aristocratic women.[41] We notice, in the second place, that the *Book of Cerne* had prayers to God the Father and God the Son as well as to saints and martyrs.[42] Anselm's collection also contains these. Third, the *Book of Cerne* is considered to be 'a meditation upon the communion of saints' wherein the user could 'invoke the intercession of all the faithful on his behalf' and thereby contribute to 'the common good of all'.[43] Interestingly, Evans has commented on Anselm's prayers to the saints that 'never is the saint allowed to stand between the soul at prayer and its creator'.[44] She furthermore highlights Anselm's incredible sense of being part of a community of love, friendship and mutual help.[45]

As mentioned above, it is difficult to tell the precise influences on Anselm's devotional writing, but the convergences and commonalities between prominent Carolingian and Anglo-Saxon prayer collections and Anselm's cannot be easily dismissed; especially when we know that some, such as the *Book of Cerne*, 'continued to be consulted throughout the Anglo-Saxon period and even after the conquest'.[46] If we combine this information with the fact that the move towards private devotion can be traced as far back as the seventh century,[47] and that the eleventh century witnessed an ever-increasing emphasis on individual piety in conjunction with the transformation of the Mass from a community event to an almost exclusive activity of the priesthood,[48] we can understand why Anselm wrote his collection of prayers for the laity and, more specifically, why he wrote a prayer to prepare the reader to receive the body and blood of Christ.

What is particularly interesting about Anselm's collection of prayers, and is certainly true of early compilations, is that they provide the reader with an aid to understanding the profundity of the truth of Scripture. This certainly entailed elucidating the mysteries of the faith, but more than that, it involved illuminating the beauty of truth and its expression found in revelation. It is in this capacity that Anselm was most closely mimicking liturgical style in general. As he 'juxtaposed texts that came from different biblical books' he was involved in the creation of 'a unique aesthetic genre'.[49]

Developing Devotion in Proportion

Anselm's second prayer to Christ is exemplary of this pattern.[50] Compare, for example, the opening stanza:[51]

> Domine Jesu Christe, redemptio <u>mea</u>, misericordia <u>mea</u>, salus <u>mea</u>; te laud<u>o</u>, tibi gratias ag<u>o</u>. <u>Quamvis</u> valde impares tuis beneficiis, <u>quamvis</u> multum expertes dignae devotionis, <u>quamvis</u> nimis macras a desiderata pinguedine dulcissimi tui affectus: tamen <u>qualescumque</u> laudes, <u>qualescumque</u> gratias, non quales scio me debere; sed sicut potest conari, tibi persolvit anima mea.

> Lord Jesus Christ, my redeemer, my mercy, my salvation; I praise you, I give you thanks. Yet how immensely unequal are these in comparison to your beneficence, and how much more does the worthiness of devotion demand, for how great is the leanness of my desire and abundant the sweetness of your love: nevertheless, by some sort of praise, by some sort of thanks, not equal to what I know I owe; but as I am able, my soul will pay its debt to you.

I have juxtaposed the original with my translation to highlight the fact that there is much in the original which is lost in translation.[52] The words and letters I have underlined show the beauty of Anselm's construction. The repetition of *mea*, the rhyming of *laudo* and *ago*, the anaphoric use of *quamvis*, and the duplication of *qualescumque* all contribute to give Anselm's prose a poetic quality. There is a definite aesthetic appeal to the reader. This is not just another addition to an already elaborate liturgy, but a genuine attempt to reflect the beauty of the one to whom he is directing our attention. He says, for instance, 'quamvis nimis macras a desiderata pinguedine dulcissimi tui affectus'. Benedicta Ward translates the passage in this way, 'but although I requite so poorly the sweet riches of your love'.[53] While this certainly communicates the thrust of the intention, it misses a subtle word play. Anselm has used the words 'macras' and 'pinguedine' to describe both the poverty of his love and the immensity of God's love. But there is more here than just a comparison. 'Macras' denotes leanness or slimness and 'pinguedine' denotes fatness or abundance. The image here is of the reader as a lean, malnourished, Christian who has not fed on the meat of the Word in the way he ought, nor indeed is he able to feed on that Word in a way which is required by the magnanimity of God's love. The combination 'pinguedine' with the superlative 'dulcissimi' emphasizes the immensity of God's love and affection not only in their own right, but especially in comparison to the pusillanimity of the love of the Christian.

Now as beautiful and carefully constructed as Anselm's opening lines are, they are not merely a lesson in appealing prose. Anselm ends this stanza by promising to offer praise and thanks to God, 'not equal to what I know I owe; but as I am able, my soul will pay its debt to you.' It is instructive to know that this prayer was probably one of a number written long after the productive decade of the 1070s. It is entirely possible that it was not written until around 1104 since this is the first time we read of its existence in a letter to Countess Matilda.[54] The significance of this date is that it is after the completion of the *Cur Deus Homo*. In that work one of Anselm's chief objectives was to instil his readers with the knowledge that no human has the means whereby he or she may appease God's judgement for the dishonour they have shown.[55] The reason for the necessity of the God-Man is that humanity is utterly unable to restore the honour we have marred. Consequently, the degree to which we are required to make reparation is a degree to which we have no hope of attaining. Thus, despite our knowledge of what should be, we can offer only what can be.

The purpose of including this in the prayer is to reinforce the complete dependence the reader has on God. This point is, of course, made in the first set of claims that Jesus is our redeemer and mercy and salvation. What is achieved then, is a form of *inclusio*. At the outset the reader is implicitly acknowledging the contingency of his position before God on the activity of Jesus. At the end of the stanza, the reader is explicitly confessing the inadequacy of his ability apart from the effectual work of Christ. This inability is elaborated further in the second stanza where Anselm begins by outlining his 'powerless weakness'.[56]

The connection between this stanza and the *Cur Deus Homo* does not end here. There is another comparison that we can make which, while true of these lines, is more broadly true of the *Prayers and Meditations* as a whole.

In Book 1, Chapter 15 of the *Cur Deus Homo* Anselm says that 'when a rational being does not wish for what is right, he dishonours God, with regard to himself, since he is not willingly subordinating himself to God's governance, and is disturbing, as far as he is able, the order and beauty of the universe.'[57] Part of the destructive nature of sin is that it disturbs the innate order and beauty of God's creation. I will argue later that much of what Anselm has to say on the atonement centres around this notion of beauty and the restoration of order, but I think it is interesting that part of the purpose of salvation, as perceived by Anselm, is to restore the beauty and order of creation. The possibility of this restoration is realized first in the person and work of Jesus Christ, but is then reflected in the life of the believer who, in seeking the will of God, makes every effort to conform his will and action to God's. When we read these prayers, therefore, one wonders if the attention to language, words, rhetorical devices, and other aspects of prosaic perfection is the practical outworking of the mandate to restore the beauty sin has disturbed.

To date, there are two main interpretations of the reason for Anselm's attention to detail. The first, and by far the more widely accepted, has been propounded by R.W. Southern and Benedicta Ward. They contend that Anselm's play on words and use of rhetorical devices aid his attempts to conjure compunction in the hearts of his readers. While at times they perceive Anselm's prose to be somewhat overworked, in the end they affirm that his efforts are for no mean task, 'but for the freeing of the soul from itself for God'.[58] The second interpretation of Anselm's prose comes from Mary Carruthers. As noted earlier, she argues that the play on words and the 'love of a jingle' are what makes the text memorable, for 'without memory there is no meditation.'[59] My contention is that while these two interpretations are correct and, indeed, mutually corroborating, they fail sufficiently to account for the intimate relationship between what is said and how it is said, particularly in light of Anselm's wider corpus.[60]

Sin has disturbed the beauty and pattern of the created order and thereby imposed incompleteness. This is why Anselm laments in the *Proslogion*,

> How wretched man's lot is when he has lost that for which he was made! Oh how hard and cruel was that Fall! Alas, what has man lost and what has he found? What did he lose and what remains to him? He lost the blessedness for which he was made, and he found the misery for which he was not made … Once man ate the bread of angels, for which now he hungers; now he eats the bread of sorrow, which then he knew nothing of. Alas the common grief of mankind, alas the universal lamentation of the children of Adam! He groaned with fullness; we sigh with hunger. He was prosperous; we go begging. He in his happiness had possessions and in his misery abandoned them; we in our unhappiness go without and miserably do we yearn and, alas, we remain empty.[61]

This same sentiment is echoed throughout the *Prayers*, but let us note for now its presence in the prayer to Christ. In the second stanza Anselm cries out, 'Hope of my heart, strength of my soul, help of my weakness, by your powerful kindness complete what in my powerless weakness I attempt. My life, the end to which I strive, although I have not yet attained to love you as I ought, still let my desire for you be as great as my love ought to be.'[62] Subsequently Anselm asks, 'Perfect what you have begun, and grant me what you have made me long for, not according to my deserts but out of your kindness that came first to me.'[63] Anselm is acutely aware of the distortion of God's beauty in his life and in the world. He desires and longs for God to restore that order, and to that end, as far as he is able, the prayers are a reflection of the beauty of God's re-creation.

Indeed, it is with re-creation that Anselm is pre-eminently occupied in this prayer to Christ. After imploring his Saviour to complete that which is wanting, Anselm appeals to the nature of God and to his act of redemption in its entirety. In his appeal to God's nature Anselm provides a catalogue of attributes and qualities. God is merciful, gentle, loving, good, patient and gracious.[64] God is all that Anselm is not. Anselm appeals to God's mercy to revive the lukewarm love in his heart, to his gentleness to spur on fervent prayer, to his mercy in combination with his goodness to cleanse what sin has marred, to his grace to breathe in his soul that he might lead a better life. But all of this is only possible because of the accomplishment of redemption as outlined in the next stanza. Moving swiftly, though carefully, through the events of Christ's work Anselm guides the reader's mind through the sweep of salvation history and begins with God as the creator, and him as the sinner. Anselm stirs up no small amount of compunction at this point as he expresses his thirst, hunger, desire, sighs and coveting thoughts for that which he has lost. Again, at a crucial moment in the prayer, Anselm's form reflects his content: 'Domine meus, creator meus, tolerator et nutritor meus, esto adiutor meus. Te sitio, te esurio, te desidero, ad te suspiro, te concupisco.'[65]

The repetition of *meus* and *te* highlights the contrast between the one speaking and the one being addressed. The assonance of the verbs propels the reader from one to the next. Even the syllables have a role to play as almost all the expressions of longing have five syllables (with the exception of the first which has four). The artistry of these lines is all the more emphasized when we consider their cardinal position. The first line refers back to and is a short summary of what has been written so far. The second line flows out of the first, but begins the introduction of the material that follows. To this point, Anselm has been seeking the aid of God so that he might have what is incomplete and imperfect restored. He has recognized the distortion of beauty because of sin, and now he is beginning the work of pursuing the presence of the one who alone can make restitution.

Thus it is with 'weeping and wailing' that Anselm draws his readers into the presence of God so that together they may discover the beauty of his plan and the glory of its fulfilment. To this end Anselm writes,

sic et ego non quantum debeo, sed quantum queo,
memor passionis tuae, memor alaparum tuarum, memor flagellorum, memor crucis, memor vulnerum tuorum,
memor qualiter pro me occisus es, qualiter conditus, qualiter sepultus,
simul memor gloriosae tuae resurrectionis et admirabilis ascensionis.[66]

For the one who has spent much time preparing for worship, who is surrounded with reminders of the biblical themes through reading, listening, talking and praying, who longs to experience the restorative power of God's recreating activity, these words pierce the heart.[67] Anselm has spent much time in this and other prayers reminding the reader about his sin and dwelling on the insufficiency of humanity in the light of perfect deity. With characteristic style and verve Anselm has sought to make the reader's presence with God all the more real. Notice how *memor* is not only repeated for effect, but is also the key noun on which each of the extended phrases turns.[68] Surely Anselm's duplication is there to serve a purpose. It is there to conjure the compunction necessary to appropriately appreciate our place before a redeeming Lord.

This practice of using well-formed prose to summon the soul to sorrow is also easily identified throughout the rest of the prayer. In a repeated series of questions Anselm asks why he was not with Christ at his death,[69] why he was unable to look upon Jesus on the cross,[70] why he lacks due horror at the crucifixion of his Lord,[71] why he is 'not drunk with bitter tears when they gave [Jesus] bitter gall to drink',[72] and why he has failed to share in the sufferings of Mary.[73] With relentless energy Anselm continues to probe deeper into the passion of Christ and to identify ever more with its intensity,[74] the culmination of which is a succession of quotations from the Psalms that mourn the loss of the physical presence of Christ, but, equally, look forward to his return.[75]

Here we have a remarkable insight into eschatology. To be sure, Anselm's eschatology was not well developed, but there is a definite sense of Christ's work inaugurating a foretaste of the last day. At the end of this prayer Anselm asks God to show him his face, display his presence, and reveal his glory. Three times Anselm tells God how his soul thirsts for an experience of divine presence, an experience which God alone will grant to those who seek him. We cannot tell if Anselm received the vision of God that he sought, but we do know that he accomplished this goal at other times. The end of the *Proslogion*, for example, is an extended doxology praising God for the revelation of his person. There, Anselm began his journey with prayer and meditation, and, after much supplication, he received an understanding of God which permitted him entrance into the presence of God.[76] The moment of belief is simply the beginning of salvation. For the rest of Anselm's life there was a constant seeking, a continual pursuit to satisfy his ever-present need to maintain and develop that relationship until its fruition when, without tarrying, his redeemer would come.[77]

In addition to revealing something about his eschatology, Anselm's prayer to Christ also reflects parts of his doctrine of the atonement. In the midst of his perambulations through the passion of Christ, Anselm adds, almost as an aside, that 'sponte moriebatur'.[78] Christ died willingly. No one forced Christ to die, nor did he do so because of any contingency.[79] Indeed, Anselm contends in the *Cur Deus Homo* that not even God the Father made Christ die. Anselm's conclusion on the reason for Christ's death is that he was acting in accord with the 'demands of his obedience'.[80] Since Christ was sinless, Anselm goes on to explain, God could not demand death from him. Although God the Father could instruct Christ to die for the sin of the world, he could not compel him to do so because that would be unfitting. Anselm adds text upon text of Scripture to support this view as he explains that Christ was utterly free in his actions and was thereby killed neither because the Father compelled him, nor because he was helpless before his accusers. Placing this reference[81] in the middle of his contemplation of salvation accomplished, Anselm adds weight to the reader's amazement at the wonder of salvation applied. How much greater is God's redemption in the light of the absence of contingency?

The effect of these reverberations of theology demonstrates again how Anselm is attempting to redress the loss of beauty and order in creation. The eschatology emphasizes the eternal presence of Christ both in the heights of glory and the depths of humanity. The distance between the two has been narrowed, obliterated in fact, by the inauguration of Christ's salvation. Granted, that salvation has yet to be perfected in the eschaton, and is in that sense not yet complete, but Anselm is driving his readers towards that final day with relentless effort as he spurs them on to seek earnestly after that presence which they will one day know without mediation. With respect to the atonement, the connection with the *Cur Deus Homo* almost speaks for itself. The voluntary death of Christ is the only fitting means whereby the dishonour paid to God and distortion of the original beauty of God's creation could be restored. The nature of God as outlined in the *Proslogion* and the nature of humanity as outlined in the *Cur Deus Homo* and most vividly in the *Prayers* demands the free will of a Saviour who, in death, could restore life and loss.

Form and Content: Sustaining the Symmetry

The theology of the *Prayers*, however, does not end here. There are two more prayers that are placed at the beginning of the collection, and for good reason. The first is the 'Prayer before receiving the body and blood of Christ' and the second is the 'Prayer to the holy cross'. The first of these is particularly interesting because, in conjunction with the first two (prayers to God and to Christ), it sets out Anselm's belief of the source of his salvation. In the prayer to God, the Father is entreated for forgiveness and mercy.[82] In the prayer to Christ, the Son is clearly identified as the sole means of salvation.[83] In this third prayer before participating in the Mass the reader's attention is directed primarily to the death of the Son, but in connection with the 'Father's plan' and the 'working of the Holy Spirit'.[84] Each person of the Trinity has a part to play in salvation.[85] Anselm again affirms Christ's free will in death,[86] stresses the necessity of salvation in the light of the sinfulness of humanity, and ends with a number of quotations and allusions to Scripture. In many ways this prayer is a précis of the first two. It does not seem to expand anything presented in those prayers nor indeed to introduce new material. And yet, it is imperative that we recognize the obvious: Jesus is Anselm's Saviour. The reason we must stress this point is that as we move on to examine his prayers to saints we must take great care not to assume that Anselm believes his salvation to derive, in any way, from those people.

The second of the two prayers mentioned above, the prayer to the cross, is more interesting. Here we have what appears to be a transitional prayer. On the one hand it is a prayer about the salvation Christ achieved on the cross, while on the other hand it seems to venerate the cross itself. How ought we to understand the opening words, 'Sancta crux, per quam nobis ad memoriam crux illa reducitur'?[87] Benedicta Ward has maintained that 'this prayer is in the liturgical tradition and very far from idolatry.'[88] She contends that Anselm is using the cross as a sign or symbol through which to view and appreciate Christ's work. This prayer is, she says, closely related to the *Cur Deus Homo* because it honours the cross in a way that denies it the shame unbelievers would heap on it.[89] In the *Cur Deus Homo*, Boso begins his line of questioning by stating that the Christian doctrine of God is derided by unbelievers because it belittles his very nature. Among the specific difficulties, Christ's crucifixion, indeed the whole passion narrative, is highlighted. Anselm addressed this problem in the *Cur Deus Homo* in a theological manner, but in the *Prayers* we see the same problem addressed in a very different manner. The tight arguments of logic and reason are temporarily set aside and Anselm concentrates on the instrument which, ironically, became the means of glory.

Although it is certainly the case that this prayer does not engage in the same kind of indagation as the *Cur Deus Homo*, they are not as far apart as one might first assume. Anselm says in his prayer that

> They chose you that they might carry out their evil deeds;
> he chose you that he might fulfil the work of his goodness.
> They that by you they might hand over the righteous to death;
> he that through you he might save sinners from death.
> They that they might kill life;
> he that he might destroy death.
> They that they might condemn the Saviour;
> he that he might save the condemned.
> They that they might bring death to the living;
> he to bring life to the dead.
> They acted foolishly and cruelly;
> he wisely and mercifully.[90]

In this passage there is a remarkable resonance with the *Cur Deus Homo*. In the *Cur Deus Homo*, as we will see, there is a tremendous emphasis on beauty, especially as manifest in order and pattern. Here, we see the same emphasis. With stunning insight Anselm reflects the irony of the crucifixion. That which was intended for evil and destruction became the very means of good and restoration. That which was chaotic and distorted became ordered and beautiful. In all of this the pattern of God's plan of redemption is powerfully portrayed. Anselm reflects this resplendent rhetoric in the next stanza where he says that

> By you the world is renewed and made beautiful with truth,
> governed by the light of righteousness.
> By you sinful humanity is justified,
> the condemned are saved,
> the servants of sin and hell are set free,
> the dead are raised to life.
> By you the blessed city in heaven is restored and made perfect.[91]

Once again Anselm demonstrates his awareness of the order and pattern that is being restored through Christ. The beauty and appeal of his prose is not intended simply as a memory aid, nor just to channel the reader's mind to the divine, but to render the restoration of creation in such a way that even his writing mimics that beauty of truth as it imposes its own order and pattern. And in so far as Anselm achieves this goal, the reader too is caught up into that beatific vision and is incorporated into the recreation of redemption wrought by Christ.

But as close as this prayer is to the *Cur Deus Homo* there remains the question of its potentially idolatrous perspective. By personifying the cross in his prayer is it accurate to charge Anselm with glorifying the object above God? As mentioned above, Ward denies this claim. In her estimation the cross is merely a symbol of redemption and is thereby venerated only in that capacity. To support this supposition Ward refers to the resonances Anselm's prayer has with 'the introit for the feast of the Holy Cross' as well as with parts of the liturgy used on Maundy Thursday, not to mention its connection with the Byzantine *Crucem Tuam* which is also used 'in the Western Veneration of the Cross'.[92] Furthermore, these liturgical traditions employ parts of Scripture which Anselm could arguably be following. In Galatians 6:14, for example, Paul declares that he boasts in nothing except the 'cross of our Lord Jesus Christ'. In Philippians 3:18, Paul describes those who continue in unbelief as enemies 'of the cross of Christ'. At least with respect to the biblical and liturgical data Anselm appears to be well within the bounds of accepted practice.

Greater force can, moreover, be added to Anselm's case if we return to the above considerations. We noted that some of Anselm's words personify the cross, but to what end? In both quotations Anselm's attention is not on the power of the cross, nor the glory of the cross, but on the cross as the instrument which was transformed by Christ. In the first quotation the cross is the passive recipient in a scenario which depicts the struggle between Christ and his assailants. There we saw how Christ refashioned that which was twisted for his own glorious purposes. The focus is on the activity of Christ, not the veneration of the cross. Similarly, the second quotation echoes the first not as a chorus of praise to the cross, but in the marvel of the irony of what Christ was able to achieve. In fact, the rest of that stanza turns the reader's attention to God the Father and God the Son. The beauty of the language and the beauty of the content coalesce to converge on the work of Christ accomplished on the cross. The final stanza bears this out:

> Sit itaque per te et in te gloria mea, sit per te et in te vera spes mea. Per te peccata mea deleantur, per te anima mea a vita veteri mortificetur, et in novam vitam iustitiae resuscitetur. Fac, obsecro, fac ut, sicut me in baptismo mundasti a peccatis, in quibus fui conceptus et natus, ita me remundes ab eis quae contraxi, postquam sum renatus, ut per te ad ea bona perveniam ad quae homo est creatus, praestante eodem Domino nostro Iesu Christo, qui sit benedictus in saecula. Amen.[93]

The opening lines appear to have the cross in view yet again, but when we arrive at the end of the stanza we discover that all that Anselm has desired and all that he describes in relation to the achievement of salvation is ascribed to 'our Lord Jesus Christ' on account of his superiority.

The opening four prayers – to God, Christ, the cross and before receiving the body and blood of Christ – set the stage for what is to come. The reader has been attuned to the beauty of salvation, in its many facets, through Anselm's sculptured presentation of its harmony and symmetry. Furthermore, he has reinforced this emphasis by incorporating crucial aspects of Christian doctrine including the sinfulness of humanity, Christ as the only means of salvation, and the tension between what has already been achieved in the life of the believer and what has yet to be completed. The significance of recognizing these characteristics in Anselm's prayers will become all the more apparent as we turn to consider his prayers to saints.

Prayer Within the Community of Saints

Why Anselm should write a number of prayers to saints has, to some extent, already been answered in the first half of this chapter. We noted there that Christians in the Middle Ages understood themselves to be part of a community which included the living and the dead. In Brown's discussion of the *Book of Cerne* we saw that Carolingian prayers were often written to saints because it was believed that a saint could identify with a particular part of a person's life.[94] If, for example, someone felt that they had betrayed a friend or, more seriously, God, they would likely pray to St Peter since he could readily identify with that experience. But the identification could also work the other way. One of the unique characteristics of Anselm's prayers is that he would take incidents from a saint's life and apply them to a sinner.[95] In this way Anselm was hoping to awaken in the reader an awareness of his sin that he had not known before.[96] The prayer to St Peter is instructive:

> See now, the sickly sheep, lies groaning at the shepherd's feet; he comes before the Lord of the shepherd and the sheep. The runaway returns and asks forgiveness for his errors and disobedience. He shows to the good and healing shepherd the gashes of wounds, and the bites of wolves, which he ran into when he strayed, and the neglected sore places that he has had for a long time. He begs him to have mercy while there is still life in him, and he prays more by showing his need to the merciful shepherd than by any beseeching. Peter, good shepherd, do not be difficult to access; do not turn away your merciful eyes.[97]

This time, instead of playing on Peter's dereliction, Anselm has John 21:15ff in mind where Jesus reinstates Peter as a shepherd of the sheep, a leader in the church. Using this imagery, Anselm encourages the reader to identify with the renegade or prodigal sheep. Regardless of how close the reader may think he has been to God, Anselm moves him to realize that for all his efforts he has been tainted, disfigured even, by the world (bitten by wolves). The negative effects of worldly contamination have, whether the reader is aware of it or not, brought him to the brink of death ('while there is still life'), and thus requires hospice from the shepherd of God's flock for he can turn to the Great Shepherd, 'the Lord of the shepherd and the sheep' and plead, in a special and intimate way, for the needs of the sinner.

There is, of course, a tension here. Is Peter so far above Anselm and his readers that their prayers will be lost in the cavernous space between saint and sinner? Anselm pleads, after all, that 'if the cry of my trouble does not come up as far as you, let the care of your goodness come down as far as me!'[98] But such a plea does not seem to bear the weight required to tip the scales in favour of judging the saints out of earshot when we recall that Anselm spends so much time and care addressing the saints. Would Anselm pray to someone he did not believe could hear? It is more likely that Anselm has used hyperbole to stress the fittingness of the one to whom he is praying since he is keenly aware that he was praying to a man who himself was the recipient of mercy and could thereby extend that mercy to him. He writes, 'See, here is a soul needing mercy, and here is the merciful apostle Peter before the God of mercy, who had mercy upon the apostle Peter and taught him what to do and gave him power to do it.'[99] Furthermore, Anselm is not afraid to point out Peter's shortcomings as a kind of reminder of their mutual indigence before God. He writes boldly that while the sinner 'may have strayed', 'at least it is not he who has denied his Lord and Shepherd.'[100] There can be no question that although Anselm respects Peter, as he does the other saints, he never venerates him beyond his own humanity. The saints are certainly righteous people, but they are righteous not because of anything within themselves, but because of the grace of God. On account of this, Anselm and Peter stand together at the feet of the Great Shepherd.[101]

If we look at the penultimate prayer in Anselm's collection, the Prayer for Friends, we may yet gain a better understanding of how Anselm conceives of the relation between sinner and saint. In the first place, it is interesting that Anselm should write a prayer for friends because the mere act of doing so indicates his belief that Christians can act as intercessors for one another. In fact, his Prayer for Enemies shows that this intercessory aspect of the Christian life extends to include everyone in the orbit of one's experience. But, more specifically, in the fourth stanza of Anselm's Prayer for Friends, he laments his own need for an intercessor despite God's command to intercede for others:

> I anxiously seek intercessors on my own behalf, how then shall I be so bold as to intercede for others? What shall I do, Lord God, what shall I do? You command me to pray for them and my love prompts me to do so, but my conscience cries out against me, saying that I should be concerned about my own sins, so that I tremble to speak for others.[102]

But speak for others Anselm does:

> Shall I then leave off from doing what you command because I have done what you have forbidden? No, rather since I have presumed so greatly in what is forbidden, all the more will I embrace what is commanded. So perhaps obedience may heal presumption, and charity may cover the multitude of my sins.[103]

This exhibits the importance Anselm placed on intercession. But more than that, it is a vivid display of the medieval model of reality. We have already seen, and will see again, how important was the community of saints. When we combine Anselm's avid interest in the role of saints in heaven with his clear concern for the role of Christians on earth, and consider that both categories of believers are bound up in Christ, we are again forced to grapple with a world-view which encompasses more than just the individual in relation to God. C.S. Lewis was surely accurate to posit that living in such a universe was like being 'conducted through an immense cathedral'.[104] As in a cathedral there is communication between communicants, so the medieval world-view interpreted all creation as continually in contact and interaction. As in a cathedral every participant has a place to occupy and a purpose to fulfil, so the medieval Christian lived and prayed in the knowledge that his place and purpose related to more than met the eye. As with spiritual books, so with spiritual prayers: the 'order of Grace' is paramount.[105] There is no grace which does not establish order, and there is no order without the presence of grace. As we have seen, the distortions brought by sin necessitate, for Anselm, the imposition of the order of grace. It is that imposition with which Anselm confronts his readers and, in so doing, seeks not merely to raise their minds to God, nor lower their gaze to humanity, but supremely to enclose and assimilate them into the beatific vision where sinner and saint, the living and the dead, the human and the divine join to the glory of God and the perfection of the church. Truly, few constructions of reality 'have combined splendour, sobriety and coherence in the same degree'.[106]

In addition to the 'cohesion and dynamism'[107] that sainthood provides within the Christian tradition, we should not neglect the influence of hagiography on Anselm's *Prayers*. There is a remarkable agreement among scholars of this genre of literature that while saints 'commanded reverence, honor, respect, and devotion' their main purpose in the community of believers was to 'glorify God'.[108] Rosemary Woolf adds that no matter how great the saint, there remains an 'utter reliance on God's power'.[109] In fact, 'the genius of Late Antique men lay in their ability to map out, to localize and render magnificently palpable by every device of art, ceremonial, religious practice and literature those few, clearly delineated points on which the visible and invisible worlds met on earth.'[110] One of those points was the interaction between saint and sinner, for 'in a world so sternly organized around sin and justice, *patrocinium* and *amicitia* provided a much needed language of amnesty.'[111]

Here again we have cause to reflect on the influence of eschatology on medieval piety. The life of a coenobite or a devout lay person is defined by their desire and drive to reconcile the continuing presence of sin with the past accomplishment of atonement in the light of the future permanence of grace. In Anselm's *Prayers* this takes the form of a constant accent on compunction contrasted with the sure achievement of redemption in the presence of believers who have attained a place at the throne of grace. In his prayer to Peter, Anselm repeats in vivid description the state of his sinful soul. He portrays his peccancy as 'full grown ulcers, open wounds, putrid decay'.[112] He envisions his iniquity as binding him with chains, weighing him down with a burden; his soul as 'stinking and dirty with misdeeds, torn by the wounds of devils, festering and filthy with the ulcers of crimes'.[113] And yet, he is equally able to declare that Peter ought to recognize 'a face washed and made white at the font of Christ' for he is one who 'confesses the name of Christ'.[114] Surely Evans is right to conclude that Anselm 'was conscious in his daily life of the complexities of living out the process of sanctification, and of its interpenetration with the absoluteness of justification'.[115]

When we draw all of the above discussion together we discover three things about the place and importance of saints in Anselm's *Prayers*. First, we find that the believer is encouraged to identify with the saints because they too are human and they too have experienced the temptations and shortcomings associated with imperfection. Second, our discussion has revealed that Anselm believed that his prayers to saints and his desire that they should pray on his behalf follows directly from the scriptural command that believers should pray for one another. This brings us to our third observation, that the incredibly vivid sense Anselm had of the community of believers (an understanding that transcended death) allowed him to balance, without contradiction, his prayers to saints with passages such as Acts 4:12.[116] One of the characteristics of Anselm's *Prayers* that comes through clearly, as mentioned before, is the firm belief that God is the sole provider of grace and salvation. The saints may be spiritual giants, but only in comparison to physical sinners. The saints may possess unimaginable amounts of righteousness, but the source of that righteousness is God alone. There is in these prayers an abundance of aesthetic considerations firmly rooted in a particular understanding of the relationship between divine and human. Whenever Anselm prays, he appeals to the beauty grace recreates, to the harmony in creation between saint and sinner. Anselm's *Prayers* are not just good examples of medieval monastic piety, but expressions of theological depth laden with divine truth. Now, as many examples as there are to prove this point, the greatest test of Anselm's resolve in this matter comes in his three prayers to Mary.

Testing the Limits with Marian Devotion

The three prayers Anselm wrote to the Virgin Mary are an excellent specimen of the development of Anselm's thought and writing. Based on the information we have,[117] Anselm was asked to write a prayer to Mary by one of the monks at Bec. Reluctant to fulfil this request, Anselm hesitated but eventually decided to give in and write a prayer to Mary. After he wrote the prayer he was dissatisfied with it so he put pen to paper again in a second effort. This too failed to please him so he tried once more, this time with success. R.W. Southern comments that the manuscript evidence left to us shows that the progression of thought and writing was not quite so simple. Anselm wrote a number of drafts, which do not appear in the collection, before he finally arrived at what he considered to be the final form.[118]

What strikes the reader of these three prayers is that they are the only ones which do not identify the saint with the sinner. Southern argues that the reason for this is because there was no biblical precedent. There is very little information given about Mary. The Bible is rife with information about so many of the other saints: their conversations, their beliefs, their faith, their shortcomings, and so on; but Mary remains an almost background figure who cannot easily be assigned a title or designation because the Bible does not give her any.[119] Furthermore, Anselm had to be careful about what he wrote since this was the period when the doctrine of the Immaculate Conception was being formed, and Anselm gives no evidence of agreeing with this doctrine.[120] It is no wonder, therefore, that Anselm was reluctant to write a prayer to Mary.[121]

Anselm's first prayer to Mary is a well-organized prayer that displays an obvious structure. There are five stanzas and they alternate between Mary and compunction. The first, third and fifth stanzas concentrate on Mary, her attributes, and her fittingness as an intercessor. The second and fourth stanzas focus on the individual's sin and his need for help and salvation. The prayer begins much as one would expect. Mary is addressed as holy, holier, in fact, than all the other saints, but less holy than God.[122] Mary is praised for her virginity, fertility and, ultimately, for bearing the Saviour.[123] After these designations and affirmations Anselm begins to make statements that sound somewhat unorthodox. He calls Mary the 'mother of life', the 'mother of salvation' and a 'temple of piety and mercy'.[124] He asks Mary to heal him[125] and to cure his sinful soul.[126] He constantly remarks how great is the depth and dirtiness of his sin in the light of Mary's shining holiness.[127] Statements like these are not easily dismissed nor should they be. But the final clause in this prayer is intriguing because it makes abundantly clear from where Anselm believes the power to accomplish all he has asked comes. He concludes by asking Mary to heal his soul[128] 'per virtutem benedicti fructus ventris tui, qui sedet in dextera omnipotentis Patris sui, superlaudabilis et supergloriosus in saecula, Amen'.[129]

Anselm rests his hope for all that he has asked on the one Mary bore: the Saviour of the world, the God of creation.[130] It is through Christ that Mary has the power and purity that she enjoys. In the end, although Mary is the chief of saints, second only to God, she is still second to God. When we read, therefore, Anselm's comments that Mary is the 'mother of life' and 'mother of salvation' and a 'temple of piety and mercy' we ought to read them in the light of the opening and closing statements that unequivocally assign Mary a place with the saints, not with God. She is the 'mother of salvation' because, as Anselm says a few lines earlier, she gave birth to the author of salvation.[131] Similarly, she is the 'mother of life' because she gave birth to the author of life. She is a 'temple of piety and mercy' because her body housed the God who is piety and mercy. There is certainly a tight connection between Mary and Jesus, and that connection forces Anselm to say some things that may make some modern readers feel uncomfortable, but it is that connection on which Anselm continued to build in the second and third prayers.

In Anselm's second prayer to Mary there are, at a number of points, clear indications that he thinks of Mary and Jesus in familial terms.[132] There is a natural bond, an umbilical connection between them. For this reason Anselm is constantly associating the one with the other with respect to feelings or emotions as well as, to some degree, abilities. Anselm writes, for instance, that 'by your glorious child-bearing you have brought salvation to all fruitfulness'.[133] There is a definite sense that Anselm is including Mary in the process of God's salvific purposes, but only as the instrument through which the Saviour of the world is brought. Mary is not the means of salvation, but salvation comes 'by' her. A little further on Anselm writes how Mary can 'more easily gain pardon for the accused by her intercession' because she was the one 'who gave milk to him who justly punishes or mercifully pardons all and each one'.[134] Again, Anselm has drawn on the familial connection as constitutive of Mary's special status before God.

On the basis of this connection Anselm is also able to say that he is 'the sinner who belongs to you both'.[135] We must be careful here not to think that this means that Mary is a co-redemptrix; that would impose anachronistic developments on a passage which, although leaning in that direction, is a long way from advocating that stance. After all, Anselm's work on the virgin birth makes it clear that he did not accept the doctrine of the Immaculate Conception. From any perspective Mary stood as one worthy of honour, but Anselm does not claim that she was born without sin. The closest Anselm comes to declaring Mary pure is in the *De Conceptione Virginali* in which he argues that she was pure at the time of Christ's birth, but that her purity was due to her faith (which cleanses from sin) and was still not on a par with the manner in which God is sinless.[136] And yet, there remains an uncomfortable link between Mary and Jesus. Anselm goes on to say that 'when I have sinned against the son, I have alienated the mother, nor can I offend the mother without hurting the son.'[137]

At this point we must admit that there are times when Anselm's fervency for evoking excitement overtakes him and his passions begin to possess him. The result is that he cries out to both mother and Son as though they were equal:

> The accused is carried from one to the other and throws himself between the good son and the good mother. Dear Lord, spare the servant of your mother; dear Lady, spare the servant of your son. Good son, make your servant's peace with your mother; good mother, reconcile your son to your servant ... I love the truth I confess about you [pl.], and I beg for the goodness which I hope for from you [pl.].[138]

Despite Anselm's escaping emotions at this point and others, we ought not to allow ourselves to think that this sort of language surrounding Mary is indicative of Anselm's Marian theology.[139]

It is so often the case throughout these prayers to Mary that Anselm is keen to repeat the fact that as great as Mary is, the Triune God is still above her. At this point we must either posit that Anselm was self-contradictory within the framework of a few prayers and, at times, a few stanzas, or that he was so eager to engage in hyperbole that he allowed himself to get carried away. On consideration it seems that the best way to reconcile Anselm's ecstatic expressions of praise to Mary with his insistence on her humanity is to adopt the latter approach. I take this approach because it seems the best way to resolve an obvious tension in Anselm's *Prayers* with respect to their place in his wider corpus. Consequently, I do not believe lines such as 'even the fallen angels are restored to their place'[140] are intended to be taken as strict doctrinal statements. In this particular case we can point to the *Cur Deus Homo* which vehemently opposes any but Christ as the one who is able to restore the marred perfection, beauty and order of creation.[141] Moreover, when we compare the content of the third prayer we read Anselm's plea: 'Mary, I beg you, by the grace through which the Lord is with you and you willed to be with him, let your mercy be with me.'[142]

Here we see that while Anselm is addressing Mary, his plea is grounded in the grace that Mary has first received from the Lord. Perhaps what makes it difficult for readers of these prayers to maintain the distinction between mother and Son is, besides the occasional overwrought hyperbole, the fact that a parent is so often considered superior to the child. That which a child has it has learned or inherited from its parents. That which a child has become is often the result of parental influence. This point may be lost on modern readers for whom 'family' means something different, but in the medieval context what could be predicated of the child could often, but not always, be predicated of the parent. St Augustine, in the most famous example, credits his mother's spirituality and godly perseverance in prayer as the reason for his salvation and spiritual development and maturity.[143] In a time when the bond between parent and child was especially close (how often did the child choose a different profession to his father during this period?) assigning an inherent righteousness to Mary would almost seem necessary. Still, Anselm makes many attempts to avoid this way of thinking. He makes it clear that while 'nothing equals Mary, nothing but God is greater than Mary. God gave his own Son, who alone from his heart was born equal to him, loved as he loves himself, to Mary, and of Mary was then born a Son not another but the same one.'[144]

The essence of the incarnation is not that Jesus adopted Mary's genes and was helplessly abandoned to inherit her qualities and characteristics, but that Jesus, as the second member of the Trinity, was God and, despite being born of a woman and taking on humanity in that way, received his righteousness and deity from the Father.[145] It is in the light of this that we can now carry on to read the rest of the above quote where Anselm concludes that 'one might be the Son of God and of Mary'.[146] The idea here is one of progeny, not one of deified humanity. For Anselm then says that

> All nature is created by God and God is born of Mary.
> God created all things, and Mary gave birth to God.
> God who made all things made himself of Mary,
> and thus he refashioned everything he had made.
> He who was able to make all things out of nothing refused to remake it by force,
> but first became the Son of Mary.
> So God is the Father of all created things,
> and Mary is the mother of all re-created things.
> God is the Father of all that is established,
> and Mary is the mother of all that is re-established.
> For God gave birth to him by whom all things were made
> and Mary brought forth him by whom all are saved.

God brought forth him without whom nothing is,
Mary bore him without whom nothing is good.
O truly, the Lord is with you to whom the Lord gave himself,
that all nature in you might be in him.[147]

What God created sin destroyed. What sin destroyed God desired to recreate. However, for reasons that would not be provided until he penned the *Cur Deus Homo*, Anselm tells us that God refused to recreate by simple fiat, and thus by force. Instead, he chose to restore humanity through humanity, in the form of his incarnate Son.[148] What is clear in this magnificent passage is that as integral to the institution of the incarnation as Mary is, she is still an instrument. True, she is honoured because of her place in the economy of redemption, and for this reason Anselm seems comfortable placing her near the apex of a divine progeny which includes all those who believe,[149] but Anselm is careful not to raise her to the rarified heights of Trinitarian activity. It is not what Mary does that captivates Anselm, so much as how she is used and who she produces.

But it is not enough simply to note the struggle and tension in Anselm's writing between honouring the human without transforming it into the divine. These prayers to Mary, like the rest, take their place in the wider body of Anselmian literature. We have seen so far, and we will see again, how Anselm was preoccupied with aesthetics; aesthetics, that is, as the presentation of truth and reality in the beauty of their fittingness, order and harmony. The passage from Anselm's third prayer to Mary that we have just examined is a good case in point. There we saw the meticulous presentation of delicate aspects of eternal truth presented to the reader in a way that reflects and mimics the symmetry and harmony of that truth. If we look, for instance, at the statement, 'omnis natura a Deo est creata, et Deus ex Maria est natus'[150] we can perceive a pattern. The second clause is a mirror image of the first, but not simply so, for the first two elements are inverted so as to draw attention to the subject. In other words, in the first clause the emphasis is on the creation as created by God; whereas, in the second clause, the emphasis is on God as born (created) of the creation. Ward's translation captures this sense well when she translates it in a chiastic fashion:

> A   All nature
>   B   is created
>   C   by God
> C_1 God
> B_1 is born
> A$_1$ of Mary

This subject/object inversion is repeated three times and impresses the beauty of the pattern of God's plan of salvation not only by distilling the facts of Scripture, but by organizing them in such a way that the visual and auditory components enhance the reader's appreciation of the order and perfection of redemption. This can also be seen in the second half of the passage when Anselm uses repetition and comparison to show the development and implementation of God's saving purposes.

The examples could be multiplied, but to avoid being redundant we must bring our discussion of this particular aspect of Anselm's theology to a close. All of Anselm's prayers exhibit, to one degree or another, a deep and well-developed understanding of theological issues, and a penchant to depict that knowledge in a way which recreates for meditative readers the aesthetic atmosphere in which mercy is mediated, grace is given, forgiveness is conferred, the sinner is saved, the judge becomes justifier, and the saints stand together with the suppliant as their compunction convicts their hearts, and as their penitence is proffered with pleas. There can be no doubt that the ideas incorporated in these prayers are not merely seeds, but budding saplings which are well rooted in the soil of Scripture, monastic contemplation, and patristic precepts. It is, however, not the soil to which we ought to direct our attention, but to the fruit it nourishes. For that fruit displays for our pleasure the beauty of eternal truths which, Anselm prayed, would become the morsels of the meditator's diet.

Notes

1   I have taken the second half of this title from T.S. Eliot's *A Song for Simeon* in *T.S. Eliot: Selected Poems* (1954), London: Faber & Faber. Although written for a different man in a different place and a different time, much of this poem reflects the life and longings of St Anselm himself. I particularly like the end of the poem where Simeon is made to say, 'Not for me the martyrdom, the ecstasy of thought and prayer, Not for me the ultimate vision'; none the less, 'Let thy servant depart, Having seen thy salvation.' This captures marvellously Anselm's own desire which we see so vividly in his *Prayers and Meditations*, the *Proslogion*, the *Monologion*, and in his theological treatises where he breaks out in prayer and thanksgiving. As we shall see in due course, every aspect of Anselm's thinking and theology was infused with aesthetic appreciation. Even the eschatological tension between the present experience of salvation and the future expectation of beatific glory, the attainment of satisfaction for the taste of atoning forgiveness in spite of the effulgence of God's glory known but not owned on this side of the resurrection, is described in aesthetic categories that express the passionate hope and ardent desire to know God on earth as he is in heaven.

2   It is difficult to date any of Anselm's works with certainty because we are often given no clues. The earliest evidence we have of him writing prayers for other people is a letter he wrote in 1071 (Ep. 10), but whether or not this marks the beginning of his literary career is not certain. It does seem likely considering the care Anselm took to ensure the preservation of his works and letters for his spiritual progeny, but it could also be possible that whatever Anselm did write prior to 1071 (with the exception of the *De Grammatico*) was considered unworthy for publication.

3   For a discussion on the dating of Anselm's works cf. R.W. Southern (1963), *St Anselm and his Biographer*, Cambridge: Cambridge University Press, pp. 34–42.

4   I have included the *Monologion* and the *Proslogion* along with the *Prayers and Meditations* not only because they were most likely written during the same fruitful period at Bec, but also because they too are couched in the language of prayer. In the case

of the *Proslogion* in particular the entire work is better understood as a prayer than as a theological treatise despite its dense content.

5 This is why in the *Proslogion*, which we will have the pleasure of examining more closely in a later chapter, Anselm is so adamant that if the Fool would only pay attention to the proper definition of who God is, he would have the obscurity of ignorance removed.

6 G.R. Evans (1991), *The Language and Logic of the Bible*, Cambridge: Cambridge University Press, p. 17.

7 Benedicta Ward (1973), *The Prayers and Meditations of St Anselm with the* Proslogion, London: Penguin Books, p. 19. Unless otherwise noted I will take all translations of Anselm's prayers and his meditations from this translation.

8 Ward, *Prayers*, p. 57.

9 Ward, *Prayers*, p. 57.

10 Ward, *Prayers*, p. 44.

11 We see this, for instance, in Hilary of Poitiers' *De Trinitate* 1.38 (*Nicene and Post-Nicene Fathers*, series 2, vol. 9), the *Rule* of St Benedict which is a transmission of Cassian's teaching on prayer (cf. C. Butler (1961), *Benedictine Monachism*, Cambridge: Cambridge University Press, pp. 61–7), and most especially throughout Augustine's *Confessions* (eg. 1.1).

12 Eadmer (1972), *Vita Anselmi*, trans. R.W. Southern, Oxford: Clarendon Press, p. 29, note 1 (hereafter cited as *VA*); cf. also D.P. Henry (1974), *Commentary on the* De Grammatico, Boston: D. Reidel Co. and his *The De Grammatico of St. Anselm*, Notre Dame: University of Notre Dame Press, 1964, as well as G.R. Evans (1989), *Anselm*, London: Geoffrey Chapman.

13 *VA*, p. 142.

14 *De Grammatico*, 21, 4.82 (S.1.168.3).

15 *Proslogion*, 17 (S.1.113.6–7).

16 *Proslogion*, 26 (S.1.120.23 ff).

17 Eia nunc homuncio, fuge paululum occupationes tuas, absconde te modicum a tumultuosis cogitationibus tuis. Abjice nunc onerosas curas, et postpone laboriosas distensiones tuas. Vaca aliquantulum Deo, et requiesce aliquantulum in eo. Intra in cubiculum (Matt. 6:6) mentis tuae; exclude omnia praeter Deum, et quae te juvent ad quaerendum eum, et, clauso ostio, quaere eum. Dic nunc, totum cor meum, dic nunc Deo: Quaero vultum tuum; vultum tuum, Domine, requiro (Ps. 26:8). *Proslogion*, 1 (S.1.97.4–10), my translation.

18 C.S. Lewis (1964), *The Discarded Image*, Cambridge: Cambridge University Press, p. 222.

19 *De Incarnatione Verbi*, 1 (S.2.9.2).

20 *De Incarnatione Verbi*, 1 (S.2.9.3–4).

21 *De Incarnatione Verbi*, 1 (S.2.10.1–4).

22 *De Incarnatione Verbi*, 1 (S.2.9.14 ff).

23 *The Rule of St Benedict* (1998), ed. Timothy Fry. Collegeville, MN: Vintage Spiritual Classics, chap. 18.

24 *Rule*, chap. 9.

25 Jean Leclercq (1974), *The Love of Learning and the Desire for God*, London: SPCK, p. 90.

26 Ward, *Prayers*, p. 43.

27 Leclercq, *Love*, p. 21.

28 Lewis, p. 5; cf. also the opposite opinion in Jacques Le Goff (1993), *Intellectuals in the Middle Ages*, Oxford: Blackwell, p. 8.

29 S.3.3.9–12.

30 Mary Carruthers (1998), *The Craft of Thought*, Cambridge: Cambridge University Press, p. 103.

31 S.3.5.3.

32   S.3.5.3–4.
33   *Rule*, p. 5.
34   Cf. *Rule*, chap. 9 and p. xxiii.
35   This difficult area has been addressed by Geneviève Nortier in her work, *Les Bibliothèques Médiévales des Abbayes Benedictines de Normandie*, Paris: P. Lethiesseux (1971), as part of the series, *Bibliothèque d'Histoire et d'Archéologie Chrétiennes*, esp. pp. 34–60.
36   D.M. Hope (1978), 'The Liturgical Books', in Jones, Cheslyn et al. (eds), *The Study of Liturgy*, London: SPCK, p. 66.
37   Ward, *Prayers*, p. 59.
38   Further study in this area may show a closer link between Anselm's prayers and earlier liturgical forms. Compare, for example, Wilmart's edition of the *Bobbio Missal* (London: Henry Bradshaw Society, 1917–24) where the Psalms are divided into brief sections and each section is followed by a short prayer. When we consider Anselm's exposure to the Psalms and his use of their language in his prayers one wonders if he has chosen to help develop an existing form.
39   There is a large body of literature surrounding surviving Anglo-Saxon and Carolingian liturgy and prayer books. Some of the more representative and detailed accounts, which cannot be discussed here, include, D.A. Bullough (1991), *Carolingian Renewal*, Manchester: Manchester University Press; Irenee Dalmais, Pierre Jounel and Aime Martimort (1983), *The Church at Prayer: The Liturgy and Time*, vol. 4, ed. Aime Martimort, trans. Matthew J. O'Connell, London: Geoffrey Chapman; F.W. Dillistone (1990), 'Liturgical Forms in Word and Act' in Jasper, David and R.C.D. Jasper (eds), *Language and the Worship of the Church*, London: Macmillan; John Harper (1991), *The Forms and Orders of Western Liturgy*, Oxford: Clarendon Press; John Harthan (1977), *Books of Hours*, London: Thames & Hudson; Rosamond McKitterick (1977), *The Frankish Church and the Carolingian Reforms: 784–895*, London: Royal Historical Society; J.T. McNeill and Helena M. Gamer (1990), *Medieval Handbooks of Penance*, New York: Columbia University Press.
40   Michelle Brown (1996), *The Book of Cerne*, Toronto: University of Toronto Press, p. 15.
41   Cf. Epp. 10 and 325 to Adelaide and Matilda.
42   Brown, *The Book of Cerne*, p. 136.
43   Brown, p. 148.
44   Evans, *Anselm*, p. 28.
45   Evans, p. 34.
46   Brown, *The Book of Cerne*, p. 157.
47   A.G. Herbert (1936), *Liturgy and Society*, London: Faber & Faber Ltd, p. 82.
48   D.M. Hope, 'The Medieval Western Rites', in *The Study of Liturgy*, op. cit., p. 225.
49   J. Leclercq (1986), 'Prayer and Contemplation: Western', in Bernard McGinn and John Meyendorff (eds), *Christian Spirituality: Origins to the Twelfth Century*, London: Routledge and Kegan Publishers, p. 421.
50   When this prayer was written is unknown. It first appears in the collection sent to Countess Matilda in 1104.
51   'Prayer to Christ' (S.3.6.4–9). My translation.
52   In a number of places in this chapter I will refer to stanzas in Anselm's prayers. Since Anselm did not write his prayers in poetic form this may seem a misnomer. I will argue, however, with Ward and Southern, that Anselm's prose possesses poetic qualities. Furthermore, Anselm himself divided each prayer into shorter sections. Considering, therefore, the rhetorical style and the use of divisions, it seemed to me not entirely mistaken to refer to these sections as stanzas. I should add, moreover, that I have translated some of the material in a manner more consistent with poetic form than prosaic form. I have done this to help emphasize the particular rhetorical devices employed.
53   Ward, *Prayers*, p. 93, lns 6–7.
54   Ward, *Prayers*, p. 60.

55 Cf. *Cur Deus Homo*, 1.13–1.15 (S.2.71.7–2.74.7).

56 (S.3.6.11).

57 1.15 (S.2.73.14–19).

58 Ward, *Prayers*, p. 57.

59 Carruthers, p. 104.

60 For all Southern's excitement over the *Prayers*, he maintains the distinction that 'the earliest prayers show as yet little sign of the exact and metaphysical mind which was soon to produce classics of Christian theology' while his later prayers (specifically those to Mary) do exhibit a small degree of the 'power of metaphysical analysis'. Even so, Southern claims, the only seeds we can perceive in the prayers of the later development of Anselm's 'theological system' are his 'intense horror of sin operating on a mind of exceptional power and precision' and the 'clarity of utterance' that runs 'through everything he wrote' (Southern, *St Anselm: A Portrait in a Landscape*, p. 106). While these two aspects of Anselm's writing are definitely part and parcel of all he wrote, I do not agree that the prayers fail to evince any serious signs of his 'exact and metaphysical mind'. As I have argued above, Anselm's prayers do engage the metaphysical in a way that none of his other works can. Everything that is beyond this carnal world is brought into the purview of the sinner. All that is spiritual is connected to the physical. There is a fine balance between the divine and the human that only an appreciation of the harmony that exists between the two can properly comprehend.

Thus, whether we look at Anselm's earlier prayers or his later prayers (and determining the difference between the two categories is a matter of some guesswork, especially when we consider that Anselm continued to edit and improve his works if he was not satisfied with them), we are confronted with a mind that is, from the beginning, ruminating on theological matters within an explicitly aesthetic framework. It is no wonder then that there is a high degree of correspondence between Anselm's prayers and his theological works. As for Southern's contention that the prayers show little sign of the exacting mind characteristic of Anselm's later treatises, his own analysis of the prayers is sufficient to gainsay that possibility. This is why I believe it is important to consider the impact and influence of the *De Grammatico*: it lays out the exacting and metaphysical groundwork that became the basis of the rest of Anselm's corpus.

61 *Proslogion*, 1 (S.1.98.16–25).

62 S.3.6.10–13.

63 S.3.7.19–20.

64 S.3.7.21, 22, 23, 25, 28.

65 'My Lord and my creator, you bear with me and nourish me – be my helper. I thirst for you, I hunger for you, I desire you, I sigh for you, I covet you', Ward, *Prayers*, p. 94 (S.3.7.29–30).

66 'So, as much as I can, though not as much as I ought, I am mindful of your passion, your buffeting, your scourging, your cross, your wounds, how you were slain for me, how prepared for burial and buried, and also I remember your glorious Resurrection and wonderful Ascension', Ward, *Prayers*, p. 95 (S.3.7.32–6).

67 Throughout this chapter the concept of compunction will return as it is an important and ubiquitous aspect of Anselm's prayers. And yet, as conspicuous an element as compunction is in the *Prayers*, it is all the more central in Anselm's first two meditations. In the first meditation, for example, Anselm writes in typical fashion, 'useless sinner, there is enough here to keep you continually mourning, there is enough here for you to be able to drink continual tears.' The paradox about this extreme form of self-effacement is that it is derived from a knowledge of God, and so emphasizes the separation between God and humanity, but is also the means by which Anselm expresses the need for reconciliation and, therefore, the reunion of God and humanity.

68 Benedicta Ward has, unfortunately, masked this in her otherwise very good translation, cf. *Prayers*, p. 95.

69 S.3.7.42–3.

70 S.3.7.43–4.
71 S.3.7.44–5.
72 S.3.7.45–3.8.46.
73 S.3.8.46–7.
74 S.3.8.50–55.
75 S.3.9.73–93.
76 Cf. *Proslogion*, 25–6 (S.1.118.12 ff).
77 S.3.9.96–7.
78 S.3.7.40.
79 We may note here that the deponent (*morior*) is used in Latin to express the middle voice, which, in this case, adds emphasis to the point that it was God himself who willed to die.
80 *Cur Deus Homo*, 1.8 and 1.9 (S.2.60.15–2.61.2 and 2.61.8–9).
81 It is particularly interesting that Anselm used the same adverb-verb combination in his prayer as he did in the *Cur Deus Homo*, 1.9 (S.2.61.4).
82 S.3.5.3–4.
83 S.3.6.4.
84 S.3.10.3.
85 Although no one has commented on the matter to date, it is interesting that Anselm does not offer a prayer to the Holy Spirit. It could, perhaps, be argued that there is no example of this practice in the Bible, and therefore no precedent for Anselm to follow. There is, however, no precedent in the Bible for praying to saints. While it is true that there is a strong tradition in the church of praying to saints, even in Anselm's time, this raises the interesting question of how forms of prayer could develop that did not conform to the examples and precedents set in Scripture. How is it possible, for instance, for the range of possible recipients of prayer to increase without that range including the Holy Spirit? This also raises, though tangentially, the question of why Anselm never wrote about the Trinity. He certainly believed in the Trinity (*Proslogion*, 26 – S.1.122.1–2), but he rarely addresses its nature. This may reflect a lack of interest in the period on specifically Trinitarian matters or could indicate that Anselm believed that Augustine had dealt sufficiently with the matter, or both.
86 S.3.10.4. The construction Anselm uses in this prayer is different from the construction used in the *Cur Deus Homo* and the prayer to Christ. In the latter two places Anselm used the deponent verb 'morior', but in this prayer he uses the noun 'mors'. This may seem an insignificant difference, but it lends support to the contention that in the prayer to Christ Anselm was consciously linking his thoughts to the *Cur Deus Homo*, whereas in this rather mundane prayer he is simply restating what has already been said.
87 S.3.11.3 – 'Holy cross, which calls to mind *the* cross' (italics mine).
88 Ward, *Prayers*, p. 32.
89 S.2.50.16–22, 24–8.
90 S.3.11.15–21.
91 S.3.12.27–30.
92 Ward, *Prayers*, p. 32.
93 'So let my glory be through you and in you; let my true hope be through you and in you. By you my sins are wiped out, by you my soul is dead to its old life and lives to the new life of righteousness. I beseech you, wash me by baptism from the sins in which I was conceived and born, and cleanse me again from those that I committed after I was reborn, so that by you I may come to those good things for which man was created, by the might of the same Jesus Christ our Lord who is blessed for ever and ever. Amen.' Ward, *Prayers*, p. 105 (S.3.12.49–56).
94 Cf. also Pierre Delooz (1983), 'Towards a sociological study of canonized sainthood', in Stephen Watson (ed.), *Saints and their Cults*, Cambridge: Cambridge University Press, p. 204.
95 R.W. Southern, *St Anselm: A Portrait in a Landscape*, Cambridge: Cambridge University Press, p. 102.

96 We find a similar pattern in Anselm's second meditation. There, Anselm considers 'virginity unhappily lost'. There has been some discussion over what Anselm meant. Dr Pusey, for instance, has argued that Anselm was speaking of adultery in a purely spiritual sense (cf. Pusey (1856), *Meditations and Prayers to the Holy Trinity and our Lord Jesus Christ by St Anselm of Canterbury*, Innes & Co., p. 31 as cited in Ward, *Prayers*, p. 74). Ward, on the other hand, suggests that in view of Anselm's dealings with Gunhilda (Ep. 157) during her adulterous affair with Count Alan, the possibility of physical fornication is equally valid. Whether one, both or neither of these answers is what Anselm had in mind, Anselm's vivid language invites, indeed compels, the reader to confront his or her sin. Only after forcing the sinner to identify with the baseness of sin does he summon the mercy of God.

97 S.3.30.23–3.31.30, Ward, *Prayers*, p. 136.

98 S.3.30.18–19, Ward, *Prayers*, p. 136.

99 S.3.32.66–8, Ward, *Prayers*, p. 139.

100 S.3.31.36–7, Ward, *Prayers*, p. 137.

101 Evans, *Anselm*, p. 35.

102 S.3.72.30–34.

103 S.3.72.34–6.

104 Lewis, p. 100.

105 Lewis, p. 114.

106 Lewis, p. 216.

107 Delooz, p. 212.

108 Patrick Geary (1994), *Living with the Dead in the Middle Ages*, London: Cornell University Press, pp. 22, 120.

109 Rosemary Woolf (1986), *Art and Doctrine: Essays in Medieval Literature*, London: The Hambledon Press, p. 241.

110 Peter Brown (1985), *Society and the Holy in Late Antiquity*, London: Faber & Faber Ltd, p. 5.

111 Peter Brown (1981), *The Cult of the Saints*, Chicago: University of Chicago Press, p. 65.

112 S.3.31.32–3.

113 S.3.32.61–4.

114 S.3.31.38–9.

115 Evans, *Anselm*, p. 35.

116 'Salvation is found in no other, for no other name under heaven has been given among men by which we must be saved.'

117 Cf. Ep. 28.

118 Southern, p. 107.

119 Southern, p. 108.

120 Southern, p. 108.

121 In the light of this material it may seem odd that a monk should ask Anselm to write a prayer to Mary. It is true, however, that prayers to Mary had existed since the time of Irenaeus and were becoming increasingly common. Irenaeus was, for instance, the first to make a connection between Eve and Mary; the former being the mother of created humanity, and the latter being the mother of recreated humanity. Irenaeus also introduced the notion of Mary as one possessing intercessory powers, thus giving her a place in the redemption of humanity. Much closer to Anselm's time and experience Alcuin's *Libelli Precum* and other collections of prayers in the Carolingian period include prayers to Mary. In fact, Mary held prominent place in the liturgical feasts of the Anglo-Saxon church, and, presumably, in the Norman church as well. All things considered, Anselm's time was a period of ever-increasing interest in Mary, and it is therefore not surprising that one of his monks should request that he write a prayer to her. For a more detailed discussion on the history and development of Marian devotion see especially Mary Clayton (1990), *The Cult of the Virgin Mary in Anglo-Saxon England*, Cambridge: Cambridge University Press.

122 S.3.13.4.
123 S.3.13.6.
124 S.3.13.8–9. One of the striking things about Anselm's prayers is not so much that he should call Mary the mother of life and salvation, but that he should also refer to Paul and Jesus as mothers. We find this intriguing designation in Anselm's prayer to St Paul. This is, unfortunately, another aspect of Anselm's *Prayers*, and therefore theology, which has been largely ignored. It is, however, not surprising on two counts. First, the avid attention lavished on, especially, the notion of Jesus as mother, did not develop significantly until the thirteenth and fourteenth centuries. (Cf. F. Bauerschmidt (1999), *Julian of Norwich and the Mystical Body Politic of Christ*, Notre Dame: University of Notre Dame Press.) Second, as already mentioned, Anselm's *Prayers* are rarely considered a fertile source of theology. It would be interesting, in another place, to trace the idea of the motherhood of God from the Old Testament through to the medieval period and, perhaps, beyond.
125 S. 3.13.12, 46.
126 S.3.14.26–8, 48–50.
127 S.3.14.40–41.
128 It is interesting that Ward has translated 'sana' as 'whole'. The connotation of the word clearly favours 'heal', as does the entire context of Anselm's prayer and petitions. I do, however, appreciate Ward's sensitivity to Anselm's belief that healing the soul of sin is an act which entails the restoration of the whole (cf. Chapter 5 on the *Cur Deus Homo* and earlier comments in this chapter on Anselm's definition of sin as a distortion of the order and perfection of creation). This understanding certainly fits well with Anselm's overall mentality, but, while there may be a hint of a desire for wholeness here I do not believe it is sufficient to warrant the translation 'whole'.
129 'by virtue of the blessed fruit of your womb, who sits at the right hand of his Almighty Father, and is praised and glorified above all for ever. Amen.' Ward, *Prayers*, p. 109 (S.3.14.50–51).
130 This prayer has sometimes been cited as the beginning of that tradition in theology which would be further developed in the twelfth century, that polarizes God and Mary in the economy of salvation. God is the angry judge, and Mary is the forgiving co-redemptrix. While this unfortunate development in medieval theology may be traced to interpretations of Anselm's work in later theologians, it runs counter to Anselm's scheme of salvation. Mary, along with all saints and believers, is not exempt from the necessity of God's grace.
131 S.3.13.6.
132 There is much that could be said here about the familial relation shared by Mary and Jesus. The occurrence and application of the term 'theotokos' or 'dei genetrix' could, for example, greatly delay us. Suffice it to say, I cannot be certain how thoroughly Anselm understood the fifth-century intention of these titles to indicate the humanity of Jesus rather than the divinity or saintliness of Mary in the face of christological heresy. As we will see, there is enough of a tension in Anselm's prayers to Mary to argue for either possibility. Perhaps this ambiguity reveals more about Anselm's context than has hitherto been realized. This period was, after all, a time when Marian devotion was continuing to evolve.
133 S.3.15.6, Ward, *Prayers*, p. 110.
134 S.3.15.16–18, Ward, *Prayers*, p. 110.
135 S.3.16.40, Ward, *Prayers*, p. 112.
136 Cf. *De Conceptione Virginali*, 18 (S.2.159.23–5).
137 S.3.16.41–2, Ward, *Prayers*, p. 112.
138 S.3.16.46–9 and 3.17.53–4, Ward, *Prayers*, pp. 112–13.
139 What I mean is that we need to be careful not to assume that Anselm is here suggesting equality between Mary and Christ. The idea of Mary as a co-redemptrix is not present in Anselm's thought, although he does come very close to propounding such a doctrine and, in later centuries, this kind of language would be used in support of an exalted view

of Mary. I think a suitable counter balance to this prayer is found in the *De Conceptu Virginali*, 18 (S.2.159.23–5) where Anselm identifies Mary's purity with her faith. She was a sinner 'cleansed by faith'.

140 S.3.21.82–4, Ward, *Prayers*, p. 120.

141 Cf. *Cur Deus Homo*, 1.15 (S.2.73.3–6).

142 S.3.22.108–109, Ward, *Prayers*, p. 121.

143 Cf. for example, Augustine, *Confessions*, 3.11.19 and 5.7.13 in *Nicene and Post-Nicene Fathers*, series 1, vol. 2.

144 S.3.21.93–3.22.96, Ward, *Prayers*, p. 120.

145 Cf. the cumulative force of the argument in *De Incarnatione Verbi*.

146 S.3.22.97, Ward, *Prayers*, p. 120.

147 S.3.22.97–107, Ward, *Prayers*, p. 120–21. As well as the English translation of this passage is able to convey the beauty and balance of the original, I think it is worthwhile citing the original, so that the reader might have the opportunity to thoroughly enjoy truly masterful Latin prose:

> Omnis natura a Deo est creata, et Deus ex Maria est natus. Deus omnia creavit, et Maria Deum generavit. Deus qui omnia fecit: ipse se ex Maria fecit, et sic omnia quae fecerat refecit. Qui potuit omnia de nihilo facere: noluit ea violata, nisi prius fieret Mariae filius, reficere. Deus igitur est pater rerum creatarum, et Maria mater rerum recreatarum. Deus est Pater constitutionis omnium, et Maria est mater restitutionis omnium. Deus enim genuit illum per quem omnia sunt facta, et Maria peperit illum per quem cuncta sunt salvata. Deus genuit illum sine quo penitus nihil est, et Maria peperit illum sine quo nihil omnino bene est. O vere dominus tecum, cui dedit Dominus, ut omnis natura tantum tibi deberet secum.

148 The reasons for this will become evident in Chapter 5, which deals more exclusively with the *Cur Deus Homo*.

149 Anselm continues to build and expand on his familial fascination from S.3.23.128 until the end (71 lines!), and in those lines we continue to see the tension between his desire to honour Mary as bearer of the eternal Son, and, therefore, her maternal attachment to God, and his wariness of going beyond Scripture and assigning responsibilities and characteristics to her that are inappropriate. I think it is this tension which drove Anselm to distraction in his attempts to write a prayer to Mary, and only after writing the third prayer did he stop because he was satisfied that he had balanced his competing contentions.

150 S.3.22.97–8, Ward, *Prayers*, p. 120.

Chapter 3

Words: Neither Void nor Vain[1]

In light of Anselm's desire to provide his readers with morsels of truth on which to chew as they savour the delights of divine discourse, it might seem strange that we should turn to the *De Grammatico*. The contrast between the sublimity of the *Prayers* and this dry, introductory work could hardly be more extreme. In the *Prayers* we saw the suffusion of rhetorical playfulness over the body of theological dogmas; in the *De Grammatico* we see the plain prose of dialectic expressing itself through grammar. The artistry has disappeared. But then, was it the artistry to which Anselm sought to bring our attention? Was the rich rhetoric the focus of our delight or the appropriate reflection of the substance explored? Surely the *De Grammatico* has shown us that the mutability of words does not deny us the opportunity to relate to immutable truths. Indeed, as we shall come to see in this chapter and later in Chapter 4, it is the mutability of words which affords us a multiplicity of perspectives.

It is here in the *De Grammatico* that we need to search for the first signs of germination; the developing suckers which will aid and bear up under the future propagation of theological growth and maturation. Consequently, as we look for these signs we must extend our search beyond the facts of grammar and dialectic to their source in the model of reality which propagates the method. Here we shall compare Anselm's agenda with similar works. Priscian, Alcuin and, supremely, Augustine will be among the standards we use to grapple with the programme Anselm displays before us. Only after we have looked to the past for inspiration will we have the luxury of turning to the future and considering the possible implications of our findings for the remainder of the corpus. There is no guarantee that this will be an easy task, for there is much in the *De Grammatico* that is densely packed, but those who bide their time will be rewarded as the fittingness of this work becomes increasingly apparent.

Beginning the Journey

The *De Grammatico* is described by Eadmer as 'a disputation with a disciple, whom he introduced as the other disputant, and in it he both propounded and solved many dialectical questions, and also defined and expounded the different ways in which qualities and *qualia* are to be regarded'.[2] Anselm himself had commented that he wrote three treatises which are in the form of question and answer, and that he also 'wrote a fourth in this same mode, not without its utility, I think, as an introduction to dialectic, called *De Grammatico*, but since it pertains to a different inquiry than the three just mentioned, I do not number it among them'.[3]

This is all the information we have about the writing of the *De Grammatico*. We have no idea when it was written, for whom or why. Did Anselm perceive this as an introductory text for students beginning their study of the trivium? Was this written for monks or, as Southern wonders, was it intended for other students who were not monks, but were attracted to Bec because of its reputation for learning under Lanfranc and Anselm?[4] These are not easily answered questions. There is one, however, with which we must occupy ourselves at the outset: what is its date? The reason this question demands our attention is because placing it within the wider corpus will help to determine whether this work was more formative or reflective; that is to say, whether it was an introductory piece or a work of mature reflection after a period of study and investigation. Perhaps the greatest reason for trying to determine the date of writing is that discovering something of its provenance might put us in a better position to evaluate its significance and relation to the rest of Anselm's writings.

Dating the *De Grammatico*

When we examine the work on its own a number of salient observations can be made. First, and most obviously, the *De Grammatico* is in the form of a dialogue. The student begins, the teacher responds and the interaction develops into, at times, a playful banter wherein the student's questions are probed and developed, and the teacher's answers provide fodder for further discussion in directions unrealized by the student. The reason this mode of expression is of such interest is that it is the way in which Anselm chose to frame his later theological works. As already noted, Anselm pointed out in the *De Veritate* that the *De Grammatico* was akin with the *De Veritate*, the *De Libertate Arbitrii*, and the *De Casu Diaboli* in that they all take the form of a dialogue. Furthermore, one of the latest of Anselm's works, the *Cur Deus Homo*, is written in the form of a dialogue. It might seem, therefore, that if Anselm favoured dialogue as the style of his more mature works then the *De Grammatico* could well belong to the middle or end of his writing career. Moreover, both Anselm and Eadmer choose to list the *De Grammatico* with the aforementioned three dialogues, which may also indicate when it was written.

There are, however, several mitigating factors which argue to the contrary. In the first place, Eadmer's inclusion of the *De Grammatico* with the other three dialogues cannot be considered very weighty since he mentions all these works in the same order that Anselm lists them in his preface to the *De Veritate*, and there Anselm is not concerned to record the chronology of his works, but to group together all of his writings which, to that point, have been written in 'the style of question and answer'.[5] That Anselm's aim is not chronological is also evident from his opening description where he admits that the three dialogues and the *De Grammatico* were written at '*diversis temporibus*'.[6] In addition, as Southern comments in a footnote to the *Vita Anselmi*, at the point where Eadmer enumerates Anselm's works, he is clearly only interested in those written before Anselm became the Archbishop of Canterbury.[7] It should also be added that Anselm's works cannot be so easily dated according to style or genre. Anselm's works display a remarkable aversion to categorization. The technique of employing confabulation as a vehicle for expressing truth, for instance, is representative of works written both before and after Anselm's appointment to Archbishop.[8] Works incorporating prayer with careful reasoning are also scattered throughout his lifetime.[9] Anselm appears not to have shown an affinity for developing a certain mode of expression in accord with his advancing years. An appeal to form, therefore, yields little information on the date of composition. Or does it?

One of the interesting aspects about the *De Grammatico* is that it appears to rely heavily on Aristotle's *Categoriae* and on Boethius' commentary on it.[10] The only other place where Anselm displays an explicit knowledge of Aristotle is in the *Cur Deus Homo* 2.17 where he is attempting to prove that, as Aristotle shows in his *De Interpretatione*, while all things exist of necessity, a distinction must be introduced between necessity which is compelling and necessity which is not. Apart from this brief footnote to Aristotle, though, Anselm nowhere else discusses or incorporates Aristotle's works (in an explicit manner) into his writing. Does this mean, then, that the *De Grammatico* could have been written towards the end of Anselm's life, perhaps around the time of the *Cur Deus Homo*? This proposition, for the reasons outlined above, is unlikely to be true. What is more likely the case is that Anselm's references to Aristotle in the *De Grammatico*, both implicit and explicit, indicate an early date of composition. Why? In order to answer this question we must first briefly sketch something of the development of grammar up to the eleventh century.

Preparing the Ground: The Growth of Aristotelianism

The intention here is not to trace the long history of pedagogic approaches to grammatical study during the medieval period, but merely to point to two significant factors that shaped the study of grammar in the centuries preceding Anselm's time. The first factor that demands consideration is Priscian's *Institutione Grammaticae*. Priscian's work was written in the sixth century and enjoyed a great deal of attention when it was introduced. It fell out of favour rather quickly, however, due to its cumbersome size.[11] It was then reintroduced onto the academic scene by none other than Alcuin of York. How it is that Alcuin came across it or why he should have decided that it was a worthy text to revisit is left to our imagination, but what is important for our purposes is that when Alcuin did introduce Priscian's grammar it met with great success. The eighth and ninth centuries soon became a time when Priscian's work was examined and scrutinized and a time when many commentaries and glosses were written on it.[12] But what is of even greater significance is that Alcuin's grammar, based as it was on Priscian's, set the standard for Carolingian grammar writing, and he chose to write his grammar in the form of a dialogue.[13] It was this precedent and example that inspired later Carolingian scholars, not to mention those who would follow them, to recognize the interpenetration of dialectic and grammar. Vivien Law is surely correct in her analysis that the joint development of grammar and dialectic does not belong to the mid-twelfth century as is so often supposed, but to the Carolingian period; for it was then that 'the seeds were sown by the scholars in Charlemagne's circle' which would be tended by later generations of scholars.[14]

Now it scarcely needs to be said that this sort of evidence is insufficient to support the contention that the impetus and example followed by Anselm in the *De Grammatico* is to be found in an earlier period and therefore the work was more likely to be written at an earlier period in his own life. There is, however, other evidence which may aid our case. Anneli Luhtala, for instance, has noted that there was a 'growing interest in a more philosophically coloured approach to grammar' during the ninth century.[15] Moreover, the 'philosophically oriented grammarians shared the contemporary philosophers' interest in the Aristotelian categories.'[16] When we consider that the Carolingian grammarians set the stage for grammatical discourse and scholarship for the next three centuries, and recall that they were the ones who forged a connection between grammar and dialectic, and add to that our discovery that later grammarians developed an ever-increasing interest in the relationship between grammar and Aristotelian categories, it seems somewhat less surprising to read Anselm describing the *De Grammatico* as an introduction to the study of dialectic in the form of a dialogue which incorporates Aristotelian categories.[17]

In addition to these influences we must not neglect Priscian himself. The rediscovery of Priscian was important not only because it inspired a generation of grammarians, but also because it introduced a certain way of talking about grammar in relation to Aristotelian categories. His language and terminology was, however, not entirely clear to the medieval reader. D.P. Henry explains that in Priscian's discussion of how 'quality-indicating words could be distinguished from substance-indicating words' he 'only bequeathed confusion to posterity by his choice of example.' After describing adjectives as words which join themselves to words which signify substances, he furnishes the example 'sapiens grammaticus'. Henry comments that *grammaticus* is, of course, 'one of the logicians' stock examples of paronym' (a word that has two different meanings despite the same spelling).[18]

When we compare this example from Priscian to the opening question of the student in the *De Grammatico* we find a parallel. The student says, 'I ask that you explain clearly for me whether "literate" is a substance or a quality; so that when I understand this, I will recognize how I ought to perceive other similar things which are so named.'[19] Anselm began at the place where Priscian had left his readers puzzling over ambiguity. While the nature and reason for this ambiguity are subjects which will occupy us a little later, it is worthwhile noting that Anselm was consciously drawing on past examples which maintained a certain amount of currency at the time he penned the *De Grammatico*, but which appear to have become outmoded and forgotten by the early part of the twelfth century.[20] Since, then, it was unusual for something to pass out of fashion quickly in the Middle Ages, it would seem likely that the relevance of Anselm's work would apply more aptly to an early period than a later one. In addition to this deduction, we should bear in mind Southern's belief that Lanfranc's use of Aristotle's *De Categoriae* in his work against Berengar over the nature of the body and blood of Christ influenced Anselm's thinking, but is more likely to have done so in the early years while the two men were still in close contact at Bec.[21]

Weighing all of the evidence, then, it is probable that Anselm wrote the *De Grammatico* early in his career. Indeed, when we compare it to the rest of his work this conclusion seems most sensible since it is the only one which is not overtly theological. So why study it? There are certainly more interesting aspects of Anselm's thought which provide a richer source of insight and inspiration. In fact, the general consensus on the matter is that the *De Grammatico* is a work occupied with nothing more than the benign questions associated with medieval grammar, dialectic and logic that have lost their relevance.[22] Marenbon states explicitly, and quite confidently, that the *De Grammatico* is an entirely non-religious work.[23] He also contends that 'Anselm's canon includes some pieces devoted entirely to logical analysis of concepts with no direct theological reference.'[24] In addition to these assessments Vivien Law has observed that medieval grammars 'possess no intrinsic value' and that they therefore can only be useful in as far as 'they shed light on something else.'[25] Her claim is that medieval grammars are most useful for the way in which they inform us of patterns of pedagogical practice, the emergence of new genres of literature; not to mention what good indicators they can be about 'the level of culture in a given region'.[26] The most damning castigation, though, is the widely held view that medieval grammars are 'totally unoriginal and therefore do not deserve our attention'.[27]

I beg to differ. While it may be true that most medieval grammars are uninteresting works which demonstrate little or no originality, I believe that Anselm's *De Grammatico* is a work which does bear the marks of some originality and that it is in fact a work with which the reader must come to terms if he or she hopes to appreciate fully the nature and purpose of the later theological treatises. In other words, I believe that the *De Grammatico* is foundational to the rest of Anselm's corpus, and therefore that an understanding of the *De Grammatico* is essential. Thus, my attempt to date it with respect to Anselm's other works is vital since establishing its chronologically primary position serves as a good starting point from which to argue its hermeneutical priority. I am not suggesting, though, that the *De Grammatico* is an enjoyable read, for there is much in this esoteric work which does not appeal to modern sensibilities, and the logic is not always as fluid as one might expect from an alleged introduction. It is, however, the sort of work which can divulge much information to those who take the time to study it carefully.

The Glory of Grammar

D.P. Henry is such a scholar and the only person to have devoted three books to the subject.[28] In his first book on the subject, *The* De Grammatico *of St Anselm*, Henry bemoaned the judgement that had been passed on the *De Grammatico* by previous scholars. He comments that 'few logical works can have been so forcefully condemned as has the dialogue *De Grammatico*.'[29] Drawing on the works of Cousin, Maurice, Prantl and Haureau, Henry notes that despite their slightly different interpretations, they are unanimous in proclaiming that the *De Grammatico* has nothing in common with Anselm's other works.[30] What is particularly interesting is that all of the authors cited by Henry were scholars of the nineteenth century who were not interested or intent on indagating Anselm's corpus. By and large their interests lay in expatiating on scholastic theology, of which they believed Anselm to be the forerunner. But if we look beyond the simple presentation of topics to the principles informing Anselm's hermeneutics, guided as they were by his particular model of reality, we may find that fitting Anselm into a preconceived and somewhat arbitrarily determined pattern in history does justice neither to Anselm nor to his works.

Considering the fact that Henry's 1964 monograph is the first to deal solely with the *De Grammatico* and, apart from his two later monographs published in 1974 and 1993, is the only work of its kind, the history of its interpretation alone is enough to convince us that Anselm's first work (excluding his early prayers) has been resoundingly neglected. Why, then, should Henry take such an interest? Because the *De Grammatico* is an extraordinary work which evinces 'a logical structure in which every word, every phrase, and every example, have their place, point, and complex historical background' despite the fact that 'in the absence of any system of minute cross-reference and comment ... little of this is apparent at first sight.'[31] The exceptional nature of this work is duly delineated and developed by Henry in all three of his volumes. In the first, he expounds the intricacies of paronymy. In the second, Henry further elucidates the Aristotelian and Boethian background to the *De Grammatico*, but lays particular emphasis on the significance of words for Anselm and the necessity to use them precisely. Finally, in his third monograph, Henry makes an attempt to show the relevance of the *De Grammatico* to some of Anselm's other works. It is with these volumes that we will interact in order to help illuminate the content of the *De Grammatico* – to which we now turn.

Rather than entering into an extended point-by-point summary of Anselm's work, it seems expedient to highlight just one section which is representative of the whole. To this end, Chapters 16 through 18 are the best choice.

At this point in the discussion, though it is nearing a resolution, the student is still struggling with the original problem (central concern): is *grammaticus* a quality or a substance?[32] Throughout the discourse the teacher has been trying to explain to the student that *grammaticus* can be both a substance and a quality.[33] Through diverse explanations the student is now lead to insist that it is difficult to think of *grammaticus* 'as being a quality', 'although it does signify literacy'.[34] The student elaborates that it is also difficult

> to think of man alone, that is, without literacy, as being literate; for since man can only be literate alone or with literacy, that man alone is literate follows as a consequence of the proof that man along with literacy is not literate. For although the name literate signifies literacy, nevertheless the correct answer to the question 'What is literate?' could scarcely be 'Literate is literacy' or 'Literate is a quality'. And again, since literate must participate in literacy, it follows that a man can only be a literate in conjunction with literacy.[35]

The teacher replies that the student's statement that man alone, without literacy, is a literate must be qualified and understood correctly. He explains that, 'man alone, without literacy, is indeed literate, in the sense that he alone ever participates in literacy; for literacy itself does not participate in literacy, either alone or along with man.'[36] That is to say that there is a category of words which are only signifiers when they are appellative of other words which signify substance. This is why the teacher adds the final clause that man 'alone ever participates in literacy'. As pertains to the *Categoriae*, the teacher concludes that the assertion that 'literate is a quality' is 'only correct if made in the sense which occurs in Aristotle's treatise *On the De Categoriae*'.[37]

To this the student retorts without hesitation that, when Aristotle is followed, *grammaticus* is a substance and not a quality.[38] Unshaken by the student's insightfulness, the teacher answers that we must remember that Aristotle's purpose was to show that words signify something. By means of some rather dense argumentation the student is led to realize the paronymous nature of *grammaticus*. In other words, he recognizes that a word can sound the same and look the same (allowing for different suffixes according to the rules of declension), but belong to two separate categories of grammar, and thus signify or mean two different things. Henry summarizes the situation succinctly in his second book when he writes that, '"literate" signifies a quality, ie. literacy, but refers to substance, ie. man. On the other hand the substance-word "man" is both significative precisively of, and is appellative of, everything indicated by the definition of man, and principally of the substantiality thereby implied.'[39] What is significant about Henry's summary is that he incorporates an appreciation for Anselm's desire to forge a language which will enable him to gain a degree of precision which will eliminate misunderstanding, thereby clearing the path of unnecessary obstacles so that understanding can be achieved with the utmost clarity and ease.

The Purpose of Paronymy

What Anselm was, in part, doing, and what Henry is keen to elaborate, was distinguishing between the learned use of language (as by logicians), and the common use of language. This distinction is most readily seen at the end of Section 12. There, the teacher is explaining that

> literate does not signify man, and literacy does not signify the whole; but literacy does signify itself directly [*per se*], and signifies man indirectly [*per aliud*]. For although the name literate is appellative of man, it is, nevertheless, characteristically said to signify him. However, while literate can signify literacy, it is not appellative of literacy. What I am saying is that the name of something is appellative of that thing when it is appellative of that thing itself according to common usage. For it is not in accord with the common usage to say, 'literacy is literate' or 'literate is literacy', but instead, 'the man is literate' and 'the literate is a man'.[40]

Towards the end of this section we can see that although the way in which the teacher and the student have been talking is proving helpful for their purposes, it is not the normal means of expression (*usus loquendi*). The reason that they must have recourse to such awkward or stilted constructions reflects, suggests Henry,

> the medievals' realisation that for logical or philosophical purposes certain semantical categories which are not available in non-technical speech, or which at least go unrecognized by the grammarian of ordinary language may be required. What we have here, in fact, is a semi-artificial language: something between natural language and the fully artificial languages of contemporary logic.[41]

This, it would seem, is the reason why the *De Grammatico* is the difficult read that it is. And yet, before we countenance too many complaints or criticisms about the unnecessary verbosity of such language, let us consider its utility.

Henry carries on in his discussion of Anselm's distinction between the common use of certain words and expressions and the more learned approach, to argue that this sort of language has many different benefits. He claims, for example, that Anselm's acumen in this area is something new and that he is thereby thrown into 'collision with his grammarian contemporaries'.[42] It is the differences between Anselm and his colleagues that, for various reasons, Henry believes provide a fruitful avenue of investigation. After enumerating a couple of other areas of interest, Henry declares that the cardinal point to be grasped, and that which is common to the various areas of investigation, is that 'the entire field of medieval philosophical and logical writings constitutes an almost totally unexplored territory still awaiting elucidation' but which has now been made possible by Lesniewski's logical systems.[43] It is such tools as these 'logical systems' with which we are now furnished that Henry believes he can open the floodgates of comprehension which have eluded scholars.

The Plain Meaning

While Henry's emphasis on the importance of the *De Grammatico* for understanding medieval philosophical logic may prove of some value, treating the *De Grammatico* to that end alone is rather unsatisfying.[44] How does such an approach fit with Anselm's statement in the *De Veritate* that his purpose in the *De Grammatico* was to write an introduction? Furthermore, he believed, even then, that this little work was not without its utility. Considering that this statement was made in the context of three works which he explicitly identifies as pertaining to the study of Scripture, one wonders if elucidations based on modern logical systems misses the point. To be sure, the development of technical language in conjunction with logic and dialectic cannot be ignored, but the pertinent question that is not being adequately addressed is, to what purpose is this linguistic understanding being enhanced? We are in danger of gross misjudgement if we neglect to reconcile theory with practice. A monk living in the eleventh century would not countenance writing a treatise on dialectic or grammar or logic without having some ultimate practical goal in mind. For Anselm, that pragmatic end was exegesis. Anselm intended for the reader to look beyond the content of the *De Grammatico* and concentrate on the method. In other words, Anselm was not primarily interested in pontificating on paronymy, nor even to propagate medieval philosophical logic. To be sure, these are characteristics of the *De Grammatico*, but is it possible that our lack of acquaintance with eleventh century pedagogy has left us bereft of a proper understanding of Anselm's purpose?

Take, for example, the fact that Anselm described the *De Grammatico* as an introduction. Does it not seem odd that an introduction should disillusion so many scholars? Surely, if Anselm wrote this as an introduction, for novice students, he would have made every effort to make it intelligible to them? This is what we would expect considering Anselm's sustained stress on the necessity of understanding.[45] Moreover, should we expect an introductory text to require an elaborate cross-referencing scheme without which the reader has no hope of comprehension? Furthermore, why is it that only now, after logicians have devised certain logical systems, that we are fully able to appreciate the content of the *De Grammatico*? These are the sorts of questions that make one query the modern presumption of the purpose of the *De Grammatico*. Granted, some of our misunderstanding is, as mentioned above, due to the fact that we no longer think in the same way or with the same categories as did medieval scholars and theologians. On this account it is certainly excusable if we encounter some degree of difficulty. It is, I think, a clue to our misapprehension, though, if we believe that only after applying modern categories and systems that the light of the *De Grammatico* will be revealed.

Let us consider for a moment that the *De Grammatico* is what Anselm says it is: an introduction to dialectic. Now if this work is a study of dialectic then it is not, primarily, a study of grammar and, therefore, not fundamentally intending to pontificate on paronymy. The greatest disservice Anselm ever did was to name this work by its first two words because, as is so often the case, readers are tempted to assume that the title indicates the purpose. We need but consider Anselm's next two works to discover that they were not named according to the nature of their content. The *Monologion* was so named because it was a soliloquy (talking with one's self)[46] and the *Proslogion* was so named because it was an allocution (an address to others).[47] None of the titles given to these first three works reveals anything to us about their content or purpose.

Taking the stated purpose of the *De Grammatico* then, we are left to ask what, in Anselm's day, was dialectic? The most obvious, and possibly the best, answer is that it was dialogue. From what evidence we have in the *De Grammatico*, dialectic appears to be that mode of investigation wherein the two disputants choose a mutually intriguing topic or question, the answer to which either one (or possibly both?) is ignorant. In the thrust and parry of the ensuing repartee the two disputants employ rhetoric to their advantage, but, more significantly, they also use logic. This much we have already seen in Henry's observation that Anselm was interested in defining words and constructing sentences which, although contrary to the *usus loquendi*, were still intelligible. The other form of logic Anselm adopted from Aristotle was syllogism.[48]

Is it not true, then, that the cathexis of Anselm's thought was channelled in the direction of logic? Yes, and no. Yes, Anselm was clearly interested in logical thinking and in attempting to demonstrate that in order to be logical, or careful, sometimes means creating a somewhat artificial language. No, because the means Anselm chose to express himself cannot be ignored. It was not just clear thinking that Anselm sought to impress upon his students, but clear questioning. Questions are supremely important to Anselm. Questions are a means of ascertaining the truth. It was because of a question that Anselm came to write the *Proslogion*. It was because of questions asked by his fellow monks that Anselm came to write the *Cur Deus Homo*. Even on his death-bed, Anselm continued to ruminate on questions pertaining to the origin of the soul.[49] It was a question which began the *De Grammatico*. What young students need to learn most is not the right answers, but the right questions. It is in asking the right sort of questions that a correct answer will be achieved.

Returning to Anselm's description of the *De Grammatico* as an introduction to dialectic, if Anselm is seeking to teach the art of dialogue or asking the right questions in the right way at the right time, would he not choose relatively simple material for such an exercise? In other words, if Anselm was seeking to teach his students how to interact and how to think clearly and cogently, in order to make his point and not have it camouflaged by extraneous material, would he not choose a subject which was familiar to his students? Indeed, would it not be more effective to choose a problem about which the students knew much? To be sure, selecting an issue that is too simple would defeat the purpose, but, similarly, choosing an issue which is too complex would detract from the objective. Perhaps we have made more of the complexities of the *De Grammatico* than was originally intended. Will, therefore, Anselm's *De Grammatico* reveal the intricacies of medieval philosophical logic, as Henry argues? It may or it may not, but to ask such a question of this text is to miss the point.

This brings us to the second point to which we have already alluded. Anselm chose to introduce this work as part of, though distinct from, three other dialogues which are also chiefly concerned with asking questions. Anselm includes the *De Grammatico* among these dialogues in so far as it too is written in the form of a discussion. He distinguished the *De Grammatico* from the three dialogues, however, by virtue of their content. Whereas the three dialogues were written as an example of scriptural investigation, the *De Grammatico* was written as an example of dialectical investigation. It is, apparently, the immediate aim of these two sets of works which differentiates them. But I would argue that in all four of Anselm's dialogues (the *De Grammatico*, the *De Veritate*, the *De Libertate Arbitrii*, and the *De Casu Diaboli*) he is about the business of exemplifying a method rather than setting out a ready-made answer. Marenbon recognizes this when he comments that 'it was Anselm's theological method which seems to have impressed his disciples, and which they took as their point of departure.'[50] It is no secret that, on the surface, Anselm appears to have very few disciples. And yet, it was his rigorous examples of method which were most enduring and left the greatest impression on twelfth-century scholasticism.[51] Set, as the *De Grammatico* is, in a context of works which are examples of method, it seems more than reasonable to suggest that it too ought to be valued for more than just its content. What we have in the *De Grammatico* is not merely a commentary on Aristotle or Boethius, nor simply a mimicking of Carolingian grammars, nor solely an attempt to elucidate the ambiguities of Priscian's *Institutiones*, but an example of method – an example of academic inquiry.

Strangely, this is, in part, how Southern interprets the *De Grammatico*. What is odd about Southern's view is that while he admits that Anselm was 'opening up a method of inquiry about the whole structure of reality and our thoughts about it', he denies that this treatise could have been intended for anyone but the pupils of an alleged external school.[52] He contends that 'it was written, as Anselm himself says, as an introduction to dialectic, and there are several indications in manner and subject-matter which suggest that it was made in the first place for pupils who were not monks.'[53]

The manner to which Southern is referring here is what he perceives to be the rather pugnacious character of the student. The less respectful, 'almost truculent' nature of the student grates with Southern, especially when compared to the docile, attentive students in Anselm's later treatises. It is precisely this sort of attitude that adds to Southern's opinion that the *De Grammatico* could not have been intended for members of the cloister. There are, however, several problems with this assessment. In the first place, as Southern himself admits, this is a work on dialectic, so why the surprise at the different tone of the student? The reason the student is so searching and demanding is that, as just shown, Anselm is trying to teach students how to ask questions, how to apply logic; in short, to provide an example of how to think and study. Anselm's later works are not intended as examples of dialectic, but as investigations into either theological or biblical topics. Moreover, Anselm does not describe his three dialogues as dialectic, but as dialogues. Second, why should a work on dialectic be considered so thoroughly secular that it is deemed inappropriate for the cloister? Were monks not taught to think? Did they not seek to master the lesser disciplines so that they might attain to the queen of the arts? It is puzzling that Southern should say on the one hand that the *De Grammatico* moves towards a new theological method, but should then turn around and immediately declare that it is a work which is so devoid of religious content that it cannot be considered appropriate for monks.

It is unfortunate that Southern does not elaborate on what he means when he says that the *De Grammatico* opens up a method of inquiry about the whole structure of reality. This reluctance to engage with the *De Grammatico* is to Southern's detriment, for when we trace back to what must have been among the chief motives for Anselm, Augustine (particularly his *De Magistro*, *De Doctrina Christiana*, and *De Trinitate*), we discover there a wealth of information about the sorts of ideas on which Anselm would have spent long hours meditating and which were integral in moulding his own thoughts on reality.

Augustinian Influence

The import of Augustine to Anselm can hardly be overestimated. In broad terms, Anselm writes on many of the same topics as Augustine (for example, free will, the existence of God, the definition of evil, and many more). This may not seem out of the ordinary considering that Augustine remained the pre-eminent theologian throughout the medieval West. There is, however, a rather telling comment in one of Anselm's letters to Lanfranc. After completing the *Monologion*, Anselm sent it to Lanfranc for his approval and editing. Lanfranc, noting that the work did not cite authorities (namely, the Church Fathers), challenged Anselm to state explicitly from where he was drawing his material. In response, Anselm informed Lanfranc that he did not believe that there was anything in the *Monologion* which could not be found in the 'canonical *dicta*' or 'from the words of St Augustine'. Anselm further asserts that everything he wrote had already been proved and discussed in St Augustine's *De Trinitate*.[54] Clearly Anselm has a special affinity for Augustine, even if he adamantly refuses to incorporate explicit citations. Other similarities between the two theologians have been helpfully summarized by Southern.[55]

The three works of Augustine mentioned above may, at first, seem to be sufficiently disparate as to cause the reader some perplexity. *De Trinitate*, for instance, defends and explicates the doctrine of the Trinity. *De Doctrina Christiana* is concerned with the interpretation of Scripture and how it should be explained. *De Magistro* appears to be a work which mines the depths of good pedagogy. How can any, indeed all, of these works be shown to bear upon the *De Grammatico*? In order to answer this question, let us look first at each one in turn, and then all together, for in so doing we will see just how pertinent these works are to understanding the *De Grammatico* and its repercussions.

Laying the Cornerstone

Beginning with the last work, the *De Magistro*, we discover there that the intent is not so much to ponder pedagogy, as to inquire into the nature of words. To this end Augustine begins by asking his son, 'What does it seem to you that we wish to accomplish when we speak?'[56] In spite of a number of suggestions, Augustine eventually brings his son around to recognizing that speaking has a dual intent: either to teach or to remind. And yet, Augustine claims, it is the latter of these which is foremost because it is in the memory 'within which words inhere' and it is in the mind that we recall 'the very things of which the words are signs'.[57] This statement leads us to the heart of the first part of the discussion: words as signs. In the following chapters, Augustine leads his son into a discussion very similar to that held between the teacher and student in the *De Grammatico*. The nature of nouns is investigated, and that which they signify is explored and explained. There is also some suggestion that Augustine had Aristotle's *Categoriae* on his mind when he refers to the genus of particular words which signify particular things.[58] But it is not so much what Augustine has to say about the signification of words *per se* that intrigues the reader of Anselm's *De Grammatico*; what is of interest is the direction in which Augustine guides his son *via* the discussion on words and signification.

In Chapter 8 Augustine praises his son for summing up their discussion to that point, and adds that despite the esoteric nature of what they have been considering, he wants to assure Adeodatus (Augustine's son) that there is a purpose. From the perspective of the modern reader Augustine's worries that 'it may seem that we are quibbling and so diverting the mind from earnest matters with naive questions' are better founded than he could have realized. So what is Augustine's point? To put it simply, Augustine is eager to convince his son that as important as words are, 'we should not attribute more to words than is proper.'[59] For although words are the means by which we are able to signify something, 'the cognition of things is superior to the signs of things' such that 'the cognition of things which are signified is to be preferred to the cognition of signs by means of which they are signified.'[60] To this assertion Adeodatus complains that this cannot be the case because without the signifier knowledge of the signified is impossible. Augustine responds by claiming that the reason things which are signified are more important than that which signifies them is because that which signifies something is useless unless the thing signified is already known to the individual. On this basis Augustine argues that 'thousands of things occur to the mind, which may be shown through themselves when no sign has been given.'[61] 'Therefore,' Augustine confidently concludes, 'that the sign is learned after the thing is cognized is rather more the case than that the thing itself is learned after the sign is given.'[62]

Augustine's epistemology is not, however, solely focused on sensible knowledge. He is careful to differentiate between 'sensibles' and 'intelligibles'.[63] The former are those things which are known to us through our senses – the 'carnal' realm. The latter are those things which pertain to the 'spiritual' realm. In the case of sensible things knowledge is only possible through experience. Something must be seen or heard or tasted in order to be known. We cannot merely tell someone about an orange, for example, and expect them to know it if they have never seen or tasted one. If, therefore, such a situation does arise where the speaker introduces that which the listener has not experienced or known, the listener, although unable to identify the validity of the object or statement, is still able to understand the speaker, but can only do so because he or she has accepted on trust the validity and accuracy of that which the speaker is describing. Thus there are two types of knowledge for Augustine under the category of sensible cognition: true knowledge based on experience, and accepted knowledge based on trust and awaiting confirmation through experience.

As for the second of the two types of knowledge (intelligible), this sort of knowledge comes from reasoning 'by means of the intellect'.[64] This sort of knowledge may not appear to be immediate since it is deduced or realized by the individual on the basis of other things. But this is not so. Augustine is careful to explain that 'even though I speak about true things [that is, things which are arrived at through reason], I still do not teach him who beholds the true things, for he is taught not through my words but by means of the things themselves which God reveals within the soul.'[65] Why? Because those things which are perceived in the mind, 'are said to be things which we see immediately in that interior light of truth by virtue of which he himself who is called the interior man is illumined'.[66]

Bringing these ideas together, Augustine concludes that,

now we may not only believe but also begin to understand that it has truly been written on divine authority that we are not to call anyone on earth our master because there is only one Master of all who is in heaven. But what *in heaven* means He Himself will advertise to us by means of men, through signs and outwardly, so that we may by turning inwardly to Him be made wise; whom to know and to love is the blessed life which, though all claim to seek it, few indeed may rejoice that they have found.[67]

It is in this statement that Augustine wonderfully unites the two apparently disparate kinds of knowledge. Intelligible knowledge is given to humanity through divine illumination, but because that which is imparted to us by the divine is not accessible to the senses, we must take it on trust that what is taught is true until the day when the Christian will finally perceive all that was taught in the final consummation of salvation. And yet, there is a hint of realized eschatology in Augustine because, as he argued earlier, 'there is a certain utility in believing'[68] that which is not experienced because 'if ye will not believe, ye shall not understand.'[69] It is through believing that which cannot be immediately grasped that the individual has any hope of attaining to the place where, through experiencing the truth of divine revelation, that which is believed is transformed into that which is understood. Thus we see that while Augustine propounded a view of epistemology which was thoroughly grounded in the senses, he allowed for the possibility of attaining through belief to that which by its very nature cannot be known immediately. In other words, faith is the instrument through which we are able to transcend our present state of knowledge, and divine illumination is the power that makes that instrument effective.

Building on the Foundation

We are, however, not left in the dark. As Augustine demonstrates in his *De Doctrina Christiana*, there is more to understanding than simply believing. One must first read the Bible, the revealed will of God, in order to know what it is that God wishes to impart to humanity. But reading the Bible is not a simple task; there is the matter of interpretation. Augustine recognized that no information comes to us in a vacuum. This is the reason why Augustine felt he had to write the *De Doctrina Christiana*.

Augustine begins by claiming that the interpretation of Scripture depends on two things: 'the mode of ascertaining the proper meaning' and 'the mode of making known the meaning when it is ascertained'.[70] While the 'mode of making known' what has been understood does not concern us at the moment, the 'mode of ascertaining the proper meaning' does. For when we look into this first part of the treatise we discover once again how heavily Augustine emphasizes the importance of words. He opens by averring that there is a distinction between things and signs; that words are the chief means of signification, and therefore that only a proper understanding of words can result in achieving a proper understanding of the text.[71] Words are the intermediaries between truth and understanding.

The sum total of Augustine's teaching, then, is that since words, whether written or spoken, are the means by which we are able to address, praise and meditate on the divine and divine things, it is clearly of paramount import that the reader come to grips with language. For apart from linguistic agility, syntactic acumen and grammatical appreciation there is little hope for proper interpretation and understanding. This is why Augustine concludes that dialectic, 'which deals with inferences, and definitions, and divisions, is of the greatest assistance in the discovery of the meaning'.[72]

One of the places this conviction works itself out most effectually is in Augustine's more mature work *De Trinitate*. Against the threefold errors of his adversaries, Augustine pronounces that

> in order, therefore, that the human mind might be purged from falsities ... Holy Scripture, which suits itself to babes, has not avoided words drawn from any class of things really existing, through which, as by nourishment, our understanding might rise gradually to things divine and transcendent.[73]

Here we have the final outcome of a programme of study which began with a simple investigation into the nature of words and their purpose (*De Magistro*), was further expanded with concrete examples from Scripture (*De Doctrina Christiana*), and now bears the full weight of a major theological inquiry. The *De Trinitate* is a remarkable work for many reasons, but as for our interests, its most significant contribution is the example it provides of how a theory of words can and should point beyond itself. The *De Trinitate* illumines the truth which is the star to which Augustine is able to point; not because he is able to marshal a number of different texts to support his position, nor because he can draw on established doctrines of the church (though these are important), but chiefly because he has spent the time and energy required to discern the things signified in the words of Scripture. In the passage cited above from the *De Doctrina Christiana* which highlights Augustine's esteem for dialectic as an effective means of interpretation, he goes on to warn that 'still, it sometimes happens that men find less difficulty in attaining the object for the sake of which these sciences are learnt, than in going through the very intricate and thorny discipline of such rules.'[74]

Augustine and Anselm: Variations on a Theme

When we take some of these thoughts from Augustine and compare them with Anselm's *De Grammatico*, we discover a number of points of inter-section. First, we note the preoccupation both authors have with words. In Augustine's earlier work, the *De Magistro*, we saw that he carefully defined and demarcated the nature and function of words, and yet he was not satisfied simply to leave the matter there. Towards the end of the treatise we noted how he drew the reader's attention to the fact that whether the source of knowledge was 'sensible' or 'intelligible', it was either experienced, and thus understood, or taken on trust or faith, and thus only believed. But if what is known is only believed, while it cannot pretend to genuine understanding, it does seek confirmation according to the nature of its source. If it is sensible knowledge, then the individual seeks confirmation through the sense; if it is intelligible knowledge, then the individual seeks confirmation through divine illumination in the reasoning faculties. In other words, Augustine's theory of words was itself intended for a higher purpose. The point was not to study words as such,[75] but to identify them as the primary means of indagation, the conduit through which we may perceive what is real or true.

I would argue that Anselm, Augustine's protégé in many respects, embarked on the same programme as did his mentor. Just as Augustine began with words and their purpose before he could work out a more fully fledged theory of interpretation which would come to fruition in works such as the *De Trinitate*, so Anselm needed to work out his own theory of words so that he too could shape his own hermeneutical method which could then, in turn, aid his theological studies in perpetuity. The *De Grammatico*, then, is not primarily about paronymy or about grammar, but, as argued earlier, about method. Southern was correct to suggest that the *De Grammatico* looks beyond itself; that Anselm was casting an eye beyond the immediate situation towards opening up 'a whole method of inquiry about the whole structure of reality and our thoughts about it.'[76] The difference between Anselm and Augustine is that Augustine incorporated more of the immediate application in his theoretical works than did Anselm. In the *De Magistro*, as in the *De Doctrina Christiana*, Augustine allowed us to see that what mattered to him most was arriving at a theory of interpretation which would allow him to discern and disseminate the Truth. Truth is here capitalized because whether knowledge fell into the category of the sensible or the intelligible, Augustine firmly believed that since God created the world, creation 'will lead him who follows it to God, its creator and orderer'.[77] Thus, whether it is knowledge revealed to the senses or knowledge revealed to the mind through divine illumination, God is the one who makes it possible and God is the final object of our understanding.

Why is it that Anselm never wrote another treatise like the *De Grammatico*? Because it was only the first step in a larger programme. The larger programme was the attainment of the beatific vision: the supreme form of realized eschatology. As we shall see in the chapter on the *Proslogion*, Anselm's agenda was driven by the desire for an experience of the divine, both sensually and rationally.[78] He did not seek proof for the sake of proof, nor did he seek affirmation because he lacked faith, nor yet was he concerned to demonstrate the validity of Christian logic in the face of unbelief. Anselm's goal stood higher than these; it was more noble in that it sought to climb the mountain of burning coals that surrounds the throne of God.[79] His theory of language was merely the necessary first step in a series of steps that built one upon the other. As Augustine had said, without due ability in linguistic analysis and care over dialectic, there could be no hope of understanding, and, therefore, no hope of participating in the divine nature on which all reality relies.

The theological underpinnings in the *De Grammatico* cannot be dismissed. Supporting language, logic, and all the intricacies of dialectic, is God, for when language is understood as significatory, it is understood as 'image-bearing', and therefore becomes 'a sacrament of divine truth'.[80] How apt this description is when we consider that a sacrament is an outward visible sign of an inward, invisible reality, and that, in the Christian tradition, the word, in the outward, visible form of the Bible, is the means through which the individual is transformed inwardly, and invisibly. This is what the monastic context is all about: meditating on the divine word in order to internalize the external. But there is more. It is not just the word of Scripture which transforms the individual, but the very incarnate Christ who is *the* Word, and through whom the *res* which lies beyond the *signa* is made manifest to all. It is in his capacity as the Word made flesh that Jesus 'who is divine truth, goodness, and beauty, enables man to perceive and to grasp these otherwise abstract ideas and principles and leads him to their true centre and meaning in Himself, as God and as Trinity'.[81]

Anselm's theory of words and signification says more about the way in which he viewed the world than about medieval ideas on grammar or logic. It says, albeit implicitly, more about his theology than anyone has yet to recognize. His theory of words makes no sense apart from a model in which God is the creator of all things, the originator of all reality, the instigator of all right relation of which signification is but a part. And how could Anselm hold to such a view in the light of the upheaval, degradation and chaos he witnessed in the eleventh century, unless he also believed in a God who had redeemed the world? As we will see in the chapter on the *Cur Deus Homo*, Anselm forged a theory of the incarnation and atonement which at once addressed the cry of his contemporaries for a return to order and harmony, while growing solidly out of the rich soil of his predecessors' penchant for perfection. The specifics of its theological implications will have to wait their turn, but for now it is enough to note that the *De Grammatico* is where we see the seeds of the *Proslogion*, the seeds of the *Monologion*, the seeds of the *Cur Deus Homo*, the seeds of the three dialogues 'pertaining to the study of sacred Scripture', and the seeds of the *Prayers and Meditations*.[82] This is where we see how vitally important words were to Anselm and the influence they had on his theology.

The Beauty of Language

The *De Grammatico* is a work which demonstrates the harmony and unity of all that one studies. Whether dialectic (the form of the *De Grammatico*) or grammar (the content of the *De Grammatico*), whether paronyms or logic, whether sacred or profane, whether for monks or lay people, the *De Grammatico* is a definitive declaration that there is order in the universe and that that order proceeds from the person of God. It is a declaration that because the God of the Bible exists there is unity between disciplines. It is a declaration that there is harmony between apparently disparate works.[83] Far from being the black sheep in the corpus, the *De Grammatico* stands at the forefront of Anselm's works, both chronologically and conceptually.

These truths are perhaps nowhere more transparently connected to Anselm's theological programme than in the *Monologion*[84] where he opens by stating that 'of all the things that exist, there is one nature that is supreme. It alone is self-sufficient in its eternal happiness, yet through its all-powerful goodness it creates and gives to all other things their very existence and their goodness.'[85]

God is the source of all that exists. The nature which any given thing has is due to its possessing it by divine fiat. This is why Anselm can carry on and claim that in spite of some people's professed disbelief in God or Christian doctrine he can begin at almost any point and, through reason ('si vel mediocris ingenii est'!), convince them of the truth of that which they profess is false. In other words, Anselm's first foray into theological reflection begins with the presupposition that the words and concepts that we all use to describe or even construct our own understanding of reality are the very things which are infused with divine attributes or truth precisely because apart from God language is an impossibility.

Using the example of that which is good, Anselm begins to demonstrate his point in more specific terms which reflect some of the themes of signification we have already seen while simultaneously directing our attention beyond those themes to a theology which is permeated with aesthetic appeal. The harmony in language between signifier and signified, grounded as it is in God and affirmed in the incarnation of the Word, is translated in the *Monologion* into concrete theological concepts.

Anselm begins by asking how what is good can be identified in light of the fact that there are many good things. 'Are we', he asks, 'to believe that there is some one thing through which all good things whatsoever are good? Or do different goods have their existence through different things?'[86] The same is true, argues Anselm, for justice; but in both cases a thing is either good or just *through* good (itself) or justice. Following the theory of signification in the *De Grammatico*, Anselm is claiming that something is called good because goodness is intrinsic to that object. In this way 'good' is also an example of paronymy as it too can be used as either a noun or an adjective signifying both substance and quality. But this is where Anselm begins to extend his thinking. In light of the fact that there are an 'uncountable number of good things'[87] there must be one good from which all goods derive their existence. Whereas in grammar it is enough to posit that substance is the chief category from which quality is derived and on which it depends, in theology substances are themselves dependent on something beyond themselves. For, inquires Anselm, how does that which is good come to be good? It must, he determines, be good through something else. This chain of reasoning leads Anselm to conclude that there must be a supreme good which is good in itself and through itself.[88]

In the following chapters Anselm carries on to extend his idea of supreme goodness to supreme being which he then spends some time expounding and explaining. The discussion becomes interesting for our purposes again when Anselm alights on the activity of creation and its connection to verbalization. In Chapter 12, Anselm informs his readers that 'the supreme substance has created everything through its inner verbalisation' and that 'this is true, whether it creates individual things through individual words, or everything at once by speaking one word'. Again we see the import of words for Anselm and how his preoccupation with them in the *De Grammatico* is reflected in these later theological concerns.[89] The correspondence is remarkable, especially when we take Chapter 16 of the *Monologion* into account. After introducing us to the idea of the necessity of the supreme nature[90] and the way in which he created all things and how all things, in turn, depend on him, Anselm reminds us that such affirmations as he has made via notions of goodness and justice also apply 'to everything else that can be said in the same way of the supreme nature.' And since the supreme nature is 'supreme essence, supreme life, supreme reason, supreme health, supreme justice, supreme wisdom, supreme truth, supreme goodness, supreme greatness, supreme beauty, supreme immortality, supreme incorruptibility, supreme immutability, supreme happiness, supreme eternity, supreme power, supreme unity' these self-same things are part of creation because they are found in the creator.[91] Just as a good thing is good by virtue of its being given goodness by something greater than itself, we ought to expect the same pattern between the whole of creation with respect to God's communicable attributes.

Having drawn these sorts of connections and inferences Anselm carries on and works through 'the properties of the supreme nature',[92] dealing with perceived difficulties as they arise. But even so, he remains unconvinced that he has sufficiently exposited the 'supreme nature's verbalisation, through which all things were created'[93] and so commences a more detailed discussion of 'locutione' within the divine essence which is, once more, obviously dependent on the *De Grammatico* for its foundation, yet reaches beyond it, while simultaneously expressing the fundamentally aesthetic nature of the model of reality there presented.

The Word, and Words

Words are likenesses, Anselm explains, of that which they signify and 'the degree of truth of every likeness and image depends on the degree of its imitation of its object.'[94] But, the reader is left wondering, what about *the* Word? Since all creation has its existence through the Word, 'is it, or is it not, a likeness of the things made through it?'[95] If we answer in the affirmative then we are faced with the question of how that which is mutable (the creation) relates to that which is immutable (the creator). Perceiving this dilemma to be an insurmountable obstacle, Anselm probes the negative response only to discover that the question is raised as to how the Word could then be said to be the model of creation. As the reader begins to feel the tension imposed by these seemingly insuperable questions, Anselm moves assiduously towards his own solution.

He suggests that we have been looking at the problem entirely from the wrong end. Instead of concentrating on the mutability of the creation and trying to relate that to the immutability of the creator, perhaps we should begin with the immutability of the creator while using the mutability of the creation to its advantage. Thus, suggests Anselm, we take the Word as the norm by which the creation is judged true such that 'every created nature stands at a higher stage of essence and worth the more it approximates to the Word.'[96] What this solution does is not only to affirm that mutability has a positive value (in so far as it is our mutability that enables us to continually move towards an improved approximation of the divine) and negative value (in as far as it is our mutability that separates us from the divine), but it also shifts the focus of the discussion towards God and specifically to the Word.

Now that our attention has been oriented in the appropriate direction we are able to carry on and ask two very essential questions. First, if a word is the likeness of a thing, how can *a* word apply or relate or signify (with any degree of accuracy or truth) *the* Word? Second, since words signify things (things being understood to belong necessarily to the created order), is the Word a created entity?[97] Addressing the second question first, Anselm again begins by considering the affirmative, but finds that to affirm the Word as a created entity is not only problematic, but utterly untenable. If, on the other hand, he denies that the Word was created he is still in a quandary because 'if there was not a word in the supreme spirit, then it would not say anything to itself. And if it did not say anything to itself, it would not understand anything. And if it understood nothing, then, since the supreme spirit is supreme wisdom, supreme wisdom would understand nothing. Absurd!'[98]

What, then, has Anselm left to say except that the only meaningful way we can speak about the Word is to affirm that the Supreme spirit understands and 'says' itself eternally. That is to say, the Word and God are identical; signifier and signified are coterminous so that the Word can be said to exist necessarily, internally and coeternally with the Supreme spirit.[99] To help the more lethargic among his readership, Anselm further explains this idea with an example:

So then, when the rational mind thinks itself (and so understands itself) it has an image of itself. This image is inside it; it is born from it. That is, its thinking itself is formed into its own likeness (molded, or impressed, as it were). And this image of itself is its word for itself. Who would deny, therefore, that in this way, when the supreme wisdom says itself and so understands itself, it begets its own likeness, ie. its Word? We cannot, of course, properly, or adequately enough, predicate anything of something as uniquely excellent as this. Nevertheless this word can, not inadequately, be called the image, figure and character, as well as the likeness, of supreme wisdom.[100]

Although the problem of the relation of the Word to creation and creator is solved to Anselm's satisfaction he still thinks that he has not adequately addressed how it is possible for *a* word to signify *the* Word (the first question above). This question is particularly problematic for Anselm because he has already stated his belief that the perfection and magnanimity of the Word is such that, in comparison, words do not exist.[101] How then does Anselm resolve this predicament? With customary sagacity and alacrity Anselm informs us that all things have their existence only 'in the supreme wisdom and reason'.[102] The act of locution in the Word entails perlocution in the form of creation.

This sort of logic and language, will, no doubt, raise the question in the reader's mind about the affinity of this sort of thinking with Platonic or Aristotelian philosophy. For just as Plato taught that there was a supreme good, so Anselm has been talking about a supreme good. Just as Plato taught that everything in the physical realm is an image of a transcendental in another realm which is, in turn, subsumed into the good, so Anselm's theory of signification is built on the notion of a created order imaging an uncreated order. As for Aristotle, did he not seek to reconcile the mutable with the immutable by suggesting that everything is moving towards the prime mover? These and other important questions will be dealt with shortly, but before we delve into such deliberations let us consider how close Anselm's reasoning is to the biblical material in which he and his colleagues were so thoroughly steeped.

Mastered by the Master? The Supremacy of Scripture

One of the influences for which altogether too many scholars have failed adequately to account is the biblical material. When reading parts of Anselm's work the informed reader is constantly reminded of passages in the Bible which comport well with what Anselm is saying. Chapter 34 of the *Monologion* is one such place. When Anselm says 'all created things exist in the supreme spirit, before they are created, after creation and after they have come to an end, or in any way altered', the reader is reminded of Acts 17:28 ('in ipso enim vivimus et movemur et sumus'). Furthermore, the hierarchy of goods with which Anselm begins is a hierarchy which exists only because the many goods that we recognize around us derive their goodness from *the* Good; and so with justice and all other things. The analogy with the *De Grammatico* cannot be missed. Just as a quality does not give the substance to which it is bound that which it describes,[103] but is derivative of the object to which it is appended,[104] so creation is not independent of itself nor does it participate in anything which is more truly created. For Anselm, the creation depends on the creator for existence to the degree that he deems it necessary to engage in the hyperbole seen in Chapter 34 of the *Monologion*. We live and move and have our being in God because if it were not so there would be neither life nor movement nor existence.

Anselm is building a model of reality in the *De Grammatico* and carrying it through into his theology beginning with the *Monologion* which necessitates a personal, active God in whom, on whom and through whom all creation has its existence. And yet, despite the intimate relation predicated in this view, there is a radical disjunction and separation between creator and creation. It is not immediately evident in the *Monologion* because the structure of his argument delays this discussion, but when the appropriate place does become manifest, Anselm is just as eager to accentuate the discontinuity as he was the continuity.

In Chapter 74, for instance, Anselm picks up on what should have been implicitly obvious from the beginning. If we can draw on the existence of good things around us as leading to a single, supreme good, and if each different good approximates more or less accurately to the supreme good according to the degree to which it participates in and emulates the supreme good, then does that not mean that there is a discontinuity or even separation between any given good and the supreme good? Anselm responds that it is absolutely certain that 'the creator, supremely just and supremely good, unjustly deprives nothing of that good for which it was made, and everyone must exert themselves to attain this good by love and desire, with all their heart, all their soul, and all their mind.'[105] Later, in Chapter 76, Anselm again affirms our need to 'progress towards the supreme essence'. But lest we think that he has begun to take up a Neoplatonic stand let us note that it is 'by faith' that the individual is able to progress towards God. And by this point in the work, Anselm has clearly identified the supreme essence as the triune God of the Bible. In fact, he stipulates that 'one must, therefore, have faith in the Father, in the Son and in their Spirit, equally in each individual and in all three together.'[106]

Be this as it may, there is still a tension in Anselm's writing between the essential unity of the creation with the creator and a clear and radical distinction between the two. This dichotomous presentation of reality is, as we shall see more clearly in the next chapter, a fundamental aspect of Anselm's theology. Whether in his *Prayers* or his *Proslogion*, his dialectic or his dogma, his soteriology or his syntax, there is a continual descanting between unity and plurality, continuity and discontinuity, similarity and difference. This bifidity in reality is, as we have seen over and over again and will continue to see in later chapters, grounded in Anselm's understanding of God, which informs his understanding of reality, which guides his theory of signification and interpretation, which, in the end, forms the basis upon which he develops his theological reasoning.

What is particularly marvellous about this aspect of the extension of the ideas introduced in the *De Grammatico* is that, in the *Monologion*, Anselm uses this notion of the dual character of nature and its antiphonal quality as an *inclusio* for the entire work. In the opening chapters as he is setting out to meditate on and probe the ineffability of the divine nature he concludes, without a hint of provisionality, that 'it is therefore utterly evident, beyond a shadow of a doubt, that the supreme essence alone and through itself produced so much and so many things of such beauty – things so varied, yet ordered, so different, yet concordant – and produced them out of nothing.'[107]

The creation is a reflection of the creator, and since we know that the creator is beauty itself and orderliness itself, and the essence of concord, it is only right that what we see around us and the way we think about reality and, therefore, theology should be dominated and permeated by beauty and fittingness. This is not to suggest that the rational was unimportant to Anselm – that would be foolish – but it is to suggest that Anselmian studies to date have given insufficient consideration to the balance that he sought to achieve in his thinking and writing. Reason is important, yes; but beauty is equally important.[108]

At the end of the *Monologion*, after Anselm has taken his readers through an examination of the nature of God, the person and activity of the Word (Son), the place of the Holy Spirit, and their interrelations within the Godhead, and shown us that the only way to comprehend (as much as possible) the nature of this God and his relation to creation is by faith, he offers as the conclusion that

> we have established that all things were created and are supported through the supremely good and supremely wise omnipotence of this spirit. And so it would be extremely contrary to claim that it does not dominate what it has created, that either something else, less powerful, wise and good, or nothing at all – just the entirely irrational, unstructured chaos of chance – controls what it has created.[109]

What was stated positively in the beginning is now stated negatively in the end. Anselm began by affirming that the beauty and harmony in the Godhead is reflected in all creation and therefore ought to pervade all our thinking, be it grammatical, syntactical, dialectical or theological. Now, after extended deliberation, he has shown to his own satisfaction that the nature of this deity is also such that it is impossible to think otherwise. It is impossible that this world could be under the providential hand of anyone other than the triune God. It is impossible that the reality we inhabit is dominated by anything other than a rational, orderly, purposeful creator. The 'unstructured chaos of chance' gives way to the beauty inherent in all things, and particularly in theological reflection because it is there that we see most clearly how 'the supreme essence alone is that through which anything good is good, without which nothing is good, and out of, through and in which all things exist'.[110] And when the reader has come to see this it will become 'superlatively clear that this is the only thing that all other natures ought, with all their might, to love and worship.'[111]

The reader cannot help but see, at this point, how immersed the *Monologion* is in the *De Grammatico*. At the beginning of the treatise the form of meditating on the divine reflected the ideas and model of reality forwarded in the *De Grammatico*. The participation of quality in substance was transformed into the participation of quality in *the* substance. Whereas white participated in and derived its quality from the substance man, now, by the same principle, goodness participates in and derives its quality from *the* transcendent, supreme Good who is God. This idea is then elaborated and explained in the *Monologion* in the way we have examined and is brought to the conclusion that since all things must necessarily derive their existence from the supreme essence who is the triune God we ought, in light of our distance from and discontinuity with God, seek to become better images of him. For just as the word which more accurately describes the quality of a substance can be said to more truly participate in its object, so the individual who more ardently reflects on the nature of God through 'love and worship' will attain an ever-increasing degree of participation in that divine nature.

More than Christian?

Is it not possible though, that Anselm's understanding of reality as evinced in the *De Grammatico* and the subsequent development of his theology in the *Monologion* reflect an Aristotelian or Platonic order? Surely we cannot deny the importance of Aristotelian categories after demonstrating their inclusion in the *De Grammatico*. For if Aristotle's philosophy framed Anselm's thought on language, and Anselm's theory of language is prescriptive for his theological enterprise, then does it not stand to reason that Greek philosophy is a seminal part of Anselm's thinking? While some preliminary considerations relating to this matter have already been broached, it may be of some benefit to interact further with this point by briefly comparing Anselm first to Aristotle and then to Plato.[112]

First, it is worth noting that there is general agreement that Anselm had a very limited knowledge of both Aristotle and Plato.[113] Clearly, Anselm had some knowledge of Aristotle's *Categoriae* or at least Boethius' commentary on it. What is interesting, however, is that although Anselm does interact with Aristotle in the *De Grammatico*, he does so in a way which neglects to interact with the finer points of Aristotle's philosophy. At the beginning of Chapter 17, for example, the student questions Anselm's line of argument in favour of paronymy by arguing Aristotle's point that 'everything which is, is one of either substance or quantity or quality, and so on.'[114] In other words, the common understanding of Aristotle seemed to be that everything that is has its own category. In response, Anselm states that the purpose of Aristotle's work is altogether different from theirs. The conclusion, summarized above, is that Aristotle is helpful in defining literate as a quality; but as for appellation, a category which Aristotle does not address in the way later medieval logicians did, literate is a substance.[115] The reasoning behind Aristotle's categorization is completely ignored and the teleological aspect which is so common in Aristotle is also left aside. What Aristotle seems to have passed down to Anselm, then, is little more than that words are important because they signify and that certain words can be categorized according to their function. It appears that Aristotle lends nothing directly to Anselm's theological interpretation of words, though the *Categoriae* may be perceived as a step in the right direction.

What of Plato? Again, we must stress with Brian Davies and Gillian Evans that Plato was not well known in Anselm's period. There is even uncertainty whether or not Anselm knew the *Timaeus*. The most solid proposition which can be made in favour of Platonic influence, therefore, is that Anselm derived his Platonism from Augustine. It is Augustine who admits to following Plato and Plotinus for some time before converting to Christianity, and it is Augustine who influenced Anselm most. The degree to which Augustine was Platonic or Neoplatonic cannot be explored fully here, but, in light of the works which we have already introduced that have a bearing on Anselm's *De Grammatico*, there is one consideration worthy of our attention: the incarnation. We noted above that the union of the divine and the human in the person of Jesus Christ was the basis on which Anselm was ultimately able to postulate a theory of signification. But it is also worth noting that the incarnation (as Anselm expresses it) is what radically separates Christian theology from Platonism and Neoplatonism. Whether we are addressing the ideal dualism of Platonic thought wherein nothing in this world is real until it has shed its dross of imitation, or the fluid emanations of being from the 'One', postulated by Plotinus, which requires the lower aspects of physicality to ascend and assimilate back into the 'One', there is nothing in either of these philosophies which affirms the goodness of the physical and the possibility of achieving perfection in the body.

In the person of Jesus, Augustine recognized the revolutionary break that such a revelation required between different religions and philosophies. Thus, in his *De Trinitate*, the culmination of, among other things, his theory of signification and interpretation, Augustine tells us that he is writing against those who wish to transcend the creation in one of any number of ways. It is against those philosophies, and in light of the inherent difficulties of talking about the Trinity, that Augustine falls back on his only hope: Christ. At the prospect of describing the One who is changeless and atemporal Augustine concludes that it is necessary, therefore, to purge our minds, in order to be able to see ineffably that which is ineffable; whereto not having yet attained, we are to be nourished by faith, and led by such ways as are more suited to our capacity, that we may be rendered apt and able to comprehend it. *And hence the Apostle says, that 'in Christ indeed are hid all the treasures of wisdom and knowledge'*.[116]

It is only by virtue of the incarnation that Augustine is able to begin to grasp something of the nature of the Trinity because it is in Christ that the Father is revealed and in Christ that the Spirit dwells. Thus it is in Christ that Augustine found his starting point.

The incarnation introduces a second point of departure: sin. Augustine makes it painfully clear that the divine and the human cannot be united until the human has been purged of the sin which causes separation from God.[117] In connection with this Carol Harrison points out that in the *De Trinitate* the incarnation is 'in harmony with man's discordant state and, therefore, in bringing the fragmented, discordant multiplicity which has resulted from man's neglect of divine order, into harmony and unity with Himself, the Unique One and with God's providential order and economy.'[118] What is particularly interesting about this work (*De Trinitate*) is that this is the very work Anselm asks his readers to peruse before judging the *Monologion*.[119]

There is no doubt much more that could be said about Augustine and Platonism and Neoplatonism, but with respect to Augustine's three works which we have shown bear similarities to Anselm's thinking on words, signification, epistemology and ontology, there seems to be little reason to posit anything other than a thoroughly biblical or Christian foundation for Anselm's ideas. The *De Grammatico* offers us a theory of words which suggests that while they are significant because they are the only means we have of communicating truth, they do nothing more than either signify a thing itself or that which is innate to the thing under consideration.[120] To be sure, this may sound like Aristotle, and since Anselm chose to interact with Aristotle a degree of similarity cannot be avoided, but when we compare the immense influence of Augustine and the remarkable similarities between Anselm's *De Grammatico*, and the outworking of those principles in the *Monologion*, with Augustine's *De Magistro*, *De Doctrina Christiana* and *De Trinitate*, the weight of the evidence mitigates against the formative power of Greek philosophy and in favour of the formative power of a distinctively Christian model.

And it is not only away from Greek philosophy and towards Augustine that we should look for Anselm's formative influence, but also to the Church Fathers since Anselm himself admits that 'in the course of frequent readings of this treatise I have been unable to find anything which is inconsistent with the writings of the Catholic Fathers'.[121] Was it not Hilary of Poitiers who claimed that Moses (as with the rest of us) 'could have known nothing except through God himself'?[122] Did Irenaeus not write, 'the Lord taught us that no man is capable of knowing God, unless he be taught of God; that is, that God cannot be known without God'?[123] We should not deny, of course, that pagan writings have influenced Christian writers, but neither should we blindly accept that their influence is formative for Christian theology. For Plato, as for Aristotle, as for Plotinus, the exercise of reason is the guarantor of epistemic success; whereas for Augustine and Anselm the necessity of divine intervention and human dependency on God for illumination and understanding is the 'prime condition and guarantee of its validity'.[124]

Plato had tried to harmonize the divergent parts of creation by proposing a realm of Forms which was, in turn, subsumed into the 'good'. Essentially, what he proposed was the elimination of individuation in perfection. What we see and experience in this world signifies something in another place, but where is the point of contact? Plotinus tried to improve on this problem by suggesting emanation from the 'One', but how does that which has no being, which is inanimate, explain the creation of being and animation? With obstacles such as these, on what foundation can one possibly build a model of reality which unites the immanent and the transcendent, the signifier and the signified? None, says Anselm, but the Christian model. True, there are dichotomies and paradoxes contained in the Christian interpretation of reality, but it is these antinomies which, for Anselm, support and sustain its very structure. And, as we shall see in the apogee of Anselm's theological works, it is the incarnation of the second member of the Trinity who embodies the restoration of perfection and beauty, symmetry and harmony, seminally portrayed in the *De Grammatico*. There in the *Cur Deus Homo* we shall see the union of the transcendent and the immanent; that which was signified obliquely (to use language from the *De Grammatico*), taking a form which allowed the supreme essence to be signified precisively.

Where Do We Go from Here?

We have now waded through the morass of interpretation surrounding the *De Grammatico*, and discovered that it is in fact not primarily about grammar or even logic, but about dialectic. And, we have also discovered, dialectic in Anselm's day referred to the art of dialogue and particularly to the ability of the participants to ask the right questions in the right order and to answer them in the right way. In the process we saw, furthermore, that since Anselm's aim was to teach dialectic through example the subject matter he chose was familiar to his students, and certainly understandable, otherwise the point of the exercise would be lost in a maze of content. Thus, if there is any confusion as to the arguments in the treatise, they are most likely problems resulting from our distance from the times in which the text was written.

Having arrived at these conclusions we then sided with Rosamund McKitterick's supposition that works such as the *De Grammatico* are more valuable for the information they offer about the author and the context in which he was writing than for their actual content. Taking our lead from

McKitterick (though not following the specifics of her suggestion that such works illumine only our understanding of politics, social values, and the like), we investigated the possibility that the *De Grammatico* tells us more about Anselm's theology than has hitherto been explored or believed. After expanding the search beyond the bounds of Carolingian precedents, we ventured into the works of St Augustine, Anselm's avowed mentor and chief authority, to see if there was any evidence to support the notion that Anselm had in fact drawn on Augustine.

It did not take long to identify one treatise in particular which set out the same principles as the *De Grammatico*: the *De Magistro*. There we saw that Augustine too had worked on a theory of words and signification which led more immediately than Anselm's *De Grammatico* into direct theological application. Following on from the *De Magistro*, we found a further development in Augustine's *De Doctrina Christiana*. This treatise reviewed some of the principles set out in the *De Magistro* and then elaborated on them for the explicit purpose of elucidating issues pertinent to hermeneutics and homiletics. Finally, we saw how one of Augustine's more popular doctrinal treatises, the *De Trinitate*, provided a good example of the outworking of the principles and theories introduced and examined in the previous two works.

Remarkably, though not surprisingly, we discovered that the same pattern was discernible in Anselm's corpus. Anselm, like Augustine, spent his early life thinking about and concentrating on words, their significance and how they can aid interpretation. As we noted at the very beginning of this chapter, the *De Grammatico* was the first treatise Anselm ever wrote, and as we discovered through careful examination, it is in that work that we find the seeds of a methodology and model of reality which would germinate in each of his succeeding theological monographs.

Drawing on Augustine, then, and thinking about the connections between his writing and the theological enterprise on which Anselm embarked, a sequence of deductions became clear. Once we saw that Anselm believed that words are pre-eminently important because they signify real things it became evident that the world is, therefore, necessarily assumed to have been ordered by some supreme being (the accuracy of which deduction was explored in the *Monologion*); otherwise there would be no reason to assume that our perception of reality relates to anything that is real. Tying this in with his context, it is not difficult to see how Anselm would have been conducive to writing a work like the *De Grammatico*. At a time when order, balance and harmony were not easily achieved or maintained, and when one could be certain of few things, it is hardly astonishing to discover that theologians such as Anselm should develop their thinking in a direction which affirms what could so easily be construed as ephemeral.

The task that we have now is to sift through the remainder of Anselm's works to see how his model of reality, implied and expanded as it is in his theory of signification, his emphasis on words, and his emphasis on definition guides his theological task and leads him ineluctably to an exploration and exposition of the beauty of God's activity in creation and redemption. It is to this end that we must now turn from one of the most obscure works in Anselm's output to, arguably, his most famous: the *Proslogion*. There, among the diversity of interpretation that abounds, we will see the subtle and quiet mind of a man consumed by a *weltbild* which directs his thinking into an understanding of the nature of God and thus into his very presence.

Notes

1   In the *Alliterative Morte Arthure* (ed. Larry D. Benson, Exeter: University of Exeter Press, 1995) part of the opening reads as follows, 'And wisse me to warp out some word at this time / That nother void be ne vain but worship til Himselven / Plesand and profitable to the pople that them heres.' In many respects this reflects Anselm's desire that his student would come to appreciate words, precisely because they are neither empty nor vain, but convey something of the deep structure of a reality that longs to worship its creator.

2   *VA*, pp. 28–9.

3   *De Veritate*, preface (S.1.73.5–8).

4   R.W. Southern (1995), *Saint Anselm: A Portrait in a Landscape,* Cambridge: Cambridge University Press, p. 63.

5   *De Veritate*, preface (S.1.73.3–4).

6   (S.1.73.3).

7   Cf. *VA*, p. 28, note 1.

8   Cf. the three dialogues and the *Cur Deus Homo.*

9   Cf. the *Prayers*, the *Proslogion*, the *Monologion*, and the *Meditation on Human Redemption*.

10 D.P. Henry (1974), *Commentary on the* De Grammatico, Boston: D. Reidel Co., p. 11 (hereafter referred to as Henry, *Commentary*).

11 Cf. Vivien Law (1982), *The Insular Latin Grammarians*, Woodbridge: The Boydell Press, p. 2ff.

12 Vivien Law (1994), 'The Study of Grammar', in R. McKitterick (ed.), *Carolingian Culture: Emulation and Innovation,* Cambridge: Cambridge University Press, p. 97. Compare also, Anneli Luhtala (1993), 'Syntax and Dialectic in Carolingian Commentaries on Priscian's *Institutiones Grammaticae*', in Vivien Law (ed.), *History of Linguistic Thought in the Early Middle Ages*, Amsterdam: John Benjamins Publishing Company, p. 149.

13 Law, 'The Study of Grammar', p. 95.

14 Law, 'The Study of Grammar', p. 99, and Luhtala, p. 148.

15 Luhtala, p. 152.

16 Luhtala, p. 149.

17 *De Veritate*, preface (S.1.73.5–8).

18 D.P. Henry (1964), *The De Grammatico of St Anselm*, Notre Dame, IN: University of Notre Dame Press, p. 89 (hereafter referred to as Henry, *De Grammatico*).

19 *De Grammatico*, 1 (S.1.145.4–6): 'De grammatico peto, ut me certum facias utrum sit substantia an qualitas; ut hoc cognito, quid de aliis quae similiter denominative dicuntur sentire debeam agnoscam.'

20 Evans comments that Anselm's technical skills in language 'began to seem a little dated as the study of logic and language progressed and technical terminology and principles became more sophisticated', G.R. Evans (1989), *Anselm*, London: Geoffrey Chapman, p. 107.

21 Southern, p. 63.

22 Cf. Henry, *De Grammatico*, p. 2.
23 John Marenbon (1983), *Early Medieval Philosophy*, London: Routledge & Kegan Paul, p. 102.
24 Marenbon, p. 95.
25 Vivien Law (1993), 'The Historiography of Grammar' in Vivien Law (ed.), *History of Linguistic Thought in the Early Middle Ages*, Amsterdam: John Benjamins Publishing Company, p. 3.
26 Law, 'The Historiography of Grammar', p. 8.
27 Law, 'The Historiography of Grammar', p. 19.
28 A remarkable point made all the more so in light of the fact that Southern's biography – regarded as the foremost work on Anselm – contains only three pages on the treatise.
29 Henry, *De Grammatico*, p. 1.
30 Henry, *De Grammatico*, p. 2. Compare also, D.P. Henry (1993), *The Logic of St Anselm*, Aldershot: Gregg Revivals, p. 22.
31 Henry, *De Grammatico*, p. 3.
32 *De Grammatico*, 1 (S.1.145.5).
33 *De Grammatico*, 2 (S.1.146.11–13).
34 I have adopted Henry's translation of 'literacy' and 'literate' because it seems to convey the sense of *grammaticus* and the context most accurately. For further comments cf. Henry, *De Grammatico*, p. 92.
35 *De Grammatico*, 16 (S.1.161.23–1.162.2).
36 *De Grammatico*, 16 (S.1.162.5–6) 'Homo quippe solus, id est, absque grammatica, est grammaticus; quia solus est habens grammaticam: grammatica namque, nec sola, nec cum homine habet grammaticam.'
37 *De Grammatico*, 16 (S.1.162.12–13).
38 *De Grammatico*, 17 (S.1.162.16–19).
39 Henry, *Commentary*, p. 205.
40 *De Grammatico*, 12 (S.1.157.1–8) my translation.
41 Henry, *Commentary*, p. 11.
42 Henry, *Commentary*, p. 11.
43 Henry, *Commentary*, p. 12.
44 Apparently, neither did Evans. Although she does follow Henry in his emphasis on *usus* or *consuetudo loquendi* as distance from proper or technical language, she does not follow him to the point of investing too much in the logic and syntax. She is careful to call our attention to the fact that as practical and helpful as Anselm's skills are to the philosopher, they are equally helpful 'to the reader of Scripture', p. 43.
45 Compare, for instance, *De Incarnatione Verbi* 1; *Proslogion* 1 (S.2.7.10–12 and 1.100.18–19).
46 *Proslogion*, preface (S.1.94.12).
47 *Proslogion.* preface (S.1.94.13).
48 *De Grammatico*, 1 (S.1.145.15–17).
49 *VA*, p. 141.
50 Marenbon, p. 104.
51 Evans, p. 107.
52 Southern, p. 63.
53 Southern, p. 63.
54 Ep. 77.
55 Southern, p. 80.
56 Augustine, *De Magistro*, 1 in Whitney J. Oates (ed.), *The Basic Writings of St Augustine*, vol. 1, Grand Rapids, MI: Baker Book House.
57 *De Magistro*, 1.
58 *De Magistro*, 4.
59 *De Magistro*, 14.
60 *De Magistro*, 9.

61 *De Magistro*, 10.
62 *De Magistro*, 10.
63 *De Magistro*, 12.
64 *De Magistro*, 12.
65 *De Magistro*, 12.
66 *De Magistro*, 12.
67 *De Magistro*, 14, original emphasis.
68 *De Magistro*, 13.
69 *De Magistro*, 11, quoting a version of the Vulgate on Is. 7:9.
70 Augustine, *On Christian Doctrine*, 1.1 in *Nicene and Post-Nicene Fathers*, series 1, vol. 2.
71 Cf. *On Christian Doctrine*, 1.2ff.
72 *On Christian Doctrine*, 2.37.
73 Augustine, *De Trinitate*, 1.1 in *Nicene and Post-Nicene Fathers*, series 1, vol. 3.
74 *On Christian Doctrine*, 2.37
75 Cf. *De Magistro*, 14, 'we should not attribute more to words than is proper.'
76 Southern, p. 63.
77 Augustine, *De Ordine*, 1.27 in *Patrologia Latina* 32:990. Database CD, Cambridge: Chadwyck-Healey, 1995.
78 Cf. *Proslogion*, prologue, 1, 14, 25, 26 (S.1.93.20–1.94.2; 1.97.4–10; 1.111.8–1.112.11; 1.118.20–1.120.20; 1.120.23–1.122.2).
79 Cf. *Proslogion*, 1 (S.1.93.1ff).
80 Harrison, p. 86.
81 Harrison, p. 192.
82 Definition was essential (cf. *Proslogion*, 2–4; numerous places in the *Cur Deus Homo* and three dialogues). Signification was vital (*Prayers and Meditations*; *Monologion*, *Proslogion*).
83 Cf. *On Christian Doctrine*, 2.32.50 where Augustine says something very similar.
84 The reason for this transparency is most likely due to the fact that the *Monologion* was Anselm's first theological work after the *De Grammatico*. Subsequent works, such as the *Proslogion*, also bear obvious affinities with the *De Grammatico*, but the more time that elapsed between the *De Grammatico* and any given work the less transparent the connection. In fact, it may well be that this is part of the reason why the *De Grammatico* is so often maligned. In the Anselmian corpus the two works which receive sustained attention, the *Proslogion* and the *Cur Deus Homo*, are both often, though not always, deemed as high water marks in Anselm's career, and for that reason seem to be considered apart from their place and connection to preceding and succeeding works. This is most obviously the case with the *Cur Deus Homo* which wasn't finished until the end of the eleventh century, but it is also true of the *Proslogion*. The *Proslogion*, rather than being the outgrowth of the *Monologion* which is, in turn, dependent on the *De Grammatico*, is considered to be such an immense improvement on the *Monologion* that, while deriving its basic subject matter from the ideas presented there, it is deemed essentially autonomous. If, however, Anselm's theological works are understood to derive, fundamentally, from the hermeneutical principles intimated in his *De Grammatico*, perhaps more attention will be paid to this obscure work and the coherency within Anselm's works will be better appreciated.
85 *Monologion*, 1 (S.1.13.5–7).
86 *Monologion*, 1 (S.1.14.5–9).
87 *Monologion*, 1 (S.1.14.5–6).
88 Cf. *Monologion*, 1 (S.1.15.6–7): 'It therefore follows that all the other good things are good through something other than what they themselves are, while this thing alone is good through itself.'
89 In fact, this chapter and its ensuing corollaries is reminiscent of the first chapter of Genesis and the opening chapter in John. There too we see how the Word and words are

integral to the establishment of the created order. We also see in these books a model of reality which, like Anselm's, considers the existence of God essential to right order and relation. God pronounced everything he had made as good because he had made it. The relationship between the creation (including Adam and Eve) and creator was as it should be. There was order and harmony and beauty in creation because they were created by and participated in the order, harmony and beauty that is in God.

90 Anselm is very careful with his terms at this point. So far he has only used two different words to identify God: *essentia* and *natura*.

91 *Monologion*, 16 (S.1.31.1–8).

92 *Monologion*, 29 (S.1.47.4–5).

93 *Monologion*, 29 (S.1.47.5–7): 'opportunum existimo ut de ejus locutione, per quam facta sunt omnia, si quid possim, considerem.'

94 *Monologion*, 31 (S.1.48.20–21). 'Imitation' here is part of Anselm's concept of participation. For further discussion on the idea of participation in Anselm cf. Chapter 3, footnote 40.

95 *Monologion*, 31 (S.1.48.23).

96 *Monologion*, 31 (S.1.50.12–13).

97 *Monologion*, 32 (S.1.50.21–3).

98 *Monologion*, 32 (S.1.50.28–1.51.3).

99 *Monologion*, 32 (S.1.51.15–16).

100 *Monologion*, 33 (S.1.52.13–1.53.4).

101 *Monologion*, 28 (S.1.46.26–31).

102 *Monologion*, 34 (S.1.53.18–21).

103 White, for example, does not participate in whiteness and then lend that whiteness to a substance such as a horse; rather, the white is a quality in as far as it is describing that which the substance horse already has.

104 *De Grammatico*, 20 and 21 (S.1.166.13–22; 1.166.24ff).

105 *Monologion*, 74 (S.1.83.7–8). Although not necessarily pertinent to our immediate interests, it is worth noting again how infused Anselm's language is with the words of the Bible, Matthew 22:37 in this case ('Love the Lord your God with all your heart and with all your soul and with all your mind').

106 *Monologion*, 77 (S.1.84.6–7). We should also note here that Anselm's designation of the Spirit as 'their Spirit' is not intended to convey the idea that the Spirit is a non-personal entity shared by the Father and the Son, but, as the second half of the sentence clearly shows, that the Spirit is the third member of the Trinity. The reason for this language is most likely due to Anselm's desire to emphasize the procession of the Holy Spirit from both Father and Son over and against the Eastern view.

107 *Monologion*, 7 (S.1.22.5–10).

108 Indeed, it may even be argued that Anselm would not be content with this description. A more apt description of Anselm's theological schema would be to say that on all points of doctrine we need to hold a balance of perspectives which incorporates all known attributes of God, for if our world is a reflection of God, then our understanding of that world must take as much of God into account as possible in order to attain the best and fullest appreciation of any given truth.

109 *Monologion*, 80 (S.1.87.1–5).

110 *Monologion*, 80 (S.1.87.5–7).

111 *Monologion*, 80 (S.1.87.8–10).

112 I will have cause to elaborate further on these themes, especially the Platonic influence in the chapter on the *Proslogion*, but it seems to me that an initial foray into this aspect of Anselmian studies cannot be ignored.

113 Cf. Davies, p. xxi, and Southern, p. 134.

114 *De Grammatico*, 17 (S.1.162.16–17).

115 *De Grammatico*, 18 (S.1.164.3–6).

116 *De Trinitate*, 1.1, italics mine.

117   Cf. *De Trinitate*, 4.18.
118   Harrison, p. 205; cf. also *De Trinitate*, 4.7.11.
119   *Monologion*, prologue (S.1.8.12–14): 'I ask that they first make a careful and thorough reading of the books *On the Trinity* of the aforementioned learned Augustine and then judge my little treatise on the basis of them.'
120   We may also add another way in which Anselm was breaking with Platonic thought. Anselm does argue that words, though they signify something, do not always signify a transcendental. White, for example, does not signify whiteness, rather it is appellative of man who does signify something real – a reality which is grounded in God (cf. *De Grammatico*, 20 – S.1.166.12ff).
121   *Monologion*, prologue (S.1.8.8–9).
122   Hilary of Poitiers, *De Trinitate*, 5.21 in *Nicene and Post-Nicene Fathers.* Series II.
123   Irenaeus, *Against Heresies*, 4.6.4 in *Ante-Nicene Fathers*, vol. 1.
124   Henri de Lubac (1960), *The Discovery of God*, trans. Alexander Dru, Grand Rapids, MI: William B. Eerdmans, p. 7.

Chapter 4

Justifying the Ways of God to Men[1]

The *Proslogion* is among the most famous of medieval works. Its examination and re-examination in the last one thousand years has produced a prodigious amount of scholarship. For some, this is a work of profoundly theological significance; for others, it is decidedly philosophical. In both cases, however, the centre of attention has been those five little words, 'quo nihil maius cogitari possit' (that which nothing greater can be conceived). The reason these words have caught the imagination of so many is that they alone are supposed to say something about God's existence. But how, it may be asked, can five little words express the essence of divine existence? What guarantee do we have that these words adequately reflect what lies beyond them? In order to appreciate what Anselm is doing, and why he believes his argument has force, the reader must remain continually mindful of the *De Grammatico* and the *Monologion*.

In those two works Anselm expressed his conviction that there is unity in diversity, harmony in reality, and the guarantee that the finite can represent the infinite and the immanent the transcendent because the creator has infused part of who he is into that which he has created. There is, therefore, a symmetry between the creation and the creator, though we must always bear in mind that this relationship with the creator is also proportional. We do not experience or know the totality of God's goodness, truth, beauty or any other aspect of his character. In fact, it is just this situation that gives the *Proslogion* its sense of yearning. Anselm knows that he can talk about God, know God and experience God in the present, but he longs to stretch beyond the present and reach into the eschaton where a fullness of the beatific vision will be known beyond measure. Only in this context, where a theory of signification is rooted in the knowledge of God's creative and re-creative work, will Anselm's desire to discover *unum argumentum* make any sense. Only in this context will a proper evaluation of *probare* be achieved. Only in this context will the conviction that *Deus vere est* bear any relation to the succeeding chapters so frequently ignored. The *Proslogion* must be read theologically, and for that reason, in Anselm's mind, it must embrace the aesthetic concerns mentioned above. There is, of course, a formidable amount of scholarship that disagrees.

Following Kant, Arthur McGill states that, among other problems, Anselm's proof fails in as far as it 'analyses a concept without once seeking contact with the data of sensory experience'.[2] P.J. McGrath argues in a similar vein when he says that internal coherence is insufficient reason to prove something if the object in question does not exist in the real world.[3] Robert

Brecher rejects Anselm's proof, but is kind enough to admit that while the argument is certainly not valid it is probative. That is to say, within the context of Anselm's perceived Platonic metaphysics the argument is internally coherent.[4] Ian Weeks interprets Anselm's formula in such a way as to understand that God is unlimited, which is clearly problematic because not even God can be unlimited in every way.[5] William Robinson adds his thoughts to the debate by arguing that Anselm did not sufficiently understand the difference between weak knowledge and strong knowledge. Consequently, Anselm misunderstood that positing a proof for the existence of God could not rest on the mere intelligibility of a statement or description because it could not answer the how and the why questions.[6]

In spite of this onslaught of disbelief and continued attempts to discredit Anselm's work, there are those who have defended it. The defenders of the *Proslogion* can roughly be divided into two groups. The first group are those who have chosen to respond to the objections of philosophers in kind. Alvin Plantinga and Charles Hartshorne are two of the best-known defenders in this tradition.[7] The second group, and the one with which we are primarily concerned include scholars such as Karl Barth, Anselm Stoltz and Ian Davie who have sought to elucidate Anselm's words within a theological context. These and others unashamedly stake out their territory entirely within the bounds of faith. Davie admits that, unlike so many, Anselm's proof does not flow from the human psyche or human understanding; rather, God is the very ground of Anselm's thinking.[8] Barth takes his starting point from the dictum *credo ut intelligam*, and contends that what Anselm is doing is not proving, but understanding, and that only as *intellegere* is achieved does one arrive at *probare*.[9] Stoltz takes a somewhat different tack and asserts that Anselm is not seeking to prove the existence of God but to gain an experience of the living God and to catch a vision of him.[10] What then is the reader of the *Proslogion* to do with these conflicting interpretations?

Turning to the Text

When we turn to the *Proslogion* itself, the first thing we notice is that Anselm is in search of one single argument. But what is it he wishes to prove by this argument? As noted above, the usual answer is that Anselm is hoping to prove that God really exists. The trouble with this answer, however, is not only that it glosses the Latin somewhat unfairly, but also that it does not take into consideration the rest of the sentence, nor the rest of the book. Anselm was hoping to demonstrate 'that God truly exists, *and* that he is the greatest good who depends on nothing else, *and* on whom all things depend in order to exist and exist well, *and* whatever else we believe about the divine substance' ('quia Deus vere est, et quia est summum bonum nullo alio indigens, et quo omnia indigent ut sint et bene sint, et quaecumque credimus de divina substantia').[11] This is indeed a formidable proposition, but before we delve into its riches we should be careful to note briefly that *probare* does not always mean 'to prove'. *Probare* is also commonly used to mean to probe, to search, to test or to prod. It is somewhat unfair to Anselm to assume he is offering a proof here. After all, proving so many different things by one single argument, by five little words, seems just a bit ambitious.

Vere in Anselm's Argument

With respect to the English gloss of the Latin text, Anselm's words 'Deus vere est' are usually translated 'God really exists' when in point of fact *vere* could also be translated to mean 'truly' ('God truly exists'). Such a slight nuance of translation may not at first seem significant, but upon closer inspection the translation of this word changes the connotation, and thus the interpretation, of the whole work (especially in conjunction with what was said about the semantic range of *probare*). For if we admit that Anselm's clause can be translated in the latter sense then the question arises, is Anselm seeking to prove that God actually exists? Is Anselm's purpose to convince the unbeliever that, contrary to his objections, God does exist in reality? The philosophers noted at the beginning of this chapter would certainly affirm that this is indeed Anselm's objective. I would argue the contrary, in part, on account of Anselm's choice of words.

The word 'vere' is used a total of twenty times throughout the text. In ten of the twenty cases the word is applied to God directly and the connotation is undoubtedly 'certain'.[12] Seven times the word is not applied directly to God but is used as an adverb indicating certainty.[13] In only one instance the word may not mean 'certain' but is not applied to God.[14] In the remaining two cases the word is applied to God and the connotation could go either way.[15] The ambiguity lies in one's overall interpretation of what Anselm is doing. If we assume the usual interpretation, that he is proving the fact of God's existence, then these two instances of 'vere' are less likely to indicate certainty. If, however, we believe that Anselm was seeking to say something about both the being and nature of God, then these two occurrences of the word do indicate certainty.[16] Indeed, it could be argued that even if we assume Anselm is seeking to prove the fact of God's existence the second of these two occurrences of 'vere' more than likely indicates certainty.

The second of these two occurrences appears in the title of Chapter 2. The title of the second chapter reads 'Quod vere sit Deus' ('That God truly exists'). This is the chapter in which Anselm begins his famous argument, and it is therefore in this chapter that, if the common interpretation is followed, we would not expect any more prayer or dialogue with God. This is not the case. Anselm begins Chapter 2 as he did Chapter 1: he addresses God. This time Anselm is asking that God would 'grant understanding to faith', and that he might 'understand that you exist as we believe you exist' and that 'you [God] are what we believe you to be.'[17] These are not the statements of someone who is entertaining doubts. These are the statements of a man who is sure of what he believes. His struggle is to extend his reasoning to match that which he believes based on the revelation of God.

Consequently, of the eighteen times *vere* is used with reference to God (not including its use in the prologue which is still under consideration) every instance is best understood to indicate certainty. Now seeking to prove the certainty of God's existence is altogether different from seeking to prove that he exists at all. The former determination operates on an entirely different set of premises than the latter. Were Anselm to attempt to prove God's existence apart from knowing he already existed then on what basis could he begin? How could he say anything about the nature of that which he was seeking to prove? There would be no guarantee of a reliable relationship between that which we know and that which lies beyond us. If, however, Anselm was seeking to probe (*probare*) the tradition of which he was a part, to test (*probare*) the limits of the tenets of the faith he had received and so demonstrate (*probare*) their certainty, then the presuppositions we have already explored in the *De Grammatico*, the *Monologion* and the *Prayers and Meditations* provide the backdrop against which the present investigation takes place. The harmony of reality is what gives Anselm his certainty. The proportioned symmetry between the creator and creation is what provides Anselm with the model of reality which is able to express the simplicity of divinity in *unum argumentum* because the world is ordered according to the divine being. *Vere* is not a word which, on its own, connotes aesthetic categories, but in the larger context of Anselm's stated purpose in the *Proslogion*, and across the gamut of his other treatises, God's true existence is part of a larger understanding of reality which encompasses beauty and fittingness.

This is why we must proceed cautiously when translating *vere*. If we say that Anselm is interested in arguing for the fact of God's existence then the rest of what he claims he wishes to show with his single argument (that is, that God is the supreme good and everything Christians believe about Him is true, that God's being is necessary, and that our being is contingent) becomes superfluous. It is superfluous if he fails to prove God's existence because then he would be talking about the attributes of a non-existent being.[18] And even if philosophers generally did agree that Anselm was successful in proving God's existence they would immediately recognize that a determination of the character and attributes of this being would be mere speculation apart from some kind of revelation. If, on the other hand, we say that Anselm is interested in establishing that God truly exists, that is, that God's existence is certain in so far as His nature is such that he cannot be thought not to exist, then the remaining chapters (5–26) become integral and indispensable to the overall argument. Understood in this way, an altogether different answer to the question of the focus of the *Proslogion* emerges.

The Rest of the Sentence

Most commentators believe that the locus of the argument is found some-where in Chapters 2 through 4. The problem with this is twofold. First, it neglects four-fifths of the text. Anselm wrote twenty-six chapters of material and intended that all twenty-six be taken into account. Second, focusing on Chapters 2 through 4 selectively edits out material that touches on God's person and therefore does not adequately account for Anselm's fundamental belief that there is an aesthetic unity[19] in God such that statements made about his existence (or being) cannot be adequately understood or appreciated apart from assertions about his person and character. But how do we know that Anselm believed that the being and person of God could not be separated? The answer lies in the very sentence that has sparked the intense scrutiny of so many thinkers. What is so often overlooked here is that Anselm's desire to prove that God truly exists is only the first of a string of objectives he wishes to achieve. Apparently, Anselm also wants to use his single argument to prove that God is the supreme good, and that his being is necessary and that ours is contingent, and, as he says, 'whatever else we believe about the divine nature'.[20] On first reading, the task Anselm has set for himself seems some-what overwrought. Surely a single argument could never hope to comprehend such divergent objectives – or could it? A careful reading of this sentence reveals that Anselm is seeking to talk about God in a way that comprehends his existence and his person.

It is for this reason that the appellative 'ontological' to Anselm's argument is a misnomer since he sought to argue for the reasonableness of God's ontological *and* personable qualities. Unfortunately, however, the latter of the two aspects of God is altogether too often neglected as the modern penchant to prove God's existence apart from his person continues to dominate discussions. The need for the logical necessity or modal integrity of the existence of a Supreme Being is often deemed prior to any consideration of its character. This is simply not the case for Anselm. This much is clear in Anselm's statement that 'if at times we assert by a process of reasoning a conclusion which we cannot explicitly cite from the saying of Scripture or demonstrate from the bare wording, still it is by using Scripture that we know in the following way whether the affirmation should be accepted or rejected.'[21] In short, Scripture is prescriptive for all theological discourse. Anselm's methodology did not allow for a dichotomy between reason and revelation. This dichotomy is not easy to accept, especially in a context where the Bible is rarely afforded the same esteem. But again, we must recall that Anselm believed that God communicated in 'Sacred Scripture' that he is unity in trinity, possessing all that it is better to be than not to be in due proportion. Thus it is only to Scripture that Anselm can turn when he comes to consider God, and there he finds that his ability to speak of the existence of God flows directly out of affirmations he can make about the character of God. Our findings in the *De Grammatico* are applied here more concretely. It is not only true that words in general accurately reflect reality because of the nature of the relationship between creator and creation, but it is also true that the words of Sacred Scripture reflect the reality of God's existence in a special way because they are, for Anselm, the words of God himself.

Henri de Lubac has argued this point on a much broader scale, contending that for patristic authors as well as for medieval scholars, 'all of divine revelation is contained in Scripture and, … that in the interpretation of this selfsame body of Scripture all of theological science is composed.'[22] What more could Anselm have done to elucidate this principle than to admit to a methodology of belief issuing in understanding? Even if we were to take such statements lightly or choose to detach them from our overall understanding of Anselm's theology we would have difficulty denying his transparent comments to Lanfranc: 'This was my intention throughout the whole disputation, whatever its quality, that in it I should never state anything at all unless I saw that it could readily be defended either by canonical writings or by the words of blessed Augustine.'[23]

Anselm is arguing as one possessed by a faith he is unwilling to relinquish because it is the content of that faith which supplies his arguments with vitality. He boldly opens his work by summoning the very God he desires to prove to help him and illumine him for, he admits, he is unsuitable for the task.[24] His sin is so great and God's perfection so lofty that it is a wonder that he should even contemplate the possibility that he could speak of God in any meaningful way. And yet, despite the admitted transcendence of the God who dwells in light inaccessible, Anselm still desires 'to understand [God's] truth in some way, which [his] heart believes and loves'.[25] Note here that Anselm does not seek to understand something of God apart from what has already been revealed to him. Anselm believes that he cannot understand God unless he believes in God. The very foundation of Anselm's investigation is bound up in the principles of Scripture. In a similar vein, Soren Kierkegaard has noted that

> Anselm says, 'I want to prove the existence of God. To that end I ask God to strengthen and help me' – but that is surely a much better proof of the existence of God, namely, the certainty that to prove it we need God's help. If we were able to prove the existence of God, without his help, that would be as if it were less certain that he is there.[26]

Only someone who believes in God can know God: 'For I do not seek to understand in order to believe; I believe in order to understand. For I also believe that unless I believe, I shall not understand.'[27] This is a principle that resounds throughout the *Proslogion* as well as the rest of Anselm's works and is firmly rooted in Augustine's *De Trinitate*. In that work we read of Augustine's fools who, in their carnal natures, 'for the most part prefer rather to believe that they who so speak to them have nothing to say, than that they themselves cannot understand what they have said'.[28] Augustine adds, moreover, that we do allege to them … such an account of it as to demonstrate to them how incapable and utterly unfit they are to understand that which they require of us. But they, on their parts, because they do not hear what they desire, think that we are either playing them false in order to conceal our own ignorance, or speaking in malice because we grudge them knowledge; and so go away indignant and perturbed.[29]

In Augustine's case as in Anselm's, the Fool is unable to apprehend Truth because he does not desire it; he does not desire it because he has not believed it. Belief is the indispensable prerequisite for knowing God.

This, it may be argued, is circular reasoning indeed! But, for Augustine and Anselm, how could it be otherwise? If we want to prove the existence of that than which nothing greater can be conceived we could only do so in so far as that being gave us insight. This is so because, as Anselm contemplates subsequently in the *Proslogion*, God is not only that than which a greater cannot be thought, but that which is greater than can be thought.[30] Again and again throughout the *Proslogion* God is that being whose nature – his transcendence and immanence – is the very ground for his existence. If God were not transcendent there would be no reason to assume his necessity. If God were not immanent no one could know him. Anselm's theology must rest on the revelation of God which produces both the belief necessary to understand what is signified by 'God', and the reason by which to explain it to others.

Anselm's Theological Scheme

The *Proslogion* must, then, be read theologically.[31] Any other reading fails adequately to comprehend the context, the intent or both. This is a position with which Karl Barth seems to have some affinity. In Barth's work on Anselm he begins by querying the nature of the proof which Anselm seeks. Barth contends that what Anselm is doing is not proving (*probare*) but understanding (*intellegere*):[32]

> As *intellegere* is achieved it issues in *probare*. Here we can give a general definition: what to prove means is that the validity of certain propositions advocated by Anselm is established over against those who doubt or deny them; that is to say, it means the polemical-apologetic result of *intellegere*.[33]

Barth's emphasis on understanding accords fully with Anselm's stated agenda on two counts. First, we know that Anselm believes that unless he believes he will not be able to understand. Understanding is Anselm's chief end. Why else would he begin the *Proslogion* with an entire chapter devoted to seeking God and asking him to reveal himself? Furthermore, Anselm admits in the Prologue that the *Proslogion* is a continuation of a train of thought begun in the *Monologion*. What was he doing there? He was writing down the content of a number of discussions he had with his fellow monks about how to meditate on the divine essence.[34] And what was the chief end of meditating on the divine essence? Meditation, as with study, was a means through which one came to know God.[35] The whole purpose of the monastic enterprise was to seek God and to imbibe all that He offered so that their lives might be transformed.[36]

Second, Barth's interpretation of the *Proslogion* accords with Anselm's words at the beginning of Chapter 2 where he says, 'grant that, in so far as you know it is useful for me, I may understand that you exist as we believe you exist, and that you are what we believe you to be.'[37] Again, Anselm calls on God to give him understanding; for apart from understanding there can be no proving.

Now we must at once take care to ensure that we grasp what Anselm means when he speaks about understanding. Anselm is not talking about a mere apprehension of facts. Simply knowing the contents of the Bible or the writings of the Church Fathers does not result in the kind of understanding Anselm is seeking. The understanding which concerns Anselm is that 'desired by faith'.[38] That this is so is clear from the above references to the first two chapters. Barth properly orients the order of Anselm's 'compulsion' as beginning with belief and moving on to understanding which results in proving: 'Thus on no account can the givenness or non-given-ness of the results of *intellegere* involve for faith the question of its existence.'[39] Why? Because for Anselm belief entailed a striving towards God such that the believer actually participates in God.[40] Since, therefore, one can only come to an understanding of God in as far as one participates in God, the notion of intellectual inquiry leading to doubt in the very object of one's faith is untenable.

Barth goes on to argue that for Anselm the theological enterprise was not one which was aimed at leading people to faith or confirming them in their faith or even relieving them of doubt.[41] He makes these assertions based on a number of other citations found mainly in the *Cur Deus Homo*. Barth's purpose is to remind us of the aim of Anselm's theological discourse. When we read in various places[42] that Anselm's students did not want to be led to faith or relieved of their doubts we discover that the reason for this is that they are already believers who required none of the above. Why then did they so eagerly implore Anselm to write what he did? Because they sought a more thoroughly explicit and integrated explanation for that about which they were already certain.[43] Anselm and his fellow monks were not struggling with the relationship between faith and reason as much as they were with questions of fittingness; what must be because it ought to be. This is what lies at the heart of the *Proslogion*. This is why the first chapter is indispensable. The whole tenor of the first chapter is found in Anselm's struggle between his understanding (or lack thereof) and the revelation of God in the Bible; between who God is and how he exists. It is the resolution of this endeavour which resonates throughout the remainder of the work, and it is this endeavour which is summed up well at the end of Anselm's reply to Gaunilo:

> For the import of this proof is in itself of such force that what is spoken of is proved (as a necessary consequence of the fact that it is understood or thought of) both to exist in actual reality and to be itself whatever *must be believed* about the Divine Being … It is, then, necessary that 'that-than-which-a-greater-cannot-be-thought' should be whatever *must be believed* about the Divine Nature.[44]

In both of these statements there is an emphasis on the necessity of God being as he is. Anselm uses the phrase 'must be believed' twice, and in both instances the word *oportet* is used. *Oportet* is a word which Anselm often uses to indicate fittingness, propriety or acting in accord with one's character. God is that than which nothing greater can be conceived because his nature demands it. The evidence of God's nature is taken from revelation (cf. *Proslogion* 1 and 2, for example), but the extension to the 'proof' for the existence of God is achieved by the application of reason. All of this is, of course, thoroughly grounded in faith since mere human reason is bound to falter in the face of the deeper truths of a transcendent God. This does not mean that Anselm maintained a dichotomy between faith and reason. The contents of what we believe may require reasoning in order to understand them better and more properly. Conversely, the reasoning that we apply to that which we believe will surely lead us on to greater understanding. The relationship between faith and reason may at times be paradoxical, but it can never be incredulous. Faith is the efficient cause of the ability to seek understanding, but it is not sufficient in itself as the means of sustaining the Christian. Without faith the sinful nature continues to distort reason; without reason the lingering effects of sin cannot be ferreted out. In the ordered world of creation, the relationship between signifier and signified, words and reality, immanence and transcendence, creation and creator has been thrown into chaos by sin, but can be restored by the activity of faith as the believer seeks to make clear what has been marred, establish what has disintegrated, build what has been razed, and restore what has been lost. The implicitly aesthetic nature of God revealed in the due proportion of his character as described in Chapters 6 through 24 of the *Proslogion* are the template from which Anselm's definition of God is derived, and through which the world will be renewed.

And how does revelation fit in with faith and reason? It is only by revelation that we can believe or reason correctly and so transcend our sinful situation by identifying areas of disharmony with God. If God had not revealed himself then we would have nothing in which to believe and all our reasoning about God and reality would be little more than a collection of personal opinions. Anselm conjures up the image of a man searching in a dark room for that which cannot be found.[45] The bottom line is: 'I cannot find you unless you show yourself to me.'[46] Revelation is, therefore, the very thing that enables

faith and reason to operate. However, revelation is also that which undergoes
the scrutiny of reason. The necessity of this co-dependence is again due to
Anselm's notion of original sin. We do indeed have God's revelation, but
we must always make sure that that revelation is properly interpreted and
understood. This does not imply, though, that reason determines revelation.
As Anselm says in the *De Incarnatione Verbi*:

> Indeed, no Christian ought to question the truth of what the Catholic Church
> believes in its heart and confesses with its mouth. Rather, by holding constantly
> and unhesitatingly to this faith, by loving it and living according to it he ought
> humbly, and as best he is able, to seek to discover the reason why it is true. If he is
> able to understand, then let him give thanks to God. But if he cannot understand, let
> him not toss his horns in strife but let him bow his head in reverence.[47]

Notice Anselm's progression: revelation, faith, reason. And yet, we see that
reason is applied to that which is revealed, and that which reason cannot
comprehend is not the cause of doubt and apostasy, but of a return to faith and
submissive reverence. In the light of a passage such as this, it appears that the
greatest disservice and injustice we can do to Anselm's concept of revelation,
faith and reason is to bind these concepts into logical categories. It may
seem that under certain circumstances faith is logically prior to reason, for
example, but who is to say that a different set of circumstances would not
require the opposite? It is also conceivable that while revelation is generally
a prerequisite for faith, revelation cannot be properly understood apart from
faith. Attempts to consign these three concepts to logical categories will
always prove unfruitful. There is a unity between these concepts that relates
more to aesthetic categories than logical ones; their bearing on one another
has to do with proportion and harmony. If revelation is needed (as in the
opening and closing chapters of the *Proslogion*), then revelation comes to the
fore; if reason is required (as with the third and fourth chapters), then reason
comes to the fore; if faith is necessary (as with Chapters 1 and 2), then faith
comes to the fore. Identifying exactly where each of these begins and ends is
no easy task, and one I suspect Anselm would never have attempted, for just
as the individual characteristics of God are identifiable though never properly
understood apart from God, so reason, faith and revelation are identifiable in
the *Proslogion*, though never properly understood apart from one another.

What about the Fool?

Anselm concludes his most rigorous interaction with the Fool with a prayer
to God: 'Thanks be to you, my good Lord, thanks be to you. For what I once
believed through your grace, I now understand through your illumination, so
that even if I did not want to believe that you exist, I could not fail to
understand that you exist.'[48]

In the first instance Anselm is giving thanks to God because what began as a matter of faith has now been illuminated through understanding. The principle of faith issuing in understanding has achieved its end. But what should we make of the second part of this prayer? How is it possible that the one who does not want to believe should still be able to understand? The answer is that he has given content to the word 'God'.[49] This does not mean, of course, that the Fool's knowledge is now the same as Anselm's. Belief differentiates the two. The Fool's knowledge might be described as an awareness; whereas Anselm's knowledge may be better described as personal.

Now, while the Fool's knowledge of God is little more than an awareness, by the end of the *Proslogion* it is an awareness of a personal, sentient being who is both transcendent and immanent. In other words, Anselm's *probare* for God's existence is achieved in its fullness only when the definition of God is coupled with the character of God. It is a disproportionate understanding of the *Proslogion* that assumes Anselm has accomplished his goal by the end of Chapter 4. Granted, Anselm admits in Chapter 4 that the Fool (or indeed anyone) must understand that God exists, but it is not enough for Anselm to leave the matter there. He immediately moves on in Chapter 5 to ask, 'What are you?' This begins the second section of the *Proslogion*, where Anselm delves into the character of God.[50]

But how exactly did Anselm overcome the difficulty between the ignorance of the Fool and his understanding of God? In a word, the answer is equivalence. Anselm believed that the 'furnishings' in his mind would be equivalent to those found in other minds.[51] The words and definitions that Anselm used are accessible to all humanity, and in as far as they are accessible to all they provide a point of contact: a way of communicating divine reality through created means. Consequently, 'what Anselm does in chapters two through four of the *Proslogion* is simply to unfold the implications of his axiom and show that what strikes the reader from the first as self-evident contains within it a demonstration of the necessary existence of God.'[52] Here the theory of signification is raised from the quotidian colloquy of paronymy in the *De Grammatico* and applied to the more stimulating question of God's existence. In both cases there is an assumption about the relationship between creation and creator, words and reality. The assumption is also made that the language used by one person has an equivalent meaning for other people; an assumption that can only be made if a unity in the plurality of minds can be guaranteed. For Anselm, the guarantee of unity in plurality is located in the person of God. Though Anselm may not understand precisely how God is able to be one and three, the multiplicity of all that it is better to be than not to be while retaining the unity of being, his ideas repeatedly rely on a model of reality wherein creation is a reflection of the divine harmony among countless particulars.

What this means is that Anselm's view of Christian understanding is not beyond anyone's reach. There is no neutral ground between the Fool and Anselm. Barth makes this same point when he comments that 'the scientific experiment about to be undertaken will take place within the limits which God himself imposes on noetic investigation.'[53] True, there is a point of contact, the possibility of meaningful communication between the Fool and Anselm, but Anselm 'has absolutely no thought whatsoever of reaching an agreement with his opponent in the debate (or with himself in his capacity as a philosopher) over a universal minimum knowledge of God, still less of becoming involved in a movement towards his opponent's basis of argument'.[54] This is precisely where a theological–aesthetic reading of the *Proslogion* differs so radically from a philosophical reading. In the latter the rules of discussion are determined by consensus. In the former the rules of discussion are determined by God. A philosophical interpretation is not compatible with Anselm's appreciation for aesthetics.

When, therefore, we approach the *Proslogion*, we must do so realizing that Anselm was not writing a book in which he was primarily concerned to convince his readers of his position. If it achieved that end then all the better, but we should not think of the *Proslogion* as a strictly apologetic work. There are certain aspects of it which do sound like apologetics, but that is not the purpose of the *Proslogion*. If the *Proslogion* is to be considered in any way apologetic it can only be considered as such in as far as Anselm's invitation to walk with him on his journey is extended to all who read what he has written. In so doing, Anselm is not engaging the Fool as one who stands against him in opposition, but as one who comes alongside. For the unbeliever, this means that he must first at least notionally accept that group of presuppositions which is distinctively Christian. Anselm's invitation does not allow for any neutral ground. Anselm stands firmly on his own ground and refuses to carry on any discussion about God which does not take place on his/God's terms. To do otherwise would deny the only set of conditions that we can hope to help us understand that which is under examination. In other words, to talk about the existence of God outside of Christian presuppositions would be impossible because it is only in such a tradition that God has revealed himself in the way that the Fool discounts. To address the question of God's existence within the belief system of the Fool would beg the question, if one presupposes that God does not exist, how can one expect to prove that he does?[55]

This raises one of the central questions about the *Proslogion*: did Anselm consider his argument to be valid for all people? This is the question with which all contenders of Anselmian interpretation are wrestling, the answer to which is no and yes. It is, in the first place, no because, as I have outlined above, Anselm was clearly working within the bounds of Christian faith and conviction. He did not surrender his presuppositions for the sake of enlightening the Fool; instead, Anselm impressed upon him the importance of accepting his own conditions. Only in this way could the Fool hope to understand.

The kind of understanding that Anselm expected the Fool to achieve and the kind of understanding Anselm himself possessed were disparate in nature. It is clear from the first chapter (not to mention the tenor of the rest of the book or indeed the rest of his writings) that Anselm's knowledge and understanding of God issue from an active relationship between himself (the one knowing) and God (the one known).[56] This is why he states his dictum 'I do not understand in order that I might believe, but I believe in order that I might understand' so emphatically at the outset of the whole enterprise. Ian Davie has noted that Anselm's definition of God does not flow from the human psyche or some projection thereof, for it resists this entirely; rather, God's existence and Anselm's relation to him provide the very ground of his thinking.[57] This is not the case for the Fool, nor does Anselm expect that it should be by the end of Chapter 4. Consider again the concluding paragraph of Chapter 4: 'Gratias tibi, bone Domine, gratias tibi; quia quod prius credidi, te donante, jam sic intelligo, te illuminante; ut si te esse nolim credere, non possim non intelligere.'[58]

What is interesting about Anselm's summary of the kind of knowledge he expects the Fool to have achieved is that he does not use the word *vere*. If Anselm is here proposing the position of the Fool after reading what has so far been written one is left to wonder if he did not exclude the notion of certainty for a reason. Anselm's goal as interpreted in this analysis is to demonstrate the veracity of God's existence, but to do so within the bounds of faith. This last phrase (within the bounds of faith) is crucial to our study because it is only within such limits that the certainty of God's existence can be established. Herein lies the tension in Anselm's metaphysics of signification when applied to theology. While it is true that words are able to effectively communicate the transcendent to the immanent, God to humanity, there is no guarantee that knowledge derived in this way will result in belief. Anselm's knowledge of God is *vere*, it is true, it is certain because it is believed; whereas the Fool's knowledge of God, though increasingly detailed, is not *vere*, it is not certain because it is not believed. This distinction is crucial. We have already seen, and will continue to see, that there is an equivalence between the creation and the creator that not only allows the finite access to the infinite, but allows the finite to reflect the glory of the infinite. This kind of proportioned relation between God and creation, the founding of order in the world on the order in God, is integral to Anselm's theological method in the *Proslogion*, and yet none of it guarantees that what is identified will be believed. Language gives Anselm the ability to communicate truth and transcendent principles, but it does not give him the ability to reorientate the Fool's convictions.

To be sure, Anselm does expect the Fool to understand the necessity of God's existence, but he does not expect the Fool to understand the certainty of God's existence in the way that a believer does. It is in the light of this approach to the *Proslogion* that Barth has insightfully paraphrased Anselm as saying, 'While I believe, I also believe that the knowledge for which I seek, as it is demanded and rendered possible by faith, has faith as its presupposition, and that in itself it would immediately become impossible were it not the knowledge of faith.'[59] In other words, says Barth, the attainment of *intelligere* is dependent on the quality of *credere*.[60] Still, there are myriads of scholars who continue to study, evaluate, and assault the *Proslogion* and its author without due attention to any such considerations. It is to some of these scholars that we must now turn.

The *Proslogion* and Its Critics: Gaunilo

The first, and probably for that reason the most famous, of Anselm's disputants is the monk Gaunilo. Apart from this one place Gaunilo remains an anonymous character. In fact, Gaunilo's name does not even appear in some of the earlier manuscripts.[61] Whether or not Anselm knew this man personally is difficult to determine. The friendliness with which they exchange their ideas would suggest a degree of familiarity; however, the opening sentence of Anselm's reply is remarkably aloof. One cannot help but compare the opening of this response to the opening of any number of his letters. In the latter there is a warmth and amicability which is absent from the former, even when the different genres are taken into account. Despite one's position on this matter Gaunilo feels free to level a number of charges against Anselm's position.

The essence of Gaunilo's first criticism is that it is entirely possible for someone to understand something which does in fact not exist. This argument is made against Anselm's statement that 'qui ergo intelligit sic esse Deum, nequit eum non esse cogitare.'[62] Indeed, the whole tenor of Chapters 2 through 4 is that anyone who has the sufficient mental equipment to understand Anselm's definition is therefore able to understand something about God and his nature. Comprehension is, therefore, equated not only with understanding but also with reality. This, says Gaunilo, takes too much for granted. There is no reason why that which someone understands (*in intellectu*) must actually exist (*in re*). Now, says Gaunilo, let us suppose that that than which nothing greater can be conceived is of such a nature that it is of a different order than that group of things which is in fact unreal (for example, fairies). This is not the same as suggesting that such a being is understood to exist in the same way a genuine table or chair exists. The point is that when the Fool hears of this being/thing as existing he can only understand it in as far as he comprehends its actual existence.[63] But thinking of that than which a greater cannot be conceived in this manner is problematic because it changes the development of the argument. In the *Proslogion* Anselm suggested that the Fool first has the concept of God in his mind, then realizes that the nature of God is such that He must exist in reality as well as in his mind, and then draws the conclusion of the existence of God. But, says Gaunilo, even if we assume that the given definition of God does not belong to the category of false beliefs, our starting point is the comprehension of actual existence. In other words, the argument does not actually develop; instead, it starts with the conclusion and presupposes the propositions.

At first, this argument may seem convoluted at best and irrelevant at worst. Gaunilo is, however, making a subtle point here. He knows that one of

Anselm's contentions is that while God is the supreme good he is not simply the greatest in an unbroken chain of existence or being. God is of a different order (if we can use such language) to us, despite the fact that his existence is a prerequisite for ours. He is the creator and we are the creatures. Therefore, when Anselm reads the first line of objection (that that than which nothing greater can be conceived may be unreal) his probable response would be to say that the definition itself separates God from that category of things which are actually unreal. But Gaunilo has already allowed for this contingency by suggesting that that than which nothing greater can be conceived does not exist in thought in the same way that unreal things do. His statement is pre-empting Anselm's rebuttal. On this ground then, it seems to Gaunilo that the only way anyone can understand Anselm's definition is by first 'apprehending with certainty that it really exists'.[64]

Essentially Gaunilo is advocating two kinds of relationships. The first is that what exists in the understanding exists also in reality. The second is that what exists in the understanding does not exist in reality. The problem for Gaunilo is that there is insufficient reason to warrant the application of the first relationship to that than which nothing greater can be conceived; by virtue of the difference which exists between such a being and unreal entities, the second relationship is also unacceptable. Where does this leave Anselm? According to Gaunilo since one of the above relationships must apply to that than which nothing greater can be conceived the best option is the first one. What this means, however, is that understanding what Anselm is talking about relies on prior knowledge that it already exists. If this is the case then 'there would no longer be a difference here between first having this thing in the understanding and subsequently understanding this thing to exist.'[65]

To this rebuttal Anselm has a ready rejoinder. He argues that if that than which nothing greater can be conceived is neither understood nor thought of then either 'God is not that than which a greater cannot be thought or else he is neither understood nor thought, and exists neither in the understanding nor in thought.'[66] Now what is troubling about this response is that nowhere in Gaunilo's comments about the potentially fallacious character of the notion that that than which nothing greater can be conceived did he suggest that it was not in the mind. Consequently, the reader is left wondering if Anselm has understood Gaunilo's objection. After some consideration it becomes apparent that Anselm has indeed understood Gaunilo's objection and done so in a rather profound way.

What Gaunilo has said is that the conceivability of construing the being under consideration as a false notion must be considered a real possibility. To suggest this, infers Anselm, is no different from suggesting that the idea of such a being is in fact not understood or in the mind at all. If someone believes something which is false their belief bears relation neither to reality nor to truth. Similarly, if someone does not have any ideas in their mind about certain things they clearly have no relation to either reality or truth. If, for example, my idea that God is contained in a box is false, it is no better than the atheist's belief that God does not exist. Both ideas are false; both ideas bear no relation to reality or truth. The key here is to understand that for Anselm right thinking is of the utmost importance. And how does one achieve right thinking? By searching after the truth. And what is truth? 'Truth is rectitude as perceived by the mind.'[67] Indeed, as Lanfranc had taught Anselm, God is Truth.[68] And as we have seen at the beginning of the *Proslogion*, the only way to know truth is to seek God that he might deign to dispense it to us. Thus, the guard against thinking about God falsely is to take one's starting point from him.

What Anselm is denying Gaunilo is a Godless epistemology. The only reason Gaunilo could argue for a false understanding of God is on the basis of an epistemology that does not consider God's revelation as its foundation. The consequence of this is, as we have seen, that the idea of God is at best potentially false and at worst non-existent. Taking the worst-case scenario Anselm argued that either God is not what he reveals himself to be or he exists beyond our understanding. In the former case God is either a liar or Anselm has misunderstood him and he is not that than which nothing greater can be conceived, in which case God is no longer transcendent. In the latter case God is so beyond our understanding that he is no longer immanent. No matter which position Gaunilo chooses, he will be forced to deny one or more of the essential attributes of God.

The Fool may well be prepared to deny one or more of the supposed attributes of God; but note that Anselm is not addressing himself to the Fool. At the outset of his response Anselm stated that, knowing that Gaunilo was a Christian, he would address his comments 'to the Christian'.[69] As a result, Anselm admits that his arguments appeal to Gaunilo's 'faith and conscience as the most compelling argument that this is false'.[70] The point here is that Gaunilo, or anyone for that matter, can deny the presuppositions upon which Anselm is building his argument, but to do so would change the nature of the argument altogether. It would therefore no longer be Anselm's argument. His is a position firmly rooted within the bounds of faith, which is why Anselm so vigorously defends the parameters of his work and why he consistently and constantly appeals to the triad of faith, reason and revelation.

Anselm does not, however, let the matter drop there. Towards the end of his reply he returns once more to Gaunilo's charge of sophistry. Here is where Anselm is most biting in his criticism of Gaunilo for he charges Gaunilo with contradicting himself in a rather obvious way. According to Gaunilo it is possible for someone to have in his 'understanding any number of false things',[71] but it is also apparently possible for that same person to 'comprehend in genuine knowledge the fact that it [that than which nothing greater can be conceived, and that which is still assumed to be false] actually exists'.[72] What is significant for Anselm is the nature of the knowledge: it is genuine. If the knowledge that the Fool has about God's existence were indeed genuine or certain (in the sense of *vere* as discussed above) then how can it fall into the same category as those things which are false and therefore uncertain?

The second thing Gaunilo does is to contend the use of the Fool as a foil. He claims that it is ludicrous to set up such an argument against the very person who denies the premises upon which the argument is based.[73] Against this criticism Anselm makes no specific reply. Indeed, we have already noted that Anselm openly admitted that he intended his response only for the Christian since it was a Christian who was raising doubts. This is a telling comment. Anselm would have known that Gaunilo's intention was to represent the Fool, and yet Anselm refused to play along. Why? Because just as Anselm's intention in the *Proslogion* was to state his argument for the certainty of God's existence within a distinctively Christian framework, so his response is set squarely in the same framework. In the *Proslogion* the Fool is a convenient foil against which to make his point, *but not the reason for making the point*. There is a difference. This is why, in the concluding chapters of the *Proslogion*, Anselm begins by mirroring the language of Chapter 1. He summons his own and his reader's soul to revel in the joy of the God he has been seeking. The references to Scripture again become numerous. The language describing the knowledge desired and obtained is indicative of an intimate salvific knowledge at every turn: 'Let my heart love it [the truth of God as outlined in the *Proslogion*] and my mouth proclaim it. Let my soul hunger for it, my flesh thirst for it, my whole being long for it, until I enter into the joy of my Lord, who is God, Three in One, blessed for ever. Amen.'[74]

Clearly the *Proslogion* was not intended for dilettantes, but for the earnest seeker of God and of his truth. If we grasp little else from the first four chapters of this work surely we can see that Anselm chose the Fool as his foil precisely because he is the personification of the opposite to everything for which Anselm is arguing and seeking. Thus, when Gaunilo charges Anselm with insufficiently addressing the Fool's desire for indubitable proof (as the Fool would define it) Anselm responds by reaffirming who it is he intends his work to affect: 'it will be enough for me to reply to the Christian.'[75]

Third, Gaunilo argues that mere understanding of the definition fails to provide the indubitable proof that Anselm promised.[76] Based on the notion that the Fool's head could be full of dubitable thoughts and understandings, Anselm must furnish him with an indubitable proof or argument that such is not the case in this instance. Consequently, the onus has not shifted to the Fool as a challenge to his unbelief.

The answer to this problem has, in part, already been addressed by the response to the previous one. What, we must ask, is meant by indubitable and who defines it? If the Fool is the one who defines what is indubitable then Anselm's argument has indeed failed as would any other attempt. The other part to this answer is repeated over and over again throughout the reply, and it is that the definition itself, when understood, necessitates the assent that such a being exists. The first place we read of this answer is near the beginning of the first section where Anselm argues that no one who denies or doubts that something than which a greater cannot be thought exists, denies or doubts that if it did exist, it would be unable to fail to exist either in reality or in the understanding, since otherwise it would not be that than which a greater cannot be thought ... So if that than which a greater cannot be thought can be thought at all, it cannot fail to exist.[77]

What we must remember here is that Anselm is arguing for the logic of his argument within the parameters he has defined. Did Anselm consider his definition and argument to be convincing for everyone: Fool and Christian? Yes and no. Yes in as far as Anselm clearly believes that the reasonableness of his system is sufficiently clear to warrant anyone's assent that God must exist. On the other hand, Anselm is not so naïve as to believe that the Fool, having understood the definition and argument, will accept the premises and presuppositions of the argument. He is well aware that in order for the Fool to be convinced about the certainty of God's existence in the way that he is convinced, the Fool would have to completely reorientate his thinking.

It may be helpful to say one more thing about this matter before we move on. One of the hallmarks of modern scholarship, and especially scholarship in the late twentieth century, is the belief that truth is not absolute. Granted, I am speaking very broadly here, but I think it is fair to say that, on the whole, philosophers have been reticent to endorse the notion of absolute truth.[78] This, we must carefully note, was not the position held in the Middle Ages nor indeed by Anselm. For Anselm there was such a thing as absolute truth and it was accessible to humanity through participation in God. Thus, when we read the *Proslogion* we ought to bear in mind that while Anselm was addressing Christians, and while he was arguing explicitly within the context of the Christian faith, because he believed that truth was absolute and that it was accessible to him through God's revelation and the use of his divinely guided reason, he believed that what he said was equally true for all people in all times regardless of their own presuppositions or beliefs. And yet, there is a tension here. This tension is derived, as Anselm points out in Chapter 1, from the existence of sin:

> How wretched human beings are! They have lost the very thing for which they were created. Hard and terrible was their fall! Alas! ... Why did he thus shut us out from the light and cover us with darkness? ... Think whence we have been cast out, whither we have been driven; thrown down from so great a height, and buried so deep. From our homeland into exile; from the vision of God into our blindness ... I was heading for God but stumbled over myself ... Take pity upon our souls and strivings after you, for without you we can do nothing ... My sins are heaped up over my head and entangle me; like a heavy burden they weigh me down. Extricate me; lift my burdens, lest like a pit they swallow me up.[79]

Anselm's sense of sin is great, as is his sense of need for divine aid. This is a tension that resonates throughout the *Proslogion* and through his whole corpus. Anselm expects God to enlighten his mind, and the minds of his readers, but he is also painfully aware that unless the individual seek forgiveness and release from the power of sin there can be no hope of genuine, salvific knowledge. This is why it seems most prudent to argue that Anselm expected his argument to be at once convincing and unconvincing. Were Anselm to read modern critiques of his proof he would not be surprised to learn that so many of them take issue with him, but he would be sure to point out that it is only by querying his 'first principles that it is possible seriously to question his conclusions'.[80]

Anselm's use of reason is, however, not beyond reproach. Gaunilo is quick to point this out in the case of the analogy of the painter and the painting used in Chapter 2. In that chapter Anselm commented that

> it is one thing for an object to exist in the understanding and quite another to understand that the object exists [in reality]. When a painter, for example, thinks out in advance what he is going to paint, he has it in his understanding, but he does not yet understand that it exists, since he has not yet painted it. But once he has painted it, he both has it in his understanding and understands that it exists because he has now painted it.[81]

The problem, says Gaunilo, is that those things which are actually real are those things which are innate to the soul. This is why St Augustine says that 'when a carpenter is about to make a chest in reality, he first has it in his craft. The chest that exists in reality is not a living thing, but the chest that exists in his craft is a living thing, since the soul of the craftsman, in which all those things exist before they are produced, is alive.'[82]

In other words, the painting on the canvas is distinct from the painting in the mind. There is no equivalence between the two. And since there is no equivalence between the two 'paintings' this analogy does nothing to aid Anselm's case. For, in his argument, Gaunilo contends that Anselm was seeking to show that just as there is equivalence between the painting in the intellect and in reality so there is equivalence between that than which nothing greater can be conceived in the intellect and in reality: 'The real thing is different from the understanding by which it is apprehended.'[83]

Gaunilo advanced this argument further by returning to the notion of the nature of understanding itself. He avers that all human thinking and understanding is analogous. That is to say that we can only understand things with reference to known entities. He gives the example of being told of a man who does not exist. Despite the man's non-existence Gaunilo can still conceive of him because he could think of him 'in accordance with that very thing that a man is, on the basis of that knowledge of genus or species by which I know what a man is or what men are'.[84] The trouble with God is that he can only be understood with reference to the words spoken about him. To say, therefore, that that than which nothing greater can be conceived is in the understanding is not actually true since what is signified cannot be thought. True, the words are *in intellectu*, but that does not mean that the knower of these words understands what they signify. This is to say that while in the analogy of the painter and the painting the idea and the reality are comprehensible because people have the appropriate categories by which to interpret what is signified, this is not the case with God. God or that than which nothing greater can be conceived is beyond any conceptual framework in human experience and thus what is being signified by the word or concept is, in the end, unintelligible to the Fool.

When one reads the analogy with these objections in mind it seems obvious enough that the idea of the painting and the painting itself are two different things. But then, it is not Anselm's point to argue that they are the same things. In fact, Anselm is using this analogy only to demonstrate that what is understood is in the mind. Surely the point is that the kind of existence that the painting had in the mind of the painter is different from the kind of existence it now enjoys on canvas. In both instances the idea of the painting exists in the mind of the painter, but the nature of the existence of the thing itself has changed. This is why Anselm sums up his analogy by saying, 'So even the fool must admit that something than which nothing greater can be thought exists at least in his understanding, since he understands this when he hears it, and whatever is understood exists in the understanding.'[85]

Only after summing up the point of his analogy does he move on to argue for the existence *in re* of that than which nothing greater can be conceived. And how does he do this? He proceeds by referring to the nature of the definition, not with reference to the analogy:

> And surely that than which a greater cannot be thought cannot exist only in the understanding. For if it exists only in the understanding, it can be thought to exist in reality as well, which is greater. So if that than which a greater cannot be thought exists only in the understanding, then that than which a greater cannot be thought is that than which a greater can be thought. But this is clearly impossible. Therefore, there is no doubt that something than which a greater cannot be thought exists both in the understanding and in reality.[86]

The existence of that than which a greater cannot be conceived in reality does not rely on the fact that it exists in the mind. For, as Anselm says, in order for the definition to be true such a being cannot exist solely in the mind. The fact that it exists in the mind is intended to show that the being about which we are speaking is comprehensible. This is a very important step because if this were not so there would be no point in carrying on with the discussion. The fact that that than which a greater cannot be conceived exists in the mind of the Fool is best understood as a point of contact which, though not directly a step towards proving the existence of God, is still a necessary part of the whole process. If we examine Chapters 2 and 3 carefully we see that where Anselm has sought to demonstrate the existence of God and then to demonstrate his necessary existence he has done so always and exclusively with reference to the definition. It is the definition itself, as revealed to Anselm, that provides the reasoning for existence *in re* as well as *in intellectu.*[87]

Concerning the extended argument about analogous knowledge and its relation to genus and species Anselm denies that there is a problem. He argues that we can 'infer a great deal about that than which a greater cannot be thought on the basis of those things than which a greater can be thought'.[88] E.J. Butterworth comments helpfully here by pointing out that Anselm used the comparative rather than the superlative because 'without the ability to make comparisons we could possess no knowledge of anything except that which is immediately evident.'[89] To define God in the superlative, regardless of whether or not such a designation would be more accurate, would eliminate a point of contact with our intellect. In short, the use of the comparative and the dependence on analogy 'allows one to approach a limit without ever encompassing that limit.'[90] Interestingly, Anselm comments at the end of this section in his reply that this response is a sufficient refutation even to the Fool who does not accept 'sacred authority'.[91] In addition, he argues that even should the orthodox Christian deny his use of analogy he ought to consider Romans 1:20.[92]

Our analysis of Gaunilo's rebuttal and Anselm's reply to the matters raised in the *Proslogion* could be carried further, but it seems prudent to end the discussion here since the main points pertaining to both have been covered. In fact, it may be asked if altogether too much space has been devoted to this exchange. I do not think this is the case for two reasons: first, Gaunilo is the only other person with whom Anselm had prolonged interaction over the *Proslogion*; second, many of the issues raised by Gaunilo are resurrected throughout the subsequent history of the interpretation of the *Proslogion*. Dealing with some of those issues at greater length in the context of Anselm's discussions with Gaunilo will prepare us for the answers proposed against later critics.

Anselm's Other Disputants

One example of a criticism which has reared its head over and over again is the argument that Anselm has assumed his premise to be true. Gaunilo contended that there was no reason for the Fool to admit that the God about which Anselm was speaking is that than which nothing greater can be thought. He grounded this argument in the fact that there is no guarantee that that which is in the mind is not false. The great fallacy in the *Proslogion* is the belief that God exists. This quarrel with Anselm is raised as early as the thirteenth century in Aquinas' *Summa Contra Gentiles*. In that work Aquinas presents a form of Anselm's argument and then refutes it by disputing the suggestion that the name God signifies the same thing to all people.[93] When one utters the name of God the Christian will think of one set of attributes and characteristics, the pagan another and the philosopher yet another. Ultimately, it appears that Aquinas' difficulty lies in Anselm's methodology. Anselm believed that in order to prove God's existence he had to begin with God's revelation; whereas Aquinas, though not dispensing with revelation, begins with the principle that the demonstration of what may be known to us is achieved chiefly through the senses.[94]

This same sentiment was later reiterated by Kant in his *Critique of Pure Reason* in which he argued that the problem with the ontological argument is that existence is not a predicate.[95] It is simply unacceptable to begin with existence as a premise. Existence cannot be assumed, it must be proved. Similarly, McGill in his article on Anselm's argument took issue with the fact that Anselm's argument was circular. If one presupposes the existence of God then that person's position is no longer objective. The arguments forwarded are determined by the subject which is itself supposed to be under investigation.[96] P.J McGrath offers largely the same critique when he says that if the greatest conceivable being does not exist in the real world then it does not exist in any world.[97] Therefore, the premise 'if the concept of an X is internally coherent, then an X exists in some possible world' is false.[98] To this list we may add any number of other contenders, such as Brecher and Johnson who we will deal with later, but the point of this chapter is not to refute Anselm's every disputant, but to point to the fact that Anselm based the argument of the *Proslogion* on a model of reality which took the aesthetic nature of reality seriously. The shortcoming of so many of Anselm's critics is that they fail to appreciate this. For Kant, McGill, McGrath and others, the application of logic obfuscates the possibility of fittingness. This is not to say that reason has no part in Anselm's discussion, but that reason is only part of understanding. Although speaking more of objects than of God, Eco's comments on Aquinas are insightful in this regard:

> Looking at an object aesthetically means looking at its structure, physical and metaphysical, as exhaustively as possible, in all its meanings and implications, and in its proportionate relations to its own nature and to its accidental circumstances. It means, that is, a kind of *reasoning about* the object, scrutinising it in detail and in depth.[99]

Anselm's definition of God attempts to do precisely this. He is interested in discerning a way of talking about God that will allow him to explore the nature of God in as much detail as possible. And, let us not forget, Anselm spends most of his time exploring God's nature. His twenty-two chapters on God's nature are neither distinct from nor even subsequent to the argument presented in the first four chapters. Reason may demand that the argument of the first four chapters precede what might be construed as an excursus of the following twenty-two, but fittingness allows the latter to inform the former. The question of God's existence and nature does, after all, begin in the *Monologion* where Anselm starts with God's nature (specifically his goodness), and from there is able to distil the argument contained in the opening chapters of the *Proslogion* which is again expanded throughout the rest of the work. But this is what many of Anselm's detractors and critics have missed. Still, we cannot dismiss them altogether on this count alone, and must therefore at least touch on some of the more prominent thinkers who have interacted with the *Proslogion*.

Responding to the Pundits

Against those who contend that the nature of God is insufficient grounds upon which to build an argument, Anselm would remind them that the kind of existence he is talking about is altogether different from that which applies to creation. The existence of humans (cf. Kant), the existence of lost islands (cf. Gaunilo), the existence of anything that we see around us is contingent. Contingent on what? Contingent on the one whose existence is necessary, 'on whom all things depend for their being and well being'.[100] Thus, when Aquinas disagrees that the name and nature of God is sufficient to warrant a proof for his existence, Anselm replies that the name of God is, once explained,[101] sufficient to indicate enough information about his nature that his existence cannot be denied. To Kant, Anselm would argue that in the case of necessary existence, existence is a predicate. To McGill, McGrath and Aquinas, Anselm would argue that sense perception in the physical world is neither the sole nor sufficient means of comprehending all that is contained in reality.

Now, as divergent as all of these scholars' opinions may be in the particularities of their refutations of the *Proslogion*, there is a common ground which unites their concerns. Oliver Johnson sums up this commonality by suggesting that much of the argumentation surrounding the ontological argument is about whether or not existence is a predicate. To this end Johnson believes that Anselm's aim was to deduce God's existence from his essence. The consequence, says Johnson, is that the affirmation that God must exist results in arguing that existence contributes to God's perfection.[102] If, therefore, being adds value to an object, is that value positive or negative? One can imagine cases where it is positive (for example, money) and cases where it is negative (for example, headache).[103] In Anselm's argument for God's existence, existence is clearly positive; but, muses Johnson, could not the negative value of existence be attributed to Satan and thus lead us to a similar argument for his existence? Johnson resolves this dilemma by positing that the positive or negative value of existence depends on the object itself and that existence has neutral value.

This means that for Anselm to say that God's existence is greater than his non-existence makes no difference because the 'greater' relies on existence having a positive value – which has already been denied. Furthermore, if existence derives its value from the object to which it is attached then it is no longer valid to deduce God's existence from his essence since the essence to which Anselm appeals is existence.[104] The end result is that existence cannot be a predicate because it does not say anything about its subject.

On the other hand, what if existence is a predicate? If this is the case then, says Johnson, God is that which has the most number of predicates. Therefore, if he does not have existence as a predicate, a being which does would be greater. The trouble here is that even if God has the greatest number of predicates, God plus Anselm equals more than God because Anselm would have some predicates that make him what he is and not God.[105] This is the sort of sentiment with which John King-Farlow resonates when he writes that if one can conceive of God as *id quo maius* then one can also think of God and His creation existing which is to conceive of something greater than God alone.[106] The conclusion seems to arise from this that whether or not existence is a predicate, God's existence remains unprovable.

There is, however, a serious shortcoming to the above line of reasoning. In both of Johnson's arguments God's existence is seen as contributing to his being. To put this another way, God's being that than which nothing greater can be conceived (which, as Anselm has shown, implies existing in reality) is contingent on existence as a characteristic. King-Farlow refers to creation rather than existence, but the idea is the same. The difficulty is that if that than which a greater cannot be conceived is contingent for its existence at any one point, then it no longer has the quality of necessary existence. And if God does not exist necessarily then he must rely on some other being for his existence. Consequently, if the definition is to hold true, the being about whom we posit contingency is in fact not that than which nothing greater can be conceived. The only being who measures up to this definition is the one who 'in no way exists through another; nor is he posterior to or less than himself or any other thing. Therefore, the supreme nature could not come about either by his own agency or by that of some other thing, nor was he or anything else the matter from which he came about, nor did he or some other thing in any way help him to be what he was not already.'[107] According to Anselm, God does not rely on anyone or anything, including himself, for existence.[108] He is the supreme nature 'who depends on nothing else, but on whom all things depend for their being and for their well-being'.[109]

Apart from the circle of concerns raised by the above philosophers, Robert Brecher has forwarded a different approach to the *Proslogion*. He argues that Anselm's argument can only properly be understood in the light of Platonic metaphysics, and as such is valid, though not probative.[110] That Anselm's argument is essentially Platonic comes as no surprise to Brecher because he is convinced that Christianity has itself assimilated Platonic metaphysics.[111]

Brecher begins his investigation by examining what Anselm means by 'greater'. After querying the supposition that existence is necessarily greater than non-existence and arguing that existence need not be an aspect of that which is perfect, Brecher concludes that 'greater' for Anselm should be understood ontologically as meaning more real. He bases this conclusion on statements such as, 'You alone, then of all things most truly exist and therefore of all things possess existence to the highest degree; for anything else does not exist as truly, and so possesses existence to a lower degree ... You of all things exist to the highest degree.'[112] Clearly, Anselm is drawing on a Platonic metaphysic of a hierarchy of being. God is the greatest in a chain of being. Reference is also made to the *Monologion*[113] where degrees of existence again come into play. Further support is garnered from Anselm Stolz's article on true existence in the *Proslogion*. According to Stolz, Anselm was working entirely within an Augustinian framework (something Anselm himself admits in a number of places, cf. Ep. 77), and since Augustine is considered to be thoroughly Platonized how could Anselm not be?[114] Brecher adds yet another nail to the coffin of Anselm's argument by citing and developing Bonaventure's comments on the matter of Gaunilo's supposed island:

> Empirical entities and God are in different ontological classes; and whereas 'greater' in the phrase 'an island, than which *a* greater cannot be thought' serves to compare it with other members of its own class – if it serves to do anything at all – in the phrase, 'a being, than which *nothing* greater can be thought', it serves to compare that being not only with other beings, but, more importantly, the class of which that being is the sole member with all other classes.[115]

Later in his book Brecher returns to this notion of comparison and classes of beings and declares that the very reason Anselm's argument fails to establish God's existence is because 'the Judaeo-Christian God cannot be absolutely different in kind from all other things.'[116] And just in case the Christian responds by insisting that God is indeed different in kind from all other things, Brecher answers that if we posit that God has a distinct existence from our own then we still do not know what God is: 'And without an answer to this question, the assertion that there is a God has no clear sense.'[117]

As damning as Brecher's comments may already appear he carries on with his barrage in other areas. First, contrary to the claims of Barth, La Croix and Campbell, Brecher argues that that than which nothing greater can be thought is a definition. This is a crucial point for Brecher because it is only as a definition that Anselm can hope to make contact with the Fool. All Anselm needs to do is to get the Fool to admit that he is defining something, and the rest can be inferred or deduced.[118] The reason that a point of contact based on a definition is so important to Brecher is that it helps him demonstrate that the only thing that could be common between Anselm and the Fool is Platonic metaphysics. In other words, since there is no fiduciary commonality between the two, the only hope they have for an agreed basis of argument is an agreed philosophical system. Thus, to designate that than which nothing greater can be conceived as a revealed name[119] or an identifier[120] or as something unrelated to God[121] would be either to fail to make meaningful contact with the Fool (Barth and Campbell) or to deny the context out of which Anselm was arguing (La Croix). What this means is that Anselm depends on a shared metaphysics when he presents his argument to the unbelieving reader since 'something actually believed by the unbeliever is shown to imply that God exists.'[122]

The final point we should note about Brecher's critique of the *Proslogion* is the brief attention he gives to the question of God's necessity. He claims that 'Anselm does not take God's unique status to reside in his necessity.' Moreover, 'the simple point is that Anselm actually distinguishes God from other necessary beings, and not ... from other beings on account of his necessary status.'[123]

Working backwards through Brecher's comments it is surprising that this last statement should even be made. In the light of Anselm's remarks in the prologue to the *Proslogion* that God is the one 'who depends on nothing else, but on whom all things depend for their being and well-being', I wonder what other beings Brecher thinks Anselm believed to be necessary. Just as in our response to Johnson we intimated that in order for God to be that than which nothing greater could be conceived, he alone must be necessary, so here. Furthermore, Anselm makes it quite clear in Chapter 3 of the *Monologion* that he believes it is impossible for more than one being to exist necessarily.[124] Consider, for instance, what Anselm has to say in Chapters 3, 13 and 24 of the *Proslogion* to show that God's existence is of an entirely different order from the rest of creation. He states that 'if particular goods are delightful, consider intently how delightful is that good which contains the joyfulness of all goods – and not such joyfulness as we have experienced in created things, but as different from that as the creator differs from the creature.'[125] And again he says that 'indeed you alone are eternal, because you alone of all beings do not cease to exist, just as you do not begin to exist ... Therefore, Lord, you are uniquely unbounded and eternal.'[126] Again, Anselm believes that God exists so truly that 'you cannot be thought not to exist. And rightly so, for if some mind could think something better than you, a creature would rise above the creator and sit in judgment upon him, which is completely absurd. Indeed, everything that exists, except for you alone, can be thought not to exist.'[127]

What could be clearer in Anselm's thinking than that God is in a class entirely his own? There is a definite distinction between the creation and the creator. Consequently, Brecher's arguments that Anselm was either distinguishing God from other necessary beings or that he was comparing God to the chain of being in some kind of Platonic (or Neoplatonic) fashion runs counter to what Anselm openly declares. Brecher has taken Anselm's analogy too far. Notice that for Brecher the analogy begins with the creation and is then applied to the creator; whereas in Anselm the analogy begins with the creator and extends to the creation.[128] Anselm draws his analogies from revelation, not from human experience. If Anselm can say anything about existence he must of necessity use the socio-linguistic concepts with which he is familiar, but remember that the ideas to which he is attempting to apply his descriptions are divinely given. The analogy is not, existence is what we experience therefore God's existence must be that existence to the nth degree; rather it is God's existence is the existence from which and on which we derive and maintain ours. The *imago humanitate* as with the *imago mundi* is known only on account of the *imago dei*.

This is why it is remarkable that Brecher and Stolz should agree that God is, in Anselm's system, the sole member of a class[129] as well as the one who stands over and against 'the subdued being of creatures, subject to change, which contains something of non-being itself, and which is therefore not *vere*'.[130] Both of these men have hit upon the very distinction which should have led them to the conclusion that, for Anselm, God is more than the end of a chain of being. The frustration here is not so much that some scholars have identified Platonic elements in Anselm, but that they have failed to see that while the vocabulary evinces Platonic forms of expression through Augustinian influence, the content of that vocabulary has been significantly altered. True, Anselm did talk about God's existence in the *Monologion* in terms of the highest degree, but how else would an eleventh-century monk imbued with the philosophy and teaching of Augustine and his disciples be expected to express a reality with which humanity has struggled for centuries? Still, what Anselm could only describe in vaguely Platonic terms in the *Monologion*, he had, in the *Proslogion*, discovered how to address in genuinely Christian terms.[131] Anselm believed that God had revealed His name/definition/identity to him which put an end to foundering Platonic expressions.

This brings us to the last of Brecher's arguments. Is that than which nothing greater can be conceived a definition, a name, an identifier or something else? Yes. If God is, as Anselm describes him, all that he is in himself apart from the aid of anything else, including himself, then a revelation from God about himself seems to be a candidate equally for his name or a definition. This is especially the case for Anselm because both a name and a definition signify something about their subject.[132] This is the cardinal point (here we broach Brecher's concomitant concern that that than which nothing greater can be conceived must be a definition because its purpose is to find a point of contact with the Fool's Platonic metaphysics): the metaphysical correlation Anselm assumes is operative between him and the Fool is based on a theory of signification that requires God to exist in a certain way and his creation to reflect and participate in that existence in a harmoniously proportionate way. Aesthetic unity pervades every aspect of Anselm's thinking on the question of God's existence. From the use of the comparative in the definition of God which strikes a balance between God's infinite, transcendent character and the obvious difficulties that could accrue if he were to possess every possible attribute in the superlative degree, to the harmony within the Trinity which he explores in his earlier attempts in the *Monologion*, to his inclusion of a theologically adapted version of his theory of signification which is, in turn, grounded in the contingency of all creation on the necessary existence of the creator which results in a correspondence between the two, Anselm is building a case for understanding and interpreting God within a theologically informed aesthetic framework.

In addition to Brecher, Johnson and the other philosophers that we have mentioned above there remains a whole host of other scholars who have taken issue with various aspects of Anselm's argument.[133] To deal with them all would prove tedious, and take us beyond the scope of our immediate interest. Consequently, we will conclude our survey of Anselm's critics with Arthur McGill's most difficult censure.

Among his many difficulties with the *Proslogion* McGill's most fundamental is that Anselm's argument is circular. He has presupposed God's existence and so 'pre-empts the whole question of his existence'.[134] McGill goes on to quote F. Ueberweg saying that 'Every deduction from a definition is only valid hypothetically, on the assumption that the subject of the definition is real.'[135] McGill adds his own comment that 'a definition, however, cannot be used to establish this assumption.'

I agree with McGill's point. A simple definition of something is insufficient grounds to demonstrate its reality. What matters is how one arrives at the definition. Presumably McGill would be happy if Anselm defined King William as, for example, that man than which no other has superior claims to authority in England and Normandy. Any deductions Anselm may have made from that definition would certainly have had the possibility of being true according to McGill because the reality of that which is being defined can be verified. Why can the same not be true for God? Can one's knowledge of something be deemed real only if it can be seen with the eyes or otherwise observed with the senses?

Anselm would also agree with Ueberweg's and McGill's argument. In fact, Anselm was using it. Anselm began with the knowledge that his subject was real and was thus able to provide an accurate definition from which appropriate deductions could be made. The obvious difficulty between McGill, Kant and others who espouse empiricist philosophy and Anselm is that the former group deny the acceptability of revelation as the basis upon which to build a valid argument. At no point did Anselm point to something and declare, 'That is God.' This is precisely where McGill finds the greatest fault with Anselm's argument: 'it analyses a concept without once seeking contact with the data of sensory experience.'[136]

What is remarkable about this criticism, however, is that it actually strengthens part of Anselm's argument. What McGill and Kant and countless other philosophers since the late eighteenth century have argued is that that which is real (*in re*) is greater than that which exists only in the mind (*in intellectu*). If, therefore, McGill and company understand the meaning of Anselm's description of God and they accept the ontic distinction between perceived reality and actual reality, why do they have such difficulty with it? Anselm is in fact seeking contact with the data of sensory experience. In Anselm's reply to Gaunilo he quoted Romans 1:20. No one more than Anselm would have known that that passage and its surrounding verses are addressing the claim that those who have not heard the arguments for God's existence have an excuse for not believing. This, says Paul, is not true 'since what may be known about God is plain to them, because God has made it plain to them. For since the creation of the world God's invisible qualities – his eternal power and divine nature – have been clearly seen, being understood from what has been made, so that men are without excuse.' In the medieval period Scripture as well as nature were thought of as a text of which God is the author and therefore the authoritative interpreter 'even of those theological conclusions of dialectical enquiry which draw their premises either from nature and history or from Scripture'.[137] How strange that Anselm should be accused of failing to make contact with the data of sensory experience when so much of what he has to say relies on analogous relationships between creator and creation. It seems to me that the real difficulty is not with Anselm's failure to respect sensory experience, nor with his ontic distinctions between *in intellectu* and *in re*, but with the source of his definition. Here we reach the true impasse. Even if we were to trace the development of the idea of God being that than which nothing greater can be conceived from Irenaeus[138] to Augustine[139] to Boethius[140] and through countless other theologians, the unbelieving inquirer would remain unmoved because, to use Anselm's own words, understanding is not the prerequisite for belief, but belief the necessary condition for understanding.

The Rationale

Why did Anselm assume so much? He must have known that people would disagree with his presuppositions. If he was genuinely looking for a rational basis for what he believed why did he incorporate so much prayer and so many biblical allusions? The answer is that Anselm was not seeking to convert the Fool,[141] but to explore the claims of the church through the lens of theological aesthetics. In so doing Anselm fully expected to furnish his fellow monks as well as other Christians with a different way of explaining and, more importantly, meditating on God and the content of their faith.[142] In this process Anselm found it helpful to use the Fool's statement in Psalm 14:1 as a foil against which to garner the various aspects of his argument. We have noticed before now that the Fool was not allowed to speak or defend himself. We have also noticed that the bulk of the *Proslogion* is not concerned with establishing the fact of God's existence, but with expressing the character and nature of God as it flows from the discovery that he is that than which nothing greater can be conceived. Despite Southern's disparagement of Eadmer's précis[143] of the *Proslogion* as misguided, Eadmer demonstrates a profound understanding of the mind and intention of the man with whom he spent much of his life. Eadmer comments in his biography that

> Afterwards [after writing the *Monologion*] it came into his mind to try to prove by one single and short argument the things which are believed and preached about God, that he is eternal, unchangeable, omnipotent, omnipresent, incomprehensible,

just, righteous, merciful, true, as well as truth, goodness, justice and so on; *and to show how all these qualities are united in him.*[144]

Anselm's primary purpose is not to argue *that* God exists, but to show that he exists in such a way that all the aforementioned qualities are 'united' in him. Anselm's present-day biographer may have been swept up by the torrent of rationalist interpretations, but his contemporary, who shared his appreciation of the beauty of theology as expressed in the revelation of God, was careful to avoid the pitfall of eisegesis. It is particularly fascinating that Southern should dismiss Eadmer's commentary so glibly considering he believes that 'Eadmer's words at this point have almost the authority of autobiography, for there can be no doubt Anselm was their source, and he probably read, and at first approved, what Eadmer had written.'[145] If these words are supposed to have come from Anselm himself or at least have been approved by Anselm then why is Southern (and, we might add, other interpreters) so reticent to accept them?

It is interesting that a brief survey of the different scholars who have examined the *Proslogion* reveals that there are two who have themselves taken religious orders: Anselm Stolz and Benedicta Ward. What is most intriguing about them is that their estimations of Anselm's work seem to parallel more accurately its general tenor (with some noted exceptions). And yet this discovery is hardly surprising since these two commentators have shared something of the spirit and mentality that Anselm experienced. Thus, in comments that echo the prologue Stolz writes that Anselm's aim was to seek 'insight into the dogmas about God', and that such an investigation should 'lead therefore to a vision of God'.[146] Later on Stolz reiterates his point that Anselm's ultimate goal was to acquire a 'knowledge of the articles of faith about God and the immediate experience of God.'[147] This is a work in which the contents of the faith, as derived from revelation, are examined in the light of God's illuminating glory,[148] so that by the end of the investigation Anselm is caught up in what can only be described as a proleptic experience of the beatific vision where the beauty of God's existence is fully known.

Notes

1   The allusion to Milton's *Paradise Lost* (ed. Christopher Ricks (1989), Harmondsworth: Penguin) is intentional. There in the opening lines Milton appeals to the Spirit of God to help him illumine the hearts of his readers as he soars over the Mount of the Muses that he might assert who God is and how he works among humanity. This is, it seems to me, very much akin to Anselm's desire in the *Proslogion*.

2   Arthur C. McGill (1968), 'Recent Discussions of Anselm's Argument', in Hick, John and Arthur C. McGill (eds), *The Many-Faced Argument*, London: Macmillan, p. 34.

3   P.J. McGrath (1994), 'Does the Ontological Argument Beg the Question?' *Religious Studies*, 30:305–10, p. 306.

4   Robert Brecher (1985), *Anselm's Argument: The logic of divine existence*, Aldershot: Gower, p. 4.

5 Ian Weeks (1990), 'A Disproof of the Existence of God', *Sophia*, 29:21–8.
6 W.S. Robinson (1984), 'The Ontological Argument', *International Journal for Philosophy of Religion* 1:51–9, p. 56.
7 Some representative works from these two scholars include: A. Plantinga (1967), *God and Other Minds*, London: Cornell University Press; A. Plantinga (1974), *God, Freedom and Evil*, New York: Harper and Row Publishers; A. Plantinga (1975), 'Aquinas on Anselm', in Orlebeke, Clifton and Lewis Smedes (eds), *God and the Good: Essays in honor of Henry Stob*, Grand Rapids, MI: Eerdmans, pp. 122–39; C. Hartshorne (1965), *Anselm's Discovery: A Re-examination of the Ontological Proof for God's Existence*, La Salle: Open Court; C. Hartshorne (1985), 'Our Knowledge of God', in L. Rouner (ed.), *Knowing Religiously*, Notre Dame, IN: University of Notre Dame Press; C. Hartshorne (1983), 'Anselm and Aristotle's First Law of Modality', in J.C. Schnaubelt et al. (eds), *Anselm Studies: An Occasional Journal*, vol. 1, London: Kraus International Publications.
8 Ian Davie (1994), 'Anselm's Argument Re-assessed', *Downside Review*, 112:103–20, p. 103.
9 Karl Barth (1958), *Anselm: Fides Quaerens Intellectum*, London: SCM Press, p. 14.
10 Anselm Stolz (1968), 'Anselm's Theology in the *Proslogion*', in Hick, John and Arthur C. McGill (eds), *The Many-Faced Argument*, London: Macmillan Press, p. 192.
11 *Proslogion*, Prologue (S.1.93.7–9), my translation.
12 *Proslogion*, 3 (S.1.102.6, 1.103.1, 1.103.3, 1.103.7); 4 (S.1.103.16 (twice)); 6 (S.1.105.5); 9 (S.1.107.7, 1.107.9); 11 (S.1.110.1).
13 *Proslogion*, 9 (S.1.107.5, 1.108.5); 11 (S.1.109.15); 14 (S.1.112.4); 16 (S.1.112.20 (twice), 1.112.21).
14 *Proslogion*, 3 (S.1.103.9).
15 *Proslogion*, Prologue (S.1.93.7) 'Deus vere est'; 2 (S.1.101.2) 'Quod vere sit Deus'.
16 It may seem odd to speak of God's being and nature as separate, but I do this because in the literature it is commonplace to make this division. The argument is usually that Anselm has first to establish the existence of God before he can say anything about the being of God. By making reference, therefore, to Anselm's desire to say something about God's being and existence I am trying to express what I see as the unity in Anselm's thought in contradistinction to his detractors. In fact, the very suggestion that a distinction can be made in the *Proslogion* between the existence and person of God demonstrates how out of touch such arguments are with Anselm's model of reality.
17 *Proslogion*, 2 (S.1.101.3–4) as translated in Thomas Williams (1995), *Anselm: Monologion and Proslogion with the Replies of Gaunilo and Anselm*, Cambridge: Hackett Publishing Company, Inc.
18 I recognize that at this point we could launch into dialogue with Kant and his critique, but I think enough has been said so far, and more will be added, that shows how fundamentally opposed my interpretation of Anselm is to Kant's.
19 When I use the term 'aesthetic unity' here I am trying to convey more than the obvious point that God is a singular entity. I am attempting to say something about the way in which God exists. In other words, God is not infinite mercy or infinite love or infinite judgement, but, as Anselm says, 'whatever it is better to be than not to be' (cf. *Proslogion*, 5 – S.1.104.15–17). Talking about God in the comparative degree allows God to be ever more than we conceive without creating the logical difficulty of reconciling a series of statically infinite incompatible characteristics. There is a proportionality to God's being.
20 *Proslogion*, Prologue (S.1.93.9), my translation.
21 *De Concordia*, 3.6 (S.2.271.28–2.272.1), as translated in Brian Davies and G.R. Evans (1998), *Anselm of Canterbury: The Major Works*, Oxford: Oxford University Press.
22 Henri de Lubac (1998), *Medieval Exegesis: The Four Senses of Scripture*, vol. 1, trans. Mark Sebanc, Edinburgh: T&T Clark, p. 24.
23 Ep. 77 (S.3.199.17–19), as translated in Walter Frölich (1990), *The Letters of Saint Anselm of Canterbury*, Kalamazoo, MI: Cistercian Publications.

24 *Proslogion*, 1 (S.1.100.8–10).
25 *Proslogion*, 1 (S.1.100.17–18), 'aliquatenus intellegere veritatem tuam, quam credit et amat cor meum', my translation.
26 Cited in Barth, p. 39.
27 *Proslogion*, 1 (S.1.100.18–19), my translation: 'Neque enim quaero intelligere, ut credam; sed credo, ut intelligam. Nam et hoc credo quia nisi credidero, non intelligam.' Many have understood this comment to derive from Isaiah 7:9. While there is an obvious relationship between Anselm's words and the Vulgate text, the final word is different. In our modern versions of the Vulgate the text finishes with the verb *permaneo*, not *intellego* (cf. Isaiah 7:9 in *Biblia Sacra*, septima editio, Madrid: Biblioteca de Autores Cristianos, 1985). While it is certainly possible (perhaps even probable) that Anselm was working with a different version of the Vulgate that did not use *permaneo*, it seems more likely to me that Anselm was recalling the words of Augustine in, for example, his lectures on John's gospel. In lecture number forty Augustine comments, 'For we believe in order that we may know, we do not know in order that we may believe' (*Nicene and Post-Nicene Fathers*. series 1, 40.9).
28 Augustine, *De Trinitate*, 1.1 in *Nicene and Post-Nicene Fathers*, series 1.
29 Augustine, *De Trinitate*, 1.1.
30 *Proslogion*, 15 (S.1.112.14–15).
31 The sort of theological–aesthetic reading of the *Proslogion* noted briefly above follows from a theological reading because, for Anselm, a theological appreciation of the nature of God will lead the reader to understand the aesthetic unity in the Godhead which will lead them to perceive that same aesthetic presence in the nature of reality. The continuity between creator and creation (and here we must remember to include language) is made explicit in revelation. As we will see, Anselm makes this point implicitly in Chapter 4 by insisting that the Fool cannot deny the existence of God if the definition provided is comprehensible. Anselm can forward this argument because, as we have seen in the *De Grammatico* and the *Monologion*, words are signs which bear sufficient resemblance to reality that they are the means through which we can perceive ultimate truths. Countless scholars have queried Anselm's assertion in *Proslogion* 4 because they have failed to recognize the importance of Anselm's signification theory and the implications it has for his theological method.
32 This construal of Anselm's argument fits well with what we said earlier about the semantic domain of *probare*. If *probare* is a prodding or a testing or an examining of what is held to be true then the higher the degree of understanding, the greater the force of the proof for those within the community of faith. On Anselm's model of reality and revelation, then, the proof ought to hold increasing weight for the unbeliever as well (though certainly not to the same degree as for the believer) because of the aesthetic unity that exists between creator and revelation and creator and creation.
33 Barth, p. 14.
34 *Monologion*, Prologue (S.1.7.2–3).
35 Jean Leclercq (1974), *The Love of Learning and the Desire for God*, London: SPCK, p. 28.
36 Leclercq, p. 21.
37 *Proslogion*, 2 (S.1.101.3–4), trans. Williams.
38 Barth, p. 16.
39 Barth, p. 17.
40 A great deal could be said here about the medieval and ancient understanding of participation. We have already seen, for example, how Anselm followed Augustine in the belief that attaining understanding allowed someone to participate in the divine nature. But how is this possible? My suggestion, and the one which will be explored in greater detail in the following two chapters, is that participation in God is achieved as we continually appropriate God's communicable attributes in their due (divinely appointed) proportion. In this way, we become reunited and reintegrated into the divine act of

re-creation which eliminates the chaos of sin and again establishes the beauty of divine harmony.

41   Barth, p. 17.

42   Cf. *Cur Deus Homo*, 1.1 (S.2.48.16–18; 2.49.23–6).

43   *Cur Deus Homo*, 1.25 (S.2.96.6–9).

44   *Contra Gaunilo*, 10 (emphasis mine) (S.1.138.30–1.139.3), trans. Davies.

45   Cf. *Proslogion*, 1 (S.1.93.3ff).

46   *Proslogion*, 1 (S.1.100.9–10), my translation.

47   *De Incarnatione Verbi*, 1 (S.2.6.10–2.7.4) as translated in Jasper Hopkins and Herbert Richardson (1976), *Anselm of Canterbury*, vol. 3, Toronto and New York: Edwin Mellon Press.

48   *Proslogion*, 4 (S.1.104.5–7), trans. Williams.

49   This takes us back, once again, to Anselm's model of reality. God has created the world in such a way that words (language) can adequately reflect the realities to which they refer. Thus, to Anselm's way of thinking, supplying the Fool with an intelligible, coherent definition of God sufficiently communicates the existence of God.

50   In fact, it is probably best to understand the *Proslogion* as divided into four parts rather than simply two large sections. Part one comprises the first four chapters which outline the one necessary thing that Anselm is seeking to prove through his single argument. Part two comprises the description of God's character that supports the argument – that than which nothing greater can be conceived – by drawing the reader's attention to immanence. Part three comprises the description of God's character that supports the argument – something greater than can be thought – by drawing the reader's attention to transcendence. In part four, Anselm returns to some final considerations of the 'one necessary thing' and makes his concluding remarks.

51   G.R. Evans (1978), *Anselm and Talking about God*, Oxford: Clarendon Press, p. 66.

52   Evans, p. 48.

53   Barth, p. 102.

54   Barth, p. 106.

55   The contrary position comes to mind immediately: 'If one presupposes that God does exist, how can one expect to prove that he does not?' There are innumerable difficulties and objections that could be raised against the above statement, but they do not take Anselm's use of *probare* into account. Recall that Anselm is not interested in proving the *mere* existence of God apart from any statement about his person; rather, Anselm is simultaneously proclaiming that God does exist and that he exists in a certain way. Proving that a deity (whether personal or impersonal) exists is an altogether different task from proving that the God who has revealed himself in the Bible is all that he claims to be. Anselm is at no point interested in proving that *a* god exists, but that his/the God has revealed himself in a coherent way that relates meaningfully to the created order.

56   Katherin Rogers has noted that '*intellegere* is a technical term for Anselm describing the kind of understanding that brings one closer to God therefore presupposing faith', cf. Katherin Rogers (1988), 'Can Christianity be Proven? St Anselm of Canterbury on Faith and Reason' in J.C. Schnaubelt et al. (eds), *Anselm Studies: An Occasional Journal*, vol. 1, New York: Kraus International Publishers, p. 464.

57   Davie, p. 103.

58   *Proslogion*, 4 (S.1.104.5–7), 'Thanks be to you, good Lord, thanks be to you; for what I first believed by your gift, I now understand by your illumination; so that if I did not wish to believe you exist, I would be unable not to understand.' My translation.

59   Barth, p. 26.

60   Barth, p. 33.

61   *Pro Insipiente*, (S.1.125.notes).

62   *Proslogion*, 4 (S.1.104.4), 'whoever understands that God exists in such a way cannot think of Him as not existing', my translation.

63   *Pro Insipiente*, 2 (S.1.125.20–1.126.1).

64 *Pro Insipiente*, 2 (S.1.126.8–13), trans. Hopkins.
65 *Pro Insipiente*, 2 (S.1.126.1–3), trans. Hopkins.
66 *Contra Gaunilo*, 1 (S.1.130.16–18), trans. Williams.
67 *De Veritate*, 11 (S.1.191.19–20), my translation.
68 Southern, p. 42: PL 150:115.
69 'sufficere mihi potest respondere catholico' *Contra Gaunilo*, Preface (S.1.130.5).
70 *Contra Gaunilo*, 1 (S.1.130.15–16), trans. Williams.
71 *Pro Insipiente*, 2 (S.1.125.14–17), trans. Williams.
72 *Pro Insipiente*, 2 (S.1.125.20–1.126.1), trans. Williams.
73 *Pro Insipiente*, 2 (S.1.126.6–7), 'why put forward this whole argument against anyone denying or doubting that there is something of this kind?'
74 *Proslogion*, 26 (S.1.121.23–1.122.2), trans. Williams.
75 *Contra Gaunilo*, Preface (S.1.130.5), trans. Williams.
76 *Pro Insipiente*, 2 (S.1.126.8–13).
77 *Contra Gaunilo*, 63 (S.1.131.2–5), trans. Williams.
78 Cf. the discussion in Trevor Hart (1995), *Faith Thinking*, Downers Grove, London: IVP.
79 *Proslogion*, 1 (S.1.98.16–1.99.7), trans. Williams.
80 Evans, *Anselm*, p. 10.
81 *Proslogion*, 2 (S.1.101.9–13), trans. Williams.
82 *Pro Insipiente*, 3 (S.1.126.23–9), trans. Williams.
83 *Pro Insipiente*, 3 (S.1.126.25), trans. Hopkins.
84 *Pro Insipiente*, 4 (S.1.127.3–7), trans. Williams.
85 *Proslogion*, 2 (S.1.101.13–15), trans. Williams.
86 *Proslogion*, 2 (S.1.101.15–1.102.3), trans. Williams.
87 Here again we see how closely the arguments and convictions we saw in the *De Grammatico* and the *Monologion* are to the *Proslogion*. There is an order, a proportionality, a reflection of the creator in the created such that what exists *in intellectu* can apply to things *in re*.
88 *Contra Gaunilo*, 8 (S.1.137.14–18), trans. Williams.
89 E.J. Butterworth (1990), *The Identity of Anselm's Proslogion Argument for the Existence of God with the Via Quarta of Thomas Aquinas*, Queenston, Ontario, Canada: Edwin Mellon Press, p. 115.
90 Butterworth, p. 116.
91 *Contra Gaunilo*, 8 (S.1.137.29), trans. Williams.
92 There are a number of points where the reader is left to wonder about Anselm's thoughts on natural theology. He certainly had a strong sense of the presence of God in all things and was convinced of what we have called the aesthetic unity between creator and creation, but I do not think we can posit an Anselmian natural theology apart from revealed theology. It is notable, for instance, that Anselm appealed to Scripture to validate his claim for analogies from nature to the divine. Were we to delve into this topic at length, I think we would have to include, if not begin our discussion with, Augustine's *City of God*. I find it interesting that in 11.3 Augustine argues for our necessary reliance on the 'canonical' Bible in order to know what is beyond our material (what he calls 'visible') reality, and that in the very next chapter he says that 'though the voices of the prophets were silent, the world itself, by its well-ordered changes and movements, and by the fair appearance of all visible things, bears a testimony of its own, both that it has been created, and also that it could not have been created save by God, whose greatness and beauty are unutterable and invisible' (Augustine, *City of God*, 11.4 in *Nicene and Post-Nicene Fathers*, series 1, vol. 2).
93 Thomas Aquinas (1924), *The Summa Contra Gentiles*, ed. and trans. the English Dominican Fathers, London: Burns Oates and Washbourne, sect. 1.11.
94 Aquinas, sect. 1.12.
95 Cf. Immanuel Kant (1965 [1929]), *Critique of Pure Reason*, trans. Norman Kemp Smith, New York: St Martin's Press, p. 500 ff.

96   McGill, 'Recent Discussions of Anselm's Argument', p. 35.

97   For a rebuttal in a more philosophical vein see William F. Vallicella (1993), 'Has the Ontological Argument been Refuted?', *Religious Studies*, 29:97–110.

98   McGrath, 'Does the Ontological Argument Beg the Question?', p. 306.

99   Umberto Eco (1997), *The Aesthetics of Thomas Aquinas*, trans. Hugh Bredin, Cambridge: Harvard University Press, p. 196 (italics original).

100 *Proslogion*, Prologue (S.1.93.8–9), trans. Williams.

101 Note that in Aquinas' précis of Anselm's argument he thinks that reference to the different ways of understanding the name 'God' is detrimental to the proof. This is interesting because Anselm makes it clear in Chapter 4 of the *Proslogion* that part of what he is doing is explaining to the Fool just what the name should signify. Anselm recognizes that it is possible for anyone to have a wrong idea of 'God' and that is why he goes to such great lengths to define the word. Whether one is defending or meditating on what is believed, the subject of that belief must be brought into sharp focus.

102 Oliver Johnson (1965), 'God and St Anselm', *Journal of Religion*, 45:326–34, p. 327.

103 Johnson, p. 328.

104 Johnson, p. 331.

105 Johnson, p. 333.

106 John King-Farlow (1982), 'Nothing Greater can be conceived', *Sophia*, 21:19–23, p. 20.

107 *Monologion*, 6 (S.1.18.23–26), trans. Williams.

108 Cf. also John Morreall (1984), 'The Aseity of God in St Anselm', *Sophia*, 23:35–44, p. 42.

109 *Proslogion*, Prologue (S.1.93.6–7), trans. Williams.

110 Robert Brecher (1985), *Anselm's Argument: The logic of divine existence*, Aldershot: Gower, p. 4.

111 Brecher, p. 5.

112 *Proslogion*, 3 (S.1.103.7–8), trans. by Brecher, p. 10.

113 *Monologion*, 8 (S.1.22.13ff).

114 Brecher, p. 11.

115 Brecher, p. 17 (italics original).

116 Brecher, p. 81.

117 Brecher, p. 83.

118 Brecher, p. 41.

119 Barth, p. 73ff.

120 Richard R. La Croix (1972), *Proslogion II and III: A Third Interpretation of Anselm's Argument*, Leiden: E.J. Brill, p. 14ff.

121 Richard Campbell (1976), *From Belief to Understanding*, Canberra: Australian National University, p. 20ff.

122 Brecher, p. 50.

123 Brecher, p. 24.

124 *Monologion*, 3 (S.1.16.15–17), trans. Williams.

125 *Proslogion*, 24 (S.1.117.26–1.118.3), trans. Williams.

126 *Proslogion*, 13 (S.1.110.12–16), trans. Williams.

127 *Proslogion*, 3 (S.1.103.3–6), trans. Williams.

128 Cf. Benedicta Ward (1977), *Anselm of Canterbury: A Monastic Scholar*, Oxford: SLG Press, p. 7.

129 Brecher, p. 17.

130 As quoted in Brecher, p. 11.

131 *Proslogion*, Prologue (S.1.94.6–7).

132 Cf. *Proslogion*, 4.

133 Some examples of other scholars we could examine include: Thomas Losconcy (1996), 'The Anselm–Gaunilo Dispute about Man's knowledge of God's Existence: An Examination', in von Fleteren, F. and Joseph C. Schnaubelt (eds), *Twenty-four Years (1969–1994) of Anselm Studies*, vol. 3, Lewiston, NY: Edwin Mellon Press; Patrick

Grim (1982), 'In Behalf of "In Behalf of the Fool"', *International Journal for Philosophy of Religion*, 13:33–42; William S. Robinson (1984), 'The Ontological Argument', *International Journal for Philosophy of Religion*, 1:51–9; Ian Weeks (1990), 'A Disproof of the Existence of God', *Sophia* 29:21–8. Much attention could also be spent on the works of Charles Hartshorne (*Anselm's Discovery*) and Alvin Plantinga (*God, Freedom and Evil*, *The Nature of Necessity*, *God and Other Minds*) if we were to introduce the modern philosophical dimension to this discussion (particularly with reference to modality and modes of argument).

134   McGill, 'Recent Discussions of Anselm's Argument', p. 35.

135   As quoted in McGill, p. 35.

136   McGill, p. 34.

137   Alasdair Macintyre (1990), *Three Rival Versions of Moral Enquiry*, London: Duckworth, p. 94.

138   Cf. Irenaeus, *Against Heresies*, 2.1.2 in *Ante-Nicene Fathers*, vol. 1.

139   Cf. Augustine, *Confessions*, 7.4.6 in *Nicene and Post-Nicene Fathers*, series 1, vol. 1.

140   Cf. Boethius, *Consolation of Philosophy*, 3.10.

141   Cf. Anna Abulafia (1990), 'St Anselm and those outside the church', *Faith and Identity*, 6:11–37.

142   Cf. McGill, p. 64; also André Hayen (1968), 'The Role of the Fool in St Anselm and the Necessarily Apostolic Character of True Christian Character', in John Hick and Arthur C. McGill (eds), *The Many-Faced Argument*, p. 176.

143   *VA*, p. 29, note 3.

144   *VA*, p. 29 (italics mine).

145   Southern, p. 116.

146   Anselm Stolz (1968), 'Anselm's Theology in the *Proslogion*', p. 186.

147   Stolz, p. 206; cf. also Ward, *Anselm of Canterbury: A Monastic Scholar*, p. 10.

148   Cf. Alasdair Macintyre's comment concerning medieval theology that God is present in every human mind, but is not necessarily recognizable to each one because it is only in so far as God gives sufficient light to each one that it is able to see him. (*Three Rival Versions of Moral Enquiry*, p. 95.)

Chapter 5

In Dialogue with the Divine

If one were to read through the works of St Anselm in the order in which we have looked at them, the next three works would come as something of a surprise. With the exception of the *De Grammatico*, the other works have all been amply imbued with explicit and implicit references to the Bible. Even when Anselm is not directly using or referring to the Bible his language exhibits a quality that evinces a man steeped in what G.R. Evans has called the language and logic of the Bible. To be sure, the *De Grammatico* does stand out from the rest in this regard, but because of its early date and its subject matter, affording it a unique place in Anselm's wider literature seems a reasonable thing to do.

Since examining some of Anselm's works in greater detail it has, however, become apparent that there is more going on in this monk's mind than meets the eye. Anselm was certainly keen to answer his colleagues' questions, but his responses have stretched beyond a simple reply. Anselm's agenda to demonstrate the beauty of the faith recurs throughout much of his writing. Time and again, Anselm goes to great lengths to show how the specific concerns of a given question fit within the framework of Christian doctrine; something he is able to do only because of his broader understanding of the relation between God and creation and the implications that has on the nature of reality. Thus, whether it be the dry, uninteresting aspects of medieval Latin grammar and signification theory or the deeply emotive yet theologically laden *Prayers and Meditations* or the intensely personal *Monologion* and *Proslogion*, the same model of reality provides the foundation on which Anselm is able to make his claims and to which his conclusions always point.

In the light of the foregoing discussion, it will come as no surprise that I believe this pattern continues to manifest itself in Anselm's three dialogues (the *De Veritate*, *De Libertate Arbitrii* and *De Casu Diaboli*). But, as just mentioned, these three treatises are somewhat odd in that, despite the claim in the preface that they 'pertain to the study of Sacred Scripture' ('pertinentes ad studium sacrae scripturae'),[1] they do not share the same plethora of scriptural detail that the other works do. In fact, there is so little in the way of scriptural exegesis or investigation that the reader is left to wonder how exactly these three dialogues could be so classified.

I suspect that any perplexity that may accrue for the modern reader in this area is due to our present manner of interpretation. More often than not, when someone announces their intention to study a portion of the Bible any combination of hermeneutical techniques (critical or otherwise) come to mind; many of which Anselm neither knew nor used. He did not intend to write an article or prepare a sermon, but to answer questions that arose in his or his students' minds from their reading. We have seen, for instance, that the subject matter of the *Proslogion* arises in part because of the need to explain Psalm 14:1.[2] Many of Anselm's prayers derive from specific sections of Scripture, but of these three dialogues two of them appear to have no explicit beginning in Scripture. The *De Veritate*, for example, begins with a reference to the *Monologion* and the *De Libertate Arbitrii* opens with what looks like a quote from Augustine. Granted, the *De Casu Diaboli* starts with a quote from 1 Corinthians 4:7,[3] but his application of that text to angels leaves us wondering how Anselm believed his three dialogues 'pertained to the study of Scripture'.

Southern's comments offer some guidance as he notes that the student's opening words in the *De Veritate* resemble those of John 14:6.[4] Indeed, there is much in the *De Veritate* which reminds the reader of Jesus' identification of himself as God and as Truth. In the *De Libertate Arbitrii*, Southern notes that the discussion centres around the theme, 'one who can sin, can be the slave of sin, since, "he who commits sin is the slave of sin"'[5] which is a quote from John 8:34.[6] For Southern, the direct quote from 1 Corinthians 4:7 requires no explanation. He simply states that these three dialogues are all 'careful, prolonged, exhaustive examinations of the doctrine of some central Biblical texts, employing the full apparatus of logic and grammar'.[7] We are left with the impression that Anselm was in the practice of using verses from the Bible as a platform from which to launch into some deeper doctrine of consequence, 'into a new range of problems in which the relations between Liberty and Justice have a central place'.[8] The concepts of truth and justice discussed in the later portions of the treatises (the *De Veritate* in particular) are not viewed as integral aspects of the very nature and structure of reality, but only as 'internal acts' which, while recognized as relating to being, are identified as 'acts' which ultimately culminate in 'the supreme self-commitment of monastic vows'.[9]

Are we really to believe that Anselm's vision was so narrow? Can the man who had been elected Abbot of Bec and had, as part of his duties, visited England on several occasions on business, really have thought that momentous concepts such as truth, rectitude and justice applied singularly to the monastic context? I do not disagree that Anselm was faithful to his vows and was a devout monk on many counts, but the tenor and character of his writing extend beyond the confines of the cloister. If we refer back to the *De Grammatico*, for example, we find that it was Southern himself who thinks that this work was intended for some external school populated by students from outside the monastery. The *Proslogion* also provides us with an interesting case because it is, as we have seen, so often deemed an apologetic treatise intended for unbelievers. In addition, the *Prayers and Meditations* were often written and intended for those women who did not take orders. There is a panoramic component to Anselm's thinking and writing. Yes, he wrote treatises for those who asked, and those who asked were most often fellow monks, but just because Anselm spent a lot of time with his fellow monks does not mean that the spectrum of his writing faded once it spread beyond the cloister walls.

The point here is not to argue whether or not Anselm was targeting a specific audience, but that the content of his writings, and more particularly the way in which he expressed and explained his thoughts, are such that their significance transcends the monastic context. Anselm's model of reality was sufficiently comprehensive that when he wrote about truth, free will or any other matter his thoughts unfolded in a way that the explanation and application incorporated all humanity. Granted, Anselm would probably have seen the monastic life as the supreme means of achieving the experience and understanding of which he spoke, but as we have seen and shall continue to see, the range of Anselm's *weltbild* leads us to contemplate the whole diapason that resonates in a reality where God is both the root and dominant chord of creation.

This is the context in which we should seek to understand how these three dialogues 'pertain to the study of Sacred Scripture'. If grammar and logic and language are, as Anselm and his contemporaries believed, created, and if all reality has been created in unity, then the process of understanding any given aspect of creation can follow any number of different paths. There is, in other words, a broader underlying belief in Anselm that the inter-relatedness of reality is such that a statement like the one made in John 14:6 can be tied to any number of different doctrines and thus illumine those articles of faith while simultaneously revealing the nature of God. Essentially, what Anselm believed he could do in the *Proslogion* with the different attributes of God all relating to one another and leading the reader to the same God, he believes he can also achieve in more overtly scriptural matters.

The difficulty is, of course, that the untrained mind may make some errors along the way. This is exactly what has happened with the student in the *De Veritate* (and the *De Libertate Arbitrii* to a lesser extent). He has drawn the conclusion that since God is Truth, when we say anything is true we can equally say that that thing is God. Leaving the details of this for later, the main difficulty here is the misunderstanding that while there is a correspondence between God and creation, it is not a univocal correspondence. Herein lies the tension in Anselm's thinking: there is discontinuity and continuity. It is true that God's creation can reveal the nature of God because of a continuity between the creator and the creation, but it is also true that those attributes in which the creation is permitted to participate are not held in the same degree or the same way by the creation. Apart from allowing for this measure of discontinuity, Anselm's appeal to aesthetics would fail. Due proportion would not exist, for example, if the creation was on a par with the creator. We saw this very error at work in Kant's critique of the ontological argument. Unfortunately, others have followed him in their error and believed that the insurmountable difficulty in Anselm's *Proslogion* is, to use somewhat different terms, that God is not like the rest of creation.

Sometimes, the admission that God is not like creation can cause difficulty because if God is not like creation then where is the point of contact? But this is precisely where Anselm would introduce continuity, just as he did at the beginning of the *Proslogion*. And just as Anselm worked very hard to hold the continuity and discontinuity between the creator and the creation together in the *Proslogion* (as well as in the *Monologion*) and just as he deemed it necessary to demonstrate the balance that exists between the immanence and transcendence of God in order to fully explore the articles of faith that are integrally intertwined with the existence of God, so here in these three dialogues Anselm again highlights the importance of combining our understanding of the world with our understanding of God as revealed in Scripture. Thus, in his treatises on truth, free will, and the fall of the devil, Anselm again employs a biblically informed *weltbild*, as he considers questions that themselves arise from the Bible in order to show the unity of all things in the created order established by a God of beauty.

Let us turn, then, with Anselm and the student to consider the nature of truth and reflect on how it fits into the proportioned order of a harmonious reality.[10]

What is Truth?[11]

The *De Veritate* opens with the student's statement that 'we believe that God is truth and we say that truth is in many other things.' From this the question follows whether or not when we speak of the truth 'we ought to be saying that it is God of whom we speak.'[12] The reason given for the question is found in Chapter 18 of the *Monologion* where Anselm is alleged by the student to have written that since the divine nature cannot have a beginning or an end, and since truth cannot have a beginning or an end, it is the case that truth is an aspect of the divine nature. The natural corollary of this is that since truth is identified with God in such an intimate way are we not talking about God when we talk about truth? To the modern reader the relationship drawn between truth and divinity is not immediately evident, so let us briefly return to the *Monologion* where Anselm made his claims to see first, how it is that he makes this claim, and second, whether or not such a claim is viable.

The Viability of Veracity in Divinity

Anselm's initial purpose as stated in Chapter 18 of the *Monologion* is to show that the divine nature (or simple nature, as he also calls it) has no beginning or end. Through a process of elimination Anselm shows that it is impossible that a supreme nature could not exist either through something else (for then it would no longer be supreme), nor through nothing (this could not be the case because if something were created out of nothing that would require a creator and if the supreme nature were created out of nothing, and, by implication by another, then it would be inferior to that creating force). Furthermore, Anselm reasons that the supreme nature could not have come into being through itself because, as in the case of coming into existence through nothing, to come into existence through itself implies that there is some kind of distinction that can be made between the thing that brought the supreme nature into existence and the essence that existed prior to the existence of the supreme nature.

The argument is then extended to show that it is impossible that the supreme nature could have an end. The essence of the argument here is that if the supreme nature has an end then either that nature will die unwillingly, in which case it is not omnipotent nor immutable nor immortal and therefore not supreme, or it dies willingly, but to die willingly is not good and since the supreme nature is supremely good this cannot be the case. In addition to this Anselm adds one last argument. He asks the reader to think of the answer to the following question: '"X is going to happen in the future". Assuming this statement is true, when does it start being true? When was it ever false? ... when will it cease being true?' It is inconceivable, says Anselm, that a true statement can have a beginning or an end: 'There is no conceivable time "when"' this statement is true. But how is it possible that the truth of a statement can attain such a transcendent quality? It is so because 'the true cannot be true without truth.' After all, if truth has a beginning then it was true before its beginning that truth did not exist, and if truth has an end, then it remains true after its end that truth no longer exists. This, Anselm states emphatically, is 'inconvenientissimum', most unfitting.[13]

The point he is trying to make is that the very nature of truth is such that it is eternal, and since it is eternal it is possible therefore to assign it as part of the supreme nature. It is, in fact, Anselm's agenda at this point in the *Monologion* to identify those things which are part of the supreme nature.[14] Now it is crucial that we recognize that Anselm firmly denied that identifying a transcendent quality in truth, goodness, beauty or any other characteristics meant that they were somehow equal, yet separate from the nature of God. He is careful to underscore the fact that the supreme nature is not 'a composite of these many good things' but is one thing altogether which can be signified by different names.[15] This is why, to return to the *De Veritate*, the student raises the question he does. Since it is true that God is truth, that truth is just another name for God as it were, is it not also the case that whenever we say something is true we are actually saying something about God?

The 'Oughtness' of Truth

To answer this question Anselm suggests that both he and the student begin the task of trying to determine a definition of truth. In order to achieve this they decide to begin by examining 'what truth there might be in speech'.[16] In the ensuing discussion the student arrives at the working definition that 'something is true only by participating in the truth, and therefore the truth of

the true is in the true itself.'[17] The resonance here with what we have already
seen in the *Monologion* and, especially, the *De Grammatico* is unmistakable.
There Anselm followed a similar pattern of identifying quality-indicating
words as those which participate in the thing which they signify. T.F. Torrance
has also noticed Anselm's characteristic connection between words or
statements and reality, though without noting the connection with the *De
Grammatico*. He comments that

> truth is not located in the statement itself, for it depends on what is signified as its
> 'cause' or ground, but it is bound up with the fact that it signifies rightly (*recte*)
> when it signifies as it ought (*quod debet*) by signifying what is in accordance with
> the facts. Thus, truth in a statement is nothing else than its rightness (*rectitudo*)
> in referring to a condition of reality beyond itself, but in this event its truth or
> rightness will depend on the truth or rightness of that to which it refers.[18]

There is, then, a similarity between the approaches taken in the *De
Grammatico* and the *De Veritate*, in grammar and in theology, in theory and in
reality. Just as in the *De Grammatico*, the *Monologion* and the *Proslogion*,
participation was central to the model of reality on which those works were
based, so too here in the *De Veritate* we discover that, for Anselm, a particular
understanding of the nature of reality is a prerequisite for comprehending
a part of that same reality. There is in the medieval mind a unanimity
among all things, a deep order which is finely balanced, a harmony between
symmetry and asymmetry such that a question about the definition of truth
is commensurate with a question about the nature of God.[19] And this is, as
we have seen, exactly where the student begins his search and, as we will
discover now, the direction Anselm steers his companion.

Following the opening section where the student contends that a statement
is true not because of something intrinsic to itself, but because it is participating in something that lies beyond it, he continues to argue that it is the case
that when a statement signifies 'that what is is, then the truth is in it and it is
true'.[20] At this point Anselm launches into a brief repartee with his pupil for a
rather interesting purpose. Consider the following excerpt:

> TEACHER: What, therefore, seems to you to be the truth there?
> STUDENT: I know nothing else except that when it signifies that what is is, then the
> truth is in it and it is true.
> T: For what reason is an affirmation made?
> S: To signify that what is is.
> T: Is this what it ought (*debet*) to do?
> S: Yes.
> T: So when it signifies that what is is, it is signifying what it ought (*debet*)?
> S: Yes.
> T: And when it signifies what it ought (*debet*), it is signifying rightly (*recte*).
> S: Yes.
> T: But when it signifies rightly (*recte*), is its signification right (*recta*)?

S: There can be no doubt.

T: When, therefore, it signifies that what is is, is its signification right (*recta*)?

S: That follows.

T: Again, when it signifies that what is is, is its signification true (*vera*)?

S: Yes, it is both right (*recta*) and true (*vera*) when it signifies that what is is.

T: To be both right (*rectam*) and true (*veram*) is, therefore, the same thing – that is, to signify that what is is?

S: Yes indeed.

T: So it must be that truth (*veritas*) is the same as rightness (*rectitudo*).

S: I now see clearly that truth (*veritatem*) is rightness (*rectitudinem*).

T: It is similar when a statement signifies that what is not, is not.[21]

In a remarkably simple way, Anselm has led his student from affirming the bare truthfulness of a statement (it is true because it is well formed or properly constructed) to recognizing that a statement can also be judged by its relation to what it purports. When it does this, it does, as Anselm says, what it ought to do. Thus, 'the standard case is had when it [a statement] fulfils its function rather than when it does not.'[22] By adding this teleological dimension to the discussion Anselm has expanded our understanding of truth to include oughtness and rectitude.

Expanding the Definition: Truth as Rectitude and Moral Necessity

The idea of rectitude has certainly not escaped the notice of scholars. Most notably, Southern mentions that this is a part of Anselm's mature theological thinking. What is interesting is that he uses rectitude as a point of departure for demarcating the *De Grammatico* from the rest of Anselm's works. The *De Grammatico*, says Southern, 'is simply an investigation into the rules for analysing words and sentences' and bears no relation whatever to the kind of thinking evinced in the dialogues or later theological works which are characterized by a concern for rectitude, moral necessity, truth or justice.[23] And yet, what provides the *De Grammatico* with its force is Anselm's conviction that there is a certain pattern to reality, an order established by God, a unity and a symmetry which is experienced and perceptible, but is only so because it is derived from that which is transcendent and immutable. Concepts such as rectitude or justice may not have arisen in the *De Grammatico*, but as an introduction to dialectic I do not think it would be fair of us to expect them.

Anselm had a set of presuppositions, what we have referred to before as a *weltbild* or a model of reality, and it is this perspective on the nature of creation and its relation to the creator that informs everything he wrote. This is why there is a closer connection between many of Anselm's works than has heretofore been acknowledged. This is why I have argued that the *Prayers and Meditations* are not as theologically immature as some have argued. This is also why I take issue with Southern over distinguishing the *De Grammatico* from the *De Veritate* and the rest of Anselm's corpus. Granted, the concepts may be evolving and the ideas may be changing, but rectitude and truth, fittingness and moral necessity belong together in a discussion which covers signification in the way covered in the *De Grammatico* because in both works there is an underlying structure which informs the way in which any given topic will be handled.[24] That is why the reader notices the preponderant use of terms such as *convenientia*, *decet*, *debeo*, and the like. Everything that has been created has been created for a purpose, and that purpose, by virtue of its being created by God, relates to God in some way. Thus, later on in the *De Veritate*, Anselm is able to argue that there is a sense in which even fire, a non-sentient, inorganic part of creation, can be said to act truly when it gives off heat because it is doing as it ought; it is fulfilling that which it has been created to do. Notice how in the relevant deliberations truth, rectitude and oughtness are again brought together:

> TEACHER: What could be more obvious then than that the truth of action is *rectitude*? ... Consider whether every action that does what it *ought* is *fittingly* said to do the *truth* ... Do you think we would *fittingly* say that fire does the *truth*?
> STUDENT: ... I do not see where the *unfittingness* would be in saying that fire exhibits *truth* and *rectitude* when it does what it *ought*.[25]

What this combination of truth, rectitude and oughtness does is to press an old question through a familiar grid. To this point in medieval theology and philosophy questions pertaining to truth dealt almost exclusively with the truth or falsity of statements.[26] Anselm had himself noticed that 'all speak of the truth of signification, but few consider the truth that is in the essence of things.'[27] Two chapters earlier, Anselm had made the provisional claim that 'there is truth in the essence of all things, because it is by being in the highest truth that they exist.'[28] That statement is, of course, the corollary of the student's comments that 'something is true only by participating in the truth.'[29] By basing all of these comments on the supposition of the dual character of truth (that there is truth which is part of who God is, and there is derivative, created truth) Anselm was actually adding not only an ontological dimension to truth, but an ethical dimension as well.

Truly Being and Being Truly: Truth as Real

The ontological element in Anselm's concept of truth comes across most clearly in his statement in Section 9 where he tells us that truth can be found within the essence of things. Anselm elaborates further that

> it is not only those things which we are accustomed to call signs, but in all other things of which we say there is true or false signification. Since one ought to do only what he ought to do, by the very fact that someone does something, he says

and signifies that he ought to do it. And if he ought to do what he does, he calls it true.[30]

What Anselm has done here is to augment his triumvirate of truth, rectitude and oughtness by suggesting that there is some standard by which all actions are measured. There is an allusion here, based as it is on the aforementioned principle of participation, that truth is concomitant with rectitude which is bound up with moral necessity because the truth which we experience is possible only because of the truth that lies beyond us. Anselm develops this allusion more boldly in the following section where he writes that 'all foregoing rectitudes are such because they are in things which are or do what they ought, but the highest truth is not rectitude because it owes anything. All other things owe him but he owes nothing to another, nor is there any other reason why he is than that he is.'[31]

How interesting that Anselm should not only appeal to God as the ground and reason for the existence and experience of truth, but that he should also introduce this teleological aspect. Just as in the *Monologion* and the *Proslogion* Anselm appealed to goodness or some other quality with which we are familiar, so now Anselm is using the same form of argument by pointing to the presence of truth in the ambit of our experience and then claiming that since there are, as it were, particular truths and rectitudes there must be a supreme truth and rectitude from which all others derive their existence. This introduces a strong sense of the purposefulness of truth. All things that have been created have been created for a purpose; they have been located within an intricate order; they have been assigned a place and function, and they are required to act in accord with that order. The interrelation presented to the reader is incredible. When I act in a certain way I am acting truthfully if I am acting in accord with what I ought (in the way that God created me), and am thus displaying rectitude and am therefore participating in the divine nature.

Now while the line of argument here may appear clear, the keen mind will have recognized that there is no reason why that particular order could not be changed. After all, how does one know what is true until one is already participating in the divine nature (Truth) and is thereby able to determine what is truthful and what is not? When we consider that each of the elements identified with truth relies equally on each other it becomes clear that what we are looking at is not a set of logical steps which helps us define what truth is, but a kind of organic unity within which truth exists. Logical progression is not a transcendent principle under which all things are ordered. Instead, Anselm is explaining how there is an aesthetic unity which governs all things. When Anselm claims that truth, rectitude and oughtness are interchangeable,[32] he does so on the strength of the conviction that this must be the case since this is the way it is in the divine nature. Since God is not first truth, and then rectitude, and on that basis moral, but all of these things at one and the same time, we too must come to understand truth (and indeed all of reality) not as the final determination of a series of propositions that best fits our perception, but as part of a whole which depends upon and is equally depended upon by everything else that constitutes God's order of creation. The beauty here is evident in the fact that truth is revealed not as a mere philosophical conundrum, a problem that can be examined in a detached manner, but a reality that touches all aspects of life and experience (both physical and spiritual), and which has its end in God. Thus, in so far as we seek to do what is right, what is true, what we ought, we are simultaneously striving towards God as we seek to participate in the rectitude, truth and oughtness that is God. The teleology of truth which is so integral to Anselm's argument witnesses to his desire to regain the aesthetic dimension marred by sin.[33]

Ought to Be or Ought not to Be – The Question of Evil

The discussion about the nature and definition of truth has so far required Anselm and his student to consider rectitude, moral necessity, fittingness, the divine nature and the relationship between the divine nature and human nature in participation. But their investigation does not end there. Indeed, it only raises a question that has probably been raised in the minds of every subsequent reader: 'how can we say that whatever is ought to be, since there are many evil deeds which certainly ought not to be?'[34] It is all well and good to argue that truth is part of the essence of all things, and that it transcends facile analyses which pertain exclusively to propositional factuality, but does not the presence of evil or sin present an insurmountable obstacle to the above understanding of truth? Not surprisingly, Anselm is not perturbed by this question and duly proceeds to respond in kind.

   He begins by asking the student whether or not it is possible for something to happen outside of the purview of divine direction or permission. The student answers, in his dutiful way, that it is impossible that 'anything could exist in any way if God did not either make it or permit it.'[35] On the strength of that admission Anselm carries on to reaffirm the goodness and wisdom of God, but he does so in a rather interesting way. He inquires of the student if he thinks that 'anything such Goodness and Wisdom does or permits ought not to be?'[36] The student replies that no one of intelligence would dare to think the opposite. At this point it would seem that Anselm is defeating his own case even before he has begun it for if it is true that God does permit or do anything which ought not to be, and there are definitely things that we believe ought not to be, reconciling these two views does not look promising. Nevertheless, Anselm immediately turns our attention to Christ's suffering. He concedes that there is a sense in which his suffering ought not to have happened since it was unjust that the one who did not deserve death should have died at the hands of those who did deserve to die. He moves on, however, to argue that there is a sense in which Christ's suffering ought to have happened. It ought to have happened because 'he wisely and benignly and usefully wished to suffer it.'[37] This brings Anselm to the crux of his argument, that 'there are many ways in which the same thing receives contrary appraisals from different considerations.'[38]

Anselm is pleading for a change of perspective. He is suggesting that any given act can be understood in different ways depending on who is doing the interpreting. In fact, Anselm goes even further to suggest that a judgement about an action cannot be divorced from those involved in that action. Thus, if man A hits man B we should not look simply at the action of man A, but we must also consider the condition of man B. Did man B deserve to be hit? Was man A acting justly when he struck man B? This leads Anselm to contend that

> just as the striker is not without the struck, nor the struck without the striker, so strikers and striking can only be understood with one another, indeed it is one and the same thing which is signified by different names according to different parts, and therefore a blow is said to be of both the striker and the struck. Wherefore in so far as the agent and the thing acted upon are subject to the same or contrary judgement, the action itself is judged to be the same or contrary.[39]

But how does this contribute to Anselm's argument? How can the interposition of the possibility of multiple perspectives allay our questions about the persistence of evil? In order to answer this question we need to remind ourselves of exactly what the student originally asked. The question was not about the existence of evil in relation to the existence of a holy God; rather, it was about the oughtness of evil for 'there are many evil deeds which certainly ought not to be.'[40] By framing the question in this way Anselm need not concern himself with the question of the existence of evil in the broad sense, but only in so far as it pertains to the disjunction between moral requisites.

Comprehending Disorder Within Order

When viewed in this light the kind of response Anselm provides begins to make a little more sense. He is concerned with perspectives because an action can be judged differently from different perspectives; thus allowing for the possibility of what ought to be in situations where it would appear that something ought not to be. Moreover, in the above excerpt we noticed that Anselm was also keen to stress that an action cannot be considered apart from those involved. We cannot look simply at the person who strikes or at the action of striking alone; we must look at the action, the striker and the one struck in order to gain a better appreciation of the whole. The unity and comprehensive ideal we saw in Anselm's understanding of reality is seen here on a much smaller and more personal level.

Ultimately, Anselm is happy to live with the paradox that 'it can very often come about that the same action both ought to be and ought not to be under different conditions'[41] because of his fundamental conviction that we cannot 'deny that what is permitted by such Wisdom and Goodness ought to be'.[42] To some, this may seem like a very poor answer to a searching and difficult question. To others, it may appear that Anselm is doing little more than toting the biblical line that God is above us and beyond us and that his ways are not always known to us. Comparisons with the last chapters of the book of Job or Romans 9 come to mind most readily. But I think there is more going on here.

What we are seeing here is another example of how Anselm's interpretative framework informs and shapes the solutions he offers. As we have seen, his framework is built on a model of reality which embraces an aesthetic unity in all things which is derived from the aesthetic unity in God. Should we not expect, therefore, that when Anselm is faced with the problem of evil he will address that problem in a manner consonant with this *weltbild*? When he admits, therefore, that there are situations in which some actions both ought to be and ought not to be, he is being consistent with his own theological position. Although evil is an undesirable, indeed, undeniable aspect of reality, Anselm will not permit it to negate the essential unity of all things as they are bound up in God, and so subsumes it within an understanding of reality that transcends a single perspective. We see best the extent to which Anselm is willing to defend this conviction in his example of the crucifixion of Christ.

Anselm asks his student if the iron nails driven through Christ's flesh ought to have penetrated his flesh or if they ought to have caused pain. The student answers that the nails ought not to have penetrated the flesh nor should they have caused any pain, and yet they did. In other words, because Jesus Christ is the second member of the Trinity and is therefore God incarnate, there is no way that mere mortals should be able to penetrate any part of him or cause him any pain. But, paradoxically, both of these things did happen. What this rather strange example shows, according to Anselm, is the possibility 'that an action or passion ought to be according to nature which ought not to be with respect to the agent or the one acted upon, since the former ought not to act and the latter ought not to suffer it'.[43]

Anselm is eager to explicate a very straightforward point: because of his sovereignty, goodness and wisdom, God can only do or permit those things to take place which ought to take place. From our perspective it appears as though there are some actions which ought not to take place, but from God's perspective nothing takes place which does not in some way participate in the truth, goodness or wisdom of God. Thus, an evil act which, from our perspective ought not to take place may, from the divine perspective, be in keeping with truth, goodness, beauty or a myriad of other possible divine attributes.

Now to this point we have seen that the *De Grammatico* is a work concerned with signification, logic and grammar, and that none of these are possible apart from a model of reality in which the creation is guaranteed to be the way it is because of its relation to the creator. Balance and symmetry between words and concepts are possible because, and only because, reality exists in a certain way. We have also seen how the *Proslogion* is not a work which is intended to exist in a vacuum, but a treatise that draws on a model of reality which views the aesthetic nature of God as necessarily communicable to creation. Here too, in the *De Veritate*, we have already noted how truth in the particulars of life is only possible in so far as the essence of all things contains and participates in divine truth. Should it not follow then, that, in the midst of a work which falls within the same framework as the *De Grammatico*, the *Monologion*, and the *Proslogion*, the explanation of the presence of evil will also be explained as part of a balanced and unified vision of reality? In fact, it is one of the strengths of an aesthetic appreciation and understanding of reality that it is able to incorporate paradoxes without embarrassment.

Of course, even explaining Anselm's argument in this fashion does not alleviate the impression that despite his integration of multiple perspectives and the nature of God, he has avoided the question. But I think it is precisely because evil is not regarded as something that needs to be explained away, but as part of our human condition, that Anselm's answer is most helpful and consistent. God's love and God's hate, God's forgiveness and God's condemnation, God's mercy and God's judgement: there are any number of characteristics in God's nature that cannot be explained unless we incorporate proportion, balance, symmetry and other similar aesthetic categories. As we saw in the *Proslogion*, Anselm never argued that God is what he is in the superlative, but in the comparative. By using the comparative Anselm allowed God to be more than we can conceive, but prevented our understanding from transgressing the bounds of God's own freedom. Were God to have all his characteristics in the highest degree possible for each then it would be impossible for God to hold them all in harmony. How could God be infinitely merciful but infinitely just? How could God be infinitely loving but infinitely hateful of sin? Just as God is all that it is better to be than not to be in perfect proportion, so all creation has been constructed with a similar aesthetic quality. And just as God's harmony is not defeated by rebellious angels, so his creation does not lose its essentially aesthetic character through the imposition of evil.

Aesthetic Unity: The Context for Ethics

T.F. Torrance also arrives at this general conclusion as he contends that all of what Anselm has to say on truth is bound up with his conviction that the universe has been given a certain order and harmony which is bound up in the very nature of God.[44] But it is also this context that Torrance believes fuels and sustains the ethical dimension of Anselm's inquiry into the nature of truth. It is not difficult to see how Torrance arrived at this determination when we consider that not only does Anselm tie together oughtness with truth from the beginning, but he also moves very quickly towards refining his definition of truth as 'a rectitude perceptible by the mind alone'.[45]

Anselm must define truth in this way because were he not to do so he would be forced to admit that everything in creation has the potential to act equally truly or rightly. The fire that provides heat would be participating in the truth just as much as the individual who sought to act ethically. Since this situation would not reflect a world modelled on due proportion and would be an affront to any reader, Anselm had to introduce the will into the discussion and argue that 'whatever does not will rectitude, even if it has it, does not merit praise for its rectitude. One who does not know it cannot will it.'[46] This explanation introduces an interesting paradox. While any member of creation acts in accord with the truth and thus does what they ought to do when they act in a manner befitting their being (the student here offers the example of a stone which acts like a stone quite naturally) it is not the case that 'whatever does willingly what it ought is just' but that something 'is not just if it does not willingly do what it does'.[47] There may be truth in all things by virtue of their acting in accord with their created nature, but truth, in what Anselm might have called the proper sense, is only present in rational creatures: humans.

What Anselm has done here is to admit that while sin is an impediment to right action (compare the first chapter of the *Proslogion*, for example), it does not utterly destroy or inhibit our ability to act in accord with what we ought to do, which is, paradoxically, the very thing our sinful natures do not always wish to do. This paradox that exists in the will and nature of humanity on account of sin is further explored in Anselm's final work, *De Concordia*. There, Anselm tries again to satisfy himself and his colleagues as to the way in which truth, justice and rectitude are all integrally and inescapably combined and yet how they cohere in the light of God's sovereignty, foreknowledge and grace.

Although this final work of Anselm's does little to advance his discussion on truth, free will or sin, and fails to augment much of his thinking on the divine nature, it is helpful in so far as it attests once again how ardently Anselm worked to demonstrate the necessity of relating concepts to one another in a model of reality wherein the aesthetic value of proportion, unity and fittingness is a required catalyst to appreciating them in their fullest measure. In fact, it is only in this sort of ordered, proportioned, coherent world where truth, rectitude and justice are simultaneously synonymous and independent and are founded in and defined by the divine nature. God is truth, God is rectitude and God is justice, yet God is one. We know truth, we can live according to rectitude, and we can act justly, but we are many. What ties our different experiences of truth together? What reconciles our differing ideas on rectitude? What defines justice? How are the multiplicity of our experiences and knowledge united? They are united in God; and only as we seek to unite ourselves with him, to participate in his divine nature, to measure our wills against his can the truth, rectitude and justice which have been implanted in us be realized.[48]

Reality has meaning for Anselm because the created has contact with the creator, we have been touched by the transcendent, and the bond that God has made with his creation is so profound that, to the uninformed mind, it is a collection of paradoxes rather than a paradigm of proportion. And yet, when we realize the connection between the immanent and transcendent, we discover that a discussion of truth also draws us to deliberate on freedom. For what point is there in relating truth or rectitude to the will unless that will is free? Thus, just as truth leads Anselm to include rectitude and justice and oughtness and, ultimately, the relationship between the creator and creation, so, within that same framework where proportion, harmony and symmetry are paramount, we find ourselves led to consider the meaning of freedom. T.F. Torrance catches this nuance of Anselm's thinking well when he states that

> if there were only natural truth in which a thing is what it already is by sheer necessity, then there would be no freedom or room for moral obligation. But since truth in the proper sense attaches to things accidentally so that they can be in the right with the truth only if they do what they ought, there is room and freedom in the world for a man to be what he ought to be.[49]

The Truth Shall Set You Free

Now it is all very good to suggest that everyone has a free will, but what exactly does Anselm mean when he talks about free will? For Anselm, understanding the will is intimately bound up with its relation to sin. At the beginning of the the opening chapter of the *De Libertate Arbitrii* he stipulates that 'I do not think free will is the power to sin or not to sin.'[50] The reason Anselm gives for thinking about free will in this way becomes clear when he carries on to comment that any definition of free will must apply to 'God and the angels' as well as to us. Thus, to define freedom as the ability to sin or not to sin would mean that God has the ability to sin, and that is impossible. Quite apart from the theological implications of this initial premise, it is immediately obvious to us yet again just how all-encompassing Anselm is in his vision of reality.

One of the first things that strikes the reader of the *De Libertate Arbitrii* is that Anselm desires to find a definition of freedom which encompasses all reality. Unlike the philosophy or theology of the day, or indeed of general opinion, Anselm is not satisfied with defining and exploring human freedom alone.[51] Anselm is unhappy with any definition of freedom that does not account for all of creation or, more properly, all of reality. Since God made all things, and all things therefore bear the fingerprint or image of God, we should strive at all times to envisage freedom in its relation to all things. As far as a definition and understanding of freedom are concerned, the whole should apply to the particulars, but any given particular must not determine the whole.

A brief examination of Anselm's opening comments to the student suffice to bear this out. After disagreeing with his student about the definition of free will, Anselm explains that true freedom is achieved when one acts as one *ought* to act: 'Do you not see that one who is as he ought to be, and as it is expedient for him to be, such that he is unable to lose this state, is freer than one who is such that he can lose it and be led into what is indecent and inexpedient for him?'[52] On the strength of this assertion and the following one that sin always entails unfittingness (*dedecet*), Anselm concludes that 'a will that cannot fall from rectitude into sin is more free than one that can desert it ... Therefore, since the capacity to sin when added to will diminishes liberty, and its lack increases it, it is neither liberty nor a part of liberty.'[53]

How remarkably counter-intuitive. Although the student, along with the majority of his peers, had believed that the essence of free will was located in the individual, Anselm reorientates the locus of freedom in the order of creation and the telos of all things. It is not the individual who determines or has control over the definition of freedom, for the individual is but a part of a composite whole. Instead of accommodating our understanding of free will to ourselves, Anselm explains that we must accommodate ourselves to free will. Richard Campbell has summed up Anselm's position well when he states that 'for Anselm the very character of freedom essentially involves what one is free for.'[54] As with the *De Veritate*, so now in the *De Libertate Arbitrii* there is a distinct metaphysic of teleology. For 'the rightness of a thing consists in its doing what it ought, that is, acting in accordance with the proper function of its nature, as it was created to be.'[55] What is particularly striking about this approach is that it so integrally binds free will with the nature and purpose of creation that the reader is, once again, inescapably drawn towards the conclusion that freedom in general and free will in particular is a gift from God. The balance in free will does not lie in choosing well from among an array of choices, but in the life that balances justice and truth, rectitude and oughtness in due proportion.

The Language of Free Will

Continuing our investigation into the place of fittingness in the *De Libertate Arbitrii* we discover in this treatise that Anselm uses *oportet* three times, *decet* once and *dedecet* twice.[56] Over the course of the whole treatise he speaks specifically of fittingness six times (albeit, two of those times he does so by means of describing the opposite – the unfittingness (*dedecet*) of the compatibility of free will and sin), and four of those occurrences come in the first chapter where the essence of his definition of freedom is crystallized.

The other two times he denotes fittingness he uses *oportet* once in a rather nondescript way (in Chapter 6 the student says, 'I ought [*oporteat*] to admit ...') and *oportet* again in Chapter 8 at a very significant point which expands on the ideas in Chapter 1.

The significance of *oportet* in Chapter 8 is at first missed when we discover that it is used only by the student to say, 'Sic oportet fateri' (it ought to be so). When, however, we consider the preceding statement to which the student is agreeing we find that Anselm has there concluded that 'to preserve rectitude of will for its own sake is, for everyone who does so, to will what God wants him to will'. As we shall see in our discussion on the *Cur Deus Homo, oportet* is used by Anselm for describing that which is in character, that which is fitting according to the nature of someone or something. Thus, in this case, Anselm is arguing that his definition of freedom, which he outlined in the first chapter, requires that human will be in harmony with the divine will. In this context, the words Anselm puts in the student's mouth become all the more illuminating because they subtly elaborate on Anselm's by indicating that the harmony that is a necessary condition for freedom is congruent with the relationship that is required between the human and divine.

There is one other word that Anselm uses to help explain the concurrence of fittingness and freedom: *debeo*. This is a much more common term, and so care in assuming significance must be taken, but it does occur eleven times, and, in conjunction with the above evidence, it strengthens the argument for an aesthetic dimension to Anselm's concept of free will. Most of the times this word occurs in the *De Libertate Arbitrii* it does so to elucidate the point we have already explained: that all reality has been created in a certain way and with a certain order, and that each member of reality ought to or is morally obliged to act in accord with their nature. But Anselm takes the oughtness of a teleologically orientated creation further and asks 'for what purpose a rational nature ought [*debeat*] to retain that rectitude, whether for the sake of the rectitude itself, or for the sake of something else'.[57]

Like so much of the *De Libertate Arbitrii*, this line of questioning leads Anselm back to points raised in the *De Veritate*. At the end of the *De Veritate* Anselm explains that in order for signification to be meaningful, that is, in order for us to speak of rectitude or truth in a meaningful way, there must be a rectitude 'whereby signification is called correct'.[58] For if our signification of rectitude or truth depended on the truth and rectitude which is in each person, then, quite clearly, the meaning of our signification would be in constant flux and, evidently, chaotic. The aesthetic unity of reality cannot be maintained apart from the communication of the singular, transcendent unity of characteristics in God to his creation. This is how Anselm was able to claim that truth can also be equated with justice because justice is 'rectitude of will preserved for its own sake'.[59]

Here in the *De Libertate Arbitrii* Anselm repeats his conviction and, through a strikingly similar train of thought, arrives at the conclusion that 'since all liberty is a capacity, the liberty of will is the capacity for preserving rectitude of the will for the sake of rectitude itself.'[60] At first glance, this statement seems to contradict everything for which Anselm has been arguing. He has constructed an explanation of truth and now of free will which vitally depends on a certain pre-understanding of the nature of reality which is in turn dependent on the nature of God. Consequently, we were not surprised to find strong traces of teleology in Anselm's discussions because our investigation of his presuppositions and *weltbild* had revealed an interpretation of reality which identified a morally motivated movement directed towards God. But have we been mistaken? If the test of free will is that it preserves rectitude (and so also truth and justice) for its own sake, then God would seem to have been removed from the picture.

This is where some scholars have seen Anselm's programme diverge from Augustine's. Based on his discussions of freedom in numerous places[61] it is clear that Augustine remained clearly focused on God. Anselm, on the other hand, appears to deviate from this pattern. Hiroko Yamazaki argues this point when he contests that in Augustine the object of the will is always God, but for Anselm the object is 'what it ought to will'.[62] But the problem with interpreting Anselm in this way is that the whole force of the argument as it runs through the *De Libertate Arbitrii* is not taken into account.

In fact, we have already mentioned the place where the answer to this dilemma is found. In Chapter 8 we discovered that the student agreed with Anselm that preserving rectitude for its own sake is equivalent to willing what God desires that we should will.[63] At no time did Anselm ever stipulate that the will should be in harmony with anything other than God. Yamazaki's criticism that Anselm replaced God with some kind of moral imperative misunderstands Anselm entirely. Throughout the *De Veritate* and now in the *De Libertate Arbitrii*, Anselm has contended that all things can and ought to relate to God because of the unity, characterized by aesthetic concerns, that the creation shares with its creator. Only when we comprehend the harmony that characterizes the bond between divinity and humanity will we comprehend how such language is permissible.

I think there is, moreover, another reason Anselm chose to describe free will as rectitude preserved for its own sake. It may be that Anselm believed it was obvious that one can only will what one ought to when one is participating in the divine nature, but realized the potential difficulty for his students in grasping this abstract concept. What, after all, does it really mean to participate in the divine nature? This question is not unlike the one the reader of Ephesians is faced with when Paul declares that Christians are 'in Christ'. In Paul's case the explanation is provided mainly in the second half of the book. After laying out the theological reality and truth of who the people of God are, and their relation to God, he moves on to explain the practicalities. Christians are to be obedient to the law of God, to live as Christ did, to learn and adhere to the truth of the message preached to them so that they might not be deceived. Is it possible that Anselm is doing something similar? Is he helping his students and readers to understand the abstract and difficult principles of free will, rectitude, truth, justice, moral necessity and their *ne plus ultra* in God by reducing these concepts to a commonly appreciable and immanently practical level?

A third reason Anselm may have decided to define free will in these terms takes us back to the *De Veritate*. There, in Chapter 12, while Anselm and his student are attempting to define justice in the light of what they have learned about truth and rectitude, Anselm inquires whether or not the definition of justice as rectitude of will for its own sake 'can be adapted to the highest justice, in so far as we can speak of it'.[64] The student responds that such a definition is indeed most applicable to the highest justice found in God because 'it [the divine nature represented in justice] does not preserve something else but itself, and not by something else but by itself, so not for the sake of something else but for the sake of itself.'[65] What we discover then, is that defining justice or, as in the *De Libertate Arbitrii*, free will as rectitude for its own sake allows Anselm to define his terms such that they apply supremely to God, but also to creation. In this way the concepts under examination are not only shown to relate to one another and so demonstrate the unity and proportion and harmony that is essential to reality, but they are also shown to exist in God. In short, Anselm has simultaneously demonstrated the unity and diversity, continuity and discontinuity that is part of a model of reality that is at once rooted in God, but separate from him.

Anselm's definition of free will is, then, shown to be focused on God and not on fittingness or moral necessity for its own sake. In fact, by identifying free will and justice by assigning them the same definition Anselm reveals just how God-centred is his whole theology. In the *De Veritate*, truth was shown to exist only in so far as it participated in the Truth. God is the measure of what is true. Truth was also shown to be related to rectitude and justice, the latter of which was defined in terms of the former and related to the will. Thus, just as truth is rectitude of will, so justice is rectitude of will. In this way, Anselm was able to show how truth, rectitude and justice are related. Anselm did not, however, stop there. He carried on to argue that what guarded against a chaotic or individualistic interpretation of rectitude of will was that it must be maintained for its own sake. Within the context of the *De Veritate* the reader is left to assume that the reference to 'for its own sake' must have been obvious to Anselm since he does not explain it any further. Help is not long in coming, though, when we come to the *De Libertate Arbitrii* where he explains that 'for its own sake' means to will according to God's will.

Freedom According to the Will of God?

There remains, though, a serious problem. Anselm's definition of free will forces one to wonder how our freedom is possible in a system that makes human will subservient to divine will. This is one of Marilyn McCord Adams' disputes with Anselm. Although much of what she finds difficult in Anselm pertains to the *Cur Deus Homo*, she does briefly mention a point which touches on the content of the *De Libertate Arbitrii*.

In the midst of criticizing Anselm for his poor handling of honour in the *Cur Deus Homo*, Adams summarizes Anselm's position by stating that 'a man's honour consists in his being able to attain happiness by free choices.'[66] Since Anselm does not touch on honour directly in the *De Libertate Arbitrii*, following Adams' criticism may seem somewhat tangential, but it seems to me that we cannot avoid challenging some of her bigger concerns. The achievement of honour is, after all, an implication of Anselm's definition of free will (not to mention the attending concepts of truth, rectitude, justice and moral obligation).

The problem, according to Adams, is that Anselm's definition assumes what cannot be proven. Surely, argues Adams in concord with Nelson Pike, it is 'possible that God should force a man to obey him and thus deprive him of his honour while simultaneously making the man sublimely happy'.[67] In other words, suggesting that freedom of choice is the essence of happiness and the way to honour is problematic because there can be no guarantee that our choices are free. This is, in fact, the same type of argument that the student raises when he asks, 'Can even God take away rectitude from the will?'[68] Adams offers what she imagines to be Anselm's response: it would be impossible for humanity to be happy were God to take away our ability to make free choices. But then, if Anselm really wants to hold on to the sovereignty of God, it would seem that he cannot make this claim. Has Anselm led us astray? Do we need to re-examine our appraisal of his argument? No.

First, Adams' argument begins by defining honour with respect to free choice. This may not initially appear a dubious part of the statement, but the use of 'free choice' is somewhat curious. Part of the reason may be attributed to Hopkins' and Richardson's translation which tends to translate *arbitrium* as 'choice'.[69] It may be that Adams independently arrived at such a translation. Whatever the reason, it is a poor representation of what Anselm is saying. Whether in the *Cur Deus Homo*, the *De Concordia* or, chiefly, in the *De Libertate Arbitrii*, Anselm's contention is focused mainly on the will. Richard Campbell agrees with Stanley Kane on this very point when he adds that the translation 'choice' does not seem to fit Anselm's train of thought. He suggests that *arbitrium* is 'used to refer either to the will-as-instrument or to the will-as-use'.[70] In either case the will is the central concern.

If we consider the beginning of the *De Libertate Arbitrii* once again it is instructive to note that Anselm uses the same words as the student (*libertas* and *arbitrium*) but applies an entirely different definition. Instead of confining himself to a definition that depends on selecting from an array of choices, as the student had done, Anselm explains that any definition of *libertatem arbitrii* must, at the very least, eliminate sin. Approaching the question of *libertatem arbitrii* in this way immediately removes the emphasis from the prospect of choice and places it firmly on the will. What matters is the purity of the will, the degree to which it reflects the divine will. This is not to deny that choices never come within the ambit of the discussion, but that they are considered a subordinate category with respect to the primary discussion on the will as free. It is, moreover, the will as free which is defined according to rectitude and justice which are in turn related to truth. From beginning to end, the principal stress in those places where Anselm addresses *libertatem arbitrii* is located on the will, not the choice. The reason for this is that if the will is pure then choosing between what is right or wrong is no longer an issue. Just as God does not deliberate over an infinite number of right and wrong choices because his will is pure and holy, so the will which is truly free does not deliberate over choices.

What this means for Adams' argument is that to stake an individual's honour on the ability to attain happiness via free choices is misguided. It is misguided because, for Anselm, honour is not bound up in the choices themselves, but in the will which directs them. Just as Anselm holds that 'justice is not rectitude of knowledge or action, but of will', so it is true that free will is rectitude of will, over and above rectitude of knowledge or action.[71] If, however, we were to modify Adams' statement to read that 'a man's honour consists in his being able to attain happiness by a free will' she would be closer to the truth. Nothing could be more obvious in Anselm's theology than that free will leads to happiness and honour.

Aside from this technical quibble with Adams' position on honour and free will in Anselm, her agreement with Pike is also rather disturbing.[72] Quite apart from the remarkably foreign and anachronistic presuppositions these two scholars are suggesting,[73] Anselm has already responded to this charge in Chapter 8 of the *De Libertate Arbitrii* and again more elaborately in the third section of the *De Concordia*. In the *De Libertate Arbitrii*, Anselm argues that God could not will to remove rectitude of will in anyone because to do so would be tantamount to willing against his own will since rectitude of will is willing what God wills. It is, therefore, impossible 'that God should take away the rectitude of will'.[74] Anselm reaffirms this position again in the *De Concordia* where, in Section 1.6, he states emphatically that since uprightness of will is willing according to God's will, 'it is obvious that God cannot remove this uprightness from people against their will for the reason that God is unable to will anything like this.'

This is, of course, not to say that God has nothing to do with free will in humanity. Anselm is careful to delineate the place of God in the freedom of humanity even further in the *De Concordia* where he writes, 'no one preserves this received uprightness without willing it. But no one can will it without having it. And one cannot have it at all except by grace. Therefore just as no one acquires it without a prevenient grace, so too no one preserves it except by subsequent grace.'[75]

As careful as Anselm is to establish human free will, he is equally careful to denote its source and sustaining strength. It is here that we see again God's immanence in creation and how his presence invests our reality with meaning in its constituent parts. I find it intriguing that Anselm should see the need for God's grace both preveniently and subsequently as a necessary factor in human ability. What this leaves us with is a situation in which the only choice a human can make that is free in the way Pike and Adams would define freedom (that is, a choice made without any outside coercion or persuasion) is the one which abandons God's gracious gift of uprightness. But then, within Anselm's theology, that would be an act of slavery, of allowing one's self to be conquered. The will would no longer be free and therefore any choices made could not be free. Richard Southern has rightly noted that 'to choose servitude cannot be an exercise of freedom.'[76]

The challenge that Adams and Pike mount against Anselm's view of free will is similar in many respects to the sorts of criticisms levelled against the *Proslogion*. In both cases the counter-arguments are only effective if you deny the metaphysical underpinnings of Anselm's theology. One is left to wonder if part of the reason Anselm's metaphysical and theological presuppositions are challenged is because there is a coherency within the system itself that is hard to remonstrate.

Coherent, but not Complete

Finding faults in Anselm's writings and theology is, however, certainly possible. One of the things that Anselm fails to do in the *De Veritate*, for instance, is to apply his definition of truth and justice to specific situations. It may be helpful to have a general guideline or principle, but the application of the principle in complex ethical situations is rarely, if ever, a straightforward matter. Similarly, in the *De Libertate Arbitrii*, it is great to have a general rule that identifies my will with the divine will, but the history of biblical interpretation, even during Anselm's day, shows us that determining the divine will is not always simple. We could imagine Anselm responding to these sorts of criticisms by explaining that he did not intend for these works to be definitive explications of all possible situations, but as introductions which elucidate some of the difficulties that are bound to arise in the beginner's mind. He might caution us against asking more of the text than it offers. Still, one of the pitfalls of Anselm's writing on the whole is that it is written on a sufficiently cerebral level that it is not always easy for the reader to translate the ideas into experience.

Lest the reader think this assessment of monastic theology too pragmatic, recall how Anselm adopted Augustine's idea of two different types of knowledge. The first type of knowledge is true knowledge based on experience; the second type of knowledge is accepted knowledge based in trust awaiting confirmation through experience. My concern with some of what Anselm writes is that in seeking to build on his students' accepted knowledge (for that is what lies at the base of the majority of his works), he fails to adequately impart a knowledge which is grounded in experience.

This leads to a second criticism of Anselm's works: by starting his investigations with accepted knowledge, but occasionally failing to arrive at knowledge in relation to experience, Anselm sometimes finds himself delving into matters better left untouched. This is the case with the *De Casu Diaboli*. Although there is much to commend it, in the final analysis Anselm is forced to stretch the definitions he has outlined in the previous two treatises beyond what they can bear. It is in this treatise, perhaps more than any of the others, that Anselm takes his belief that a Christian ought to look into the dictates of the faith 'inasmuch as one can look for reasons' too far.[77] There will always be reason to look into something, but one wonders if the better part of wisdom requires some matters to remain mysteries.

Why the Fall of the Devil?

The fall of the Devil (and the consequent question of the origin of evil) is certainly one of those mysteries. The problem of evil was nothing new to Anselm. Among the more conspicuous theologians to tackle this Gordian knot was St Augustine and, the informed reader will observe, some of what Anselm says on the matter is directly influenced by Augustine.[78] But there is a more immediate cause for Anselm's curiosities into the fall of the Devil and the origin of evil. Since it is written as a disputation between a student and a teacher it is possible that a member of the cloister school raised the issue, but it is also possible that Anselm wrote this treatise as a result of having raised the issue himself in the *De Veritate* and the *De Libertate Arbitrii*.

When we discussed the *De Veritate* we noticed that Anselm felt it necessary to respond, be it ever so briefly, to the problem of evil.[79] There were, in addition, a number of places in the *De Libertate Arbitrii* where the reader's thoughts may well have extended beyond the limits of the immediate discussion. Take the first section, for example. When defining free will Anselm was adamant that it could not mean the power to sin or not to sin since 'the divine free will and that of the good angels cannot sin.' If the good angels cannot sin, indeed, do not have the power to sin, how it is possible that some of the angels fell? The student makes this point more compellingly in the second section when he inquires after the capacity he assumes was given to both humanity and angels to sin freely. Part of Anselm's answer includes an excursus on the fall of the *apostata angelus*. The answers provided do, however, require greater elaboration consonant with the import of the issue for theological reflection. The reason for writing on the fall of the Devil is, therefore, not entirely out of place.[80]

While it is true then that the *De Casu Diaboli* follows closely on the heels of the *De Libertate Arbitrii* which follows on from the *De Veritate*, it is also true that the arguments forwarded in this work approximate many of the arguments used in the *De Libertate Arbitrii*, the *De Veritate* as well as the *Monologion*. The impression the reader is given is that this treatise is not a work intended to stand alone, but is the capstone of a series of discussions. This is not to say that the *De Casu Diaboli* is unworthy of or unable to withstand examination, but to suggest that rather than introducing new concepts its purpose is to cement those already presented. Consequently, if the thesis is correct that aesthetic categories are paramount in Anselm's theological discourse, we would expect to find the evidence woven into the warp and woof of even this dark topic.

From the Inner Sanctum to the Den of Iniquity

The *De Casu Diaboli* opens exactly like the previous two treatises: the student asks the teacher to clarify a point of theology or scriptural interpretation. In this case the question derives directly from 1 Corinthians 4:7 ('What do you have that you have not received?'). The student desires to know if this statement applies equally to humans and angels. Very quickly, the discussion turns towards the nature of being and how it relates to God. Anselm points out that while all being flows from God, non-being does not come from God for 'just as from the highest good only good comes, so from the highest being only being comes, and all being comes from the highest being … Hence nothing and non-being do not come from God, from whom come only good and being.'[81] The attentive reader will have doubtless noticed the resonance here with some of the initial chapters in the *Monologion*. In the first nine chapters of that work Anselm goes to great lengths to make the same point. It appears as though Anselm is preparing the reader for what follows by reinforcing the connection between the creator and creation.

We discover soon enough that Anselm's preparation was not in vain when the student probes further and asks how it can be that fallen angels did not persevere if angels and men have all that they have because they have received it. The only possibility is that they must not have received the ability to persevere, for how can a fallen angel be at fault for something he could not control or be held responsible for an action he did not have the ability to carry out?[82] The dilemma is serious. If God is the source of all things that exist, including free will and the ability to preserve rectitude, how is it possible that certain angels should fail to persevere? The logic of this situation militates against the beauty and fittingness which has been so much a part of Anselm's deliberations.[83]

Anselm replies by distinguishing, first of all, between the activity of giving and the activity of receiving. According to Anselm one can only properly be said to give if the recipient actually receives what is given. Consequently, certain angels[84] were given (and received) 'the will and capacity to accept perseverance' but were not given 'the acceptance of perseverance … only the will and ability to accept it'.[85] In the Devil's case he 'had the will and the capacity to receive perseverance and the will and the capacity to persevere, [but] did not receive perseverance and did not persevere because he did not will it all the way'.[86] Here we see the second distinction in Anselm's response. There was in the Devil a dual capacity: a capacity to accept God's gift of perseverence and the capacity to reject God's perseverence. In other words, the Devil is still to blame for his fall because God gave him the ability to accept the gift of perseverence. The Devil's fault lies in his not willing to will in accord with the capacity he has been granted.

At this point the discussion begins to mirror parts of the *De Libertate Arbitrii* and *De Concordia* quite closely. In those two treatises, as we saw, Anselm emphasized two different aspects of the will. The first emphasis was on the will as free as long as it participated in the divine will. The second emphasis was on the ability to make free choices, but, as we noted, Anselm denied that any free choice should be attributed to anything but the grace of God. What this means is that, within the compass of the discussion on free will, whenever someone acts in accord with what is right and true they owe the ability for that activity to God; but whenever someone does what is wrong, they have no one to blame but themselves.[87] To put it another way, God gives us the ability or capacity to be free, but it is up to us to exercise that capacity.[88]

The same argument is used in the *De Casu Diaboli*. The Devil was given the ability to accept perseverence, but he did not exercise that ability. Anselm does not stop there, however, because his interest extends beyond the fall of the Devil to the evil that precipitated the fall of the Devil.[89] This brings us back to the *Monologion* and participation. We saw there that everything that is good is good because it participates in the goodness that is God. This principle was then expanded in the *De Veritate* where all truths are described as participating in the truth that is God. The idea was taken one step further in the *De Libertate Arbitrii* when Anselm claimed that a will is free only when it participates in and thus acts according to the divine will. In *De Casu Diaboli* the pervasiveness of participation is shown again when the teacher tells the student that 'We should hold that justice is the good whereby they are good or just, both angels and men, and that whereby the will itself is called good and just; and injustice is the evil that is only a privation of the good, and makes angels and men bad and makes their will bad.'[90]

Here we have the characteristic argument that things are not what they are in themselves, but by virtue of their participation in something beyond them. But there are two difficulties here. First, where did the first 'injustice' come from? Second, does this mean that evil is a real substance? Answering the second question first, Anselm tries to prove to the student that sin is both nothing and something.[91] This is, of course, exactly why the student began his inquiry in the way he did. He wanted to know if all things have their existence from God. Perceiving the direction of the conversation, Anselm is forced to say that sin is nothing because if sin is something and all things that have existence owe their existence to God then God created sin. Such a conclusion is patently unfitting. When Anselm claims that sin is nothing he is following a long tradition most notably upheld by St Augustine. This tradition is, however, not without its own difficulties.

One of the main difficulties is that sin is defined in terms of being. The reason for this is, as far as Anselm is concerned, because words relate to that which is real. We saw this most clearly in the *De Grammatico* where Anselm explored the meaning and signification of nouns and adjectives within a metaphysical context. This position appears again in the first section of the *De Incarnatione Verbi* where Anselm warns against 'those contemporary logicians (rather, the heretical logicians) who consider universal essences to be merely vocal emanations'. These people, he argues, are able to understand abstract concepts 'only as material substances'. Such people 'should be altogether brushed aside from discussion of spiritual questions'. Anselm's point seems to be that there is more to reality than what we can access through our bodily senses. There are realities beyond us which, though not material, are still very real. Being does not have to assume a physical form to exist. God is real, God has being, and yet God the Father and God the Holy Spirit do not maintain a physical form.

In this context the problem of evil and, consequently, of the fall of the Devil is most perplexing. How can sin, that which must be something by virtue of our being able to name it, exist without God being responsible for its existence? This is a question which can only provisionally be answered by suggesting that sin is nothing or an absence. But if sin is nothing or an absence then how is it responsible for the distortion and tribulation we see around us? The deeper one gets into this question the more the difficulties proliferate. How could nothing do so much? But what if the idea of sin as nothing, negation or absence were understood in the light of aesthetic concerns? In this situation, if sin is defined as that which is unfitting, which ought not to be done, the absence of some element of an originally balanced, ordered, proportioned part of reality, then sin can be nothing, strictly speaking, and still cause horrendous things to happen.[92] To explain this, Anselm draws two analogies. A horse without a bridle is liable to veer off course, to do what it ought not do. A ship without its pilot will eventually run aground.[93] In both cases, there was not activity as such taking place to cause the final outcome, but a lack of what ought to have been which resulted in disaster. In Letter 97 Anselm contends that 'there is no contradiction in saying that evil is nothing and that the word "evil" has significance; it refers to something by exclusion while being constitutive of nothing.'

Connecting these analogies to reality we can see Anselm's point. The world, though ordered and created in a way that reflects the beauty of God, is infested with sin. This sin is not actually an identifiable substance, nor is it part of creation because God could not have created it. What it is is an absence of what ought to be, and this absence is what causes the effects which give the appearance of the existence of evil. But how does this advance Anselm's investigation into the origin of evil? It accomplishes two things. First, it locates evil in the will of created beings. Second, it militates against the accusation that since God is the creator of all things he must be the author or source of evil. Above all, Anselm has sought to situate this discussion within his metaphysic of participation. This does, however, beg the question, 'If evil is that in which all angels and humans participate that makes them evil, does that mean evil existed prior to the Devil's decision to not accept God's gift of perseverance?' Although Anselm does not tackle this question, he would probably say, 'Yes, and no'. No, evil did not exist before the Devil made his decision because, by its very nature, evil has no existence. Yes, evil did 'exist' before the Devil made his decision because non-being or the absence of what ought to be is, barring divine fiat, always possible.

Our deliberations on this question of the origin of evil and the cause of the fall of the Devil could continue indefinitely, but our purpose in looking at this last of the three dialogues has been to examine what role aesthetics plays in an attempt to unravel the Gordian knot of the origin of sin and the fall of the Devil. What we have discovered is that rather than adding anything new, the *De Casu Diaboli* serves to cement an already well-enunciated principle that what matters in theological inquiry is fittingness and oughtness. The Devil sinned, did what was unfitting because he willed what he ought not to have willed. What is interesting about framing the problem in this way is that Anselm has described the Devil, sin and the concomitant consequences against the backdrop of order and harmony. In other words, by defining sin as nothing, as the absence of what is and ought to be, Anselm has reinforced the standard of order and beauty in his readers' minds. The aesthetic nature of God is the measure by which reality was created, and after which the world was fashioned. What is evil? The absence of what ought to be. How did the Devil fall? He desired that which he ought not to will. The challenge of disorder, disharmony and ugliness brought by evil is countered by Anselm when he places evil within the larger context of aesthetic concerns, thereby showing the paradox of evil: it can only exist within a world marked by beauty. Anselm has orientated our perspective in such a way that the tangled web of sin that confuses and perplexes student and master alike disintegrates when the glory of God's perfection is brought into focus.

Tying It All Together

At the beginning of the *De Veritate*, Anselm defended the interdependency and order of his three little treatises by arguing that they pertained to the study of Holy Scripture. We have seen that each one incorporates some part of Scripture as the ground from which to launch a series of related questions, but has something more been achieved? Anselm has orientated our thinking about the nature of truth, free will, evil and the fall of the Devil in such a way that God's goodness, truth and beauty remain intact, but are still integrally related to each other. Is this not what Scripture itself does? Does the Bible not identify areas of human experience which require intimate interaction with the divine in order to reach fulfilment? Does the Bible not define aspects of our existence in ways which orient our perspective around God and not ourselves?[94] Anselm's treatises not only 'pertinentes ad studium sacrae scripturae' because they take their lead from meditations on specific texts, but they also 'pertinentes ad studium sacrae scripturae' in the way they reflect the presuppositions and model of reality presented therein.[95]

When the reader pays careful attention to Anselm's words at the beginning of the *De Veritate*, and realizes that his three dialogues, though written over a period of time, are intended to be regarded sequentially, he discerns a uniformity amid the diversity. These are not minor works which deserve the scant attention they have received, nor are they insignificant in determining the method, structure and order of Anselm's thought. Instead, they are an integral part of a collection of works which show that more can be gleaned from Anselm than his integration of faith and reason or his stalwart devotion to monastic piety. There is a deeper, more fundamental aspect to his writing. The words, the phrases, the ideas are the external expression of an internal conviction. It is not, for Anselm, simply a matter of explaining the relations that exist between apparently divergent or disparate aspects of reality or the Christian faith, but a matter of fulfilling the mandate to explain why these relations must be.[96] This is where the aesthetic dimension comes into its own. Although fittingness and what ought to be are certainly part of aesthetic concerns, they fail to satisfy apart from a broader understanding of aesthetics which incorporates beauty, symmetry, proportion and harmony as a necessary concomitant of a transcendent God displaying his glorious character through immanence.

Notes

1 *De Veritate*, preface (S.1.173.2).
2 'The fool says in his heart, "There is no God."'
3 'What do you have that you have not received?'
4 'Jesus answered, "I am the way, the truth and the life."'
5 'qui potest peccare, servus potest esse peccati, quoniam "omnis qui fecit peccatum, servus est peccati"'.
6 R.W. Southern, *St Anselm: A Portrait in a Landscape* (1995), Cambridge: Cambridge University Press, p. 172, note 9.
7 Southern, p. 172.
8 Southern, p. 172.
9 Southern, p. 172.
10 It is worth noting here that it is possible that Anselm wanted the *De Veritate* to come first because, in many respects, it is the most important. In the *De Veritate* a lot of themes are introduced which, although sufficiently addressed, raise subsidiary questions answered more fully in the following two treatises. What this means is that while some new material is introduced in both the *De Libertate Arbitrii* and the *De Casu Diaboli*, they both depend heavily on what has been established in the *De Veritate*. Consequently, to avoid undue prolixity, the ideas and presuppositions in the *De Veritate* will not be repeated (unless necessary) in the discussion on free will or the fall of the Devil. Thus, although the section on the *De Veritate* will be longer than either of the two subsequent treatises, there is no reason to assume that they have been, for that reason, neglected.

11 A lot could be written on the date of these three dialogues and their place in the corpus, but the evidence from Ep. 100, and their convergence in both style and content would seem to argue more strongly for the mid to late 1080s.

12 *De Veritate*, 1 (S.1.176.4–6).

13 Cf. *Monologion*, 18 (S.1.33.20).

14 Cf. *Monologion*, 17 (S.1.31.13–15).

15 *Monologion*, 17 (1.31.21–3).

16 *De Veritate*, 2 (S.1.177.6–7).

17 *De Veritate*, 2 (S.1.177.16).

18 T.F. Torrance, 'Ethical Implications of Anselm's *De Veritate*', *Theologische Zeitschrift*, 24, p. 309.

19 I cannot help but wonder at the irony of Pilate's question before Jesus, 'What is truth?', in light of the fact that Jesus himself had claimed to be the truth. Sometimes with piercing irony, sometimes as part of an argument and sometimes as an off-handed comment, the authors of the Bible display a vision of the physical and the metaphysical which so obviously informed the development of medieval theology.

20 *De Veritate*, 2 (S.1.178.6–7), my translation.

21 *De Veritate*, 2 (S.1.178.5–27), my translation.

22 *De Veritate*, 2 (S.1.179.7–8).

23 Southern, p. 65.

24 Although he does not enter into the kind of detail that one might have liked to see, Gordon Leff (1980), *Medieval Thought*, London: Marlin Press, p. 100 does refer to the *De Veritate* as a work which clearly shows that reality transcends individuals.

25 *De Veritate*, 5, emphasis mine (S.1.181.27–1.182.5).

26 Edward A. Synan (1988), 'Truth: Augustine to Anselm', in Schnaubelt, J.C. et al. (eds), *Anselm Studies: An Occasional Journal*, vol. 2, New York: Kraus International Publications, p. 284.

27 *De Veritate*, 9 (S.1.188.28–9).

28 *De Veritate*, 7 (S.1.185.18–19).

29 *De Veritate*, 2 (S.1.177.16).

30 *De Veritate*, 9 (S.1.189.2–7).

31 *De Veritate*, 10 (S.1.190.1–4).

32 *De Veritate*, 2 (S.1.178.5–27).

33 A theme which will recur most poignantly in our discussion of the *Cur Deus Homo*.

34 *De Veritate*, 8 (S.1.186.7–9).

35 *De Veritate*, 8 (S.1.186.14).

36 *De Veritate*, 8 (S.1.186.18–19).

37 *De Veritate*, 8 (S.1.187.2).

38 *De Veritate*, 8 (S.1.187.2–3).

39 *De Veritate*, 8 (S.1.187.13–20).

40 *De Veritate*, 8 (S.1.186.8–9).

41 *De Veritate*, 8 (S.1.188.6–7).

42 *De Veritate*, 8 (S.1.187.30–31).

43 *De Veritate*, 8 (S.1.188.2–4).

44 Torrance, p. 313.

45 *De Veritate*, 11 (S.1.191.19–20).

46 *De Veritate*, 12 (S.1.192.30–33).

47 *De Veritate*, 12 (S.1.192.24–5).

48 *De Concordia*, 2.3 (S.2.261.14ff); 3.2 (S.2.264.15ff); 3.5 (S.2.269.2ff).

49 Torrance, p. 314.

50 *De Libertate Arbitrii*, 1 (S.1.207.11–12).

51 S.G. Kane, 'Anselm's Definition of Freedom', *Religious Studies*, 9, p. 298.

52 *De Libertate Arbitrii*, 1 (S.1.208.18–21): 'An non vides quoniam qui sic habet quod *decet*, et quod expedit, ut hoc amittere non queat; liberior est quam ille, qui sic habet hoc

ipsum, ut possit perdere, et ad hoc quod *dedecet*, et non expedit, valeat adduci?' (italics mine).

53 *De Libertate Arbitrii*, 1 (S.1.208.26–7).
54 Richard Campbell (1988), 'Freedom as Keeping Truth', in Schnaubelt, J.C. et al. (eds), *Anselm Studies: An Occasional Journal*, New York: Kraus International Publications, p. 308.
55 Campbell, p. 301.
56 He uses *dedecet* to indicate that which is lost when sin is introduced to the will.
57 *De Libertate Arbitrii*, 3 (S.1.212.11–12).
58 *De Veritate*, 13 (S.1.198.18–20).
59 *De Veritate*, 12 (S.1.196.5–8).
60 *De Libertate Arbitrii*, 3 (S.1.212.19–20).
61 Cf. for example Augustine's *De Civitate Dei*, 22.30.3 in *Nicene and Post-Nicene Fathers*, series 1, vol. 2.
62 Hiroko Yamazaki (1988), 'Anselm and the Problem of Evil', in Schnaubelt, J.C. et al. (eds), *Anselm Studies: An Occasional Journal*, vol. 2, New York: Kraus International Publications, p. 345.
63 *De Libertate Arbitrii*, 8 (S.1.220.21–2).
64 *De Veritate*, 12 (S.1.195.31–3).
65 *De Veritate*, 12 (S.1.196.7–8).
66 Marilyn M. Adams (1975), 'Hell and the God of Justice', *Religious Studies*, 11, p. 437.
67 Adams, p. 437.
68 *De Libertate Arbitrii*, 8 (S.1.220.12).
69 Campbell, p. 299; cf. also Hopkins and Richardson, *Anselm of Canterbury*, vol. 2, p. 105.
70 Campbell, p. 299; cf. also Stanley G. Kane (1981), *Anselm's Doctrine of Freedom and the Will*, Toronto: Edwin Mellon Press, p. 120ff.
71 *De Veritate*, 12 (S.1.193.12–13).
72 You will recall that Pike argued that it is 'possible that God should force a man to obey him and thus deprive him of his honour while simultaneously making the man sublimely happy'.
73 I do not intend to intimate here that arguing from a different set of presuppositions or philosophical bias is necessarily wrong, but it does seem most strange to me that Adams and Pike would choose to argue against Anselm on the grounds that God cannot be trusted. Such an argument is, I believe, not aimed at bringing a logical fallacy to light, but at undermining the supporting model of reality. It is not that I mind one world-view challenging another, what bothers me is when it is carried out surreptitiously, disguised as a legitimate reason for abandoning a particular argument.
74 *De Libertate Arbitrii*, 8 (S.1.221.8–9).
75 *De Concordia*, 3.4 (S.2.267.13–16).
76 Southern, p. 173.
77 *De Incarnatione Verbi*, 1 (S.2.7.2).
78 Cf. Augustine's *De Civitate Dei*, 22.30.3 in *Nicene and Post-Nicene Fathers*, series 1, vol. 2; cf. also G.R. Evans (1982), *Augustine on Evil*, Cambridge: Cambridge University Press.
79 Cf. *De Veritate*, 8 (S.1.186.7–9).
80 *Pace* G.R. Evans (1978), 'Why the Fall of Satan?', *Recherches de Théologie ancienne et médiévale*, 45:130–46, esp. p. 130.
81 *De Casu Diaboli*, 1 (S.1.235.1–5).
82 *De Casu Diaboli*, 2 (S.1.235.20–29).
83 Cf. Evans, 'Why the Fall of Satan?', p. 131.
84 Immediately the reader is faced with the obvious question, why only certain angels? This is one of the difficulties in Anselm's response. On what authority can he posit that some were given a certain ability and others were not? He would likely answer that this distinction is necessary in order to maintain a balance between the Devil's culpability and

God's purity. It is possible that Anselm might have referred to Romans 9:18 ('Therefore God has mercy on whom he wants to have mercy, and he hardens whom he wants to harden') in his defence. Although he used it with reference to humans in the *De Concordia*, it would not be difficult to imagine him using it with reference to angels as well.

85 *De Casu Diaboli*, 3 (S.1.237.15–19).
86 *De Casu Diaboli*, 3 (S.1.237.20; 1.238.27–8).
87 Again, the reader is presented with a quandary here. Just how is it that God is not culpable for our wrong choices? Surely, if he is the one who gives us the ability to persevere he could make our perseverence a permanent situation. But, we must remember, if that were the case, humans would be reduced to automatons. Perhaps the most significant reason this approach is so difficult to accept is that it removes glory and honour and praise from the individual and places it on God – not a naturally appealing thought.
88 Cf. especially Section 3 of the *De Concordia*.
89 Evans, p. 132.
90 *De Casu Diaboli*, 9 (S.1.246.22–5).
91 *De Casu Diaboli*, 11 (S.1.248.4ff); Ep. 97.
92 *De Casu Diaboli*, 4 (S.1.240.16ff).
93 *De Casu Diaboli*, 26 (S.1.274.19–24).
94 A remarkable example of this is the way in which humanity is distinguished from the rest of creation in Genesis 1. Humans, unlike the rest of creation, have been invested with the image of God. Regardless of precisely what this may mean, at the very least it forces us to view humanity in the light of deity.
95 I include the Latin here to draw the reader's attention to the word normally translated 'pertain'. The semantic domain of *pertineo* is sufficiently large that we should guard against interpreting it too narrowly according to modern expectations.
96 Cf. *De Incarnatione Verbi*, 1 (S.2.7.2).

Chapter 6

'Nailed to the racking cross ... So did I win a kingdom'[1]

In the *Cur Deus Homo* we see the plan of redemption unfold in all its beauty, harmony and fittingness as the transcendent God recreates and reorders sinful humanity through the immanence of the incarnation. Anselm does, however, begin the *Cur Deus Homo* much the same way he has begun a number of his other works: by ascribing the reason for writing to his fellow monks. As in the case of the *Monologion* and the *Proslogion*, Anselm's younger colleagues entreated him 'most earnestly ... to set down a written record of the reasoned explanations with which I am in the habit of answering people who put enquiries to me about a certain question of Our Faith'.[2] What is different about the request this time is that Anselm's interlocutors make it explicit that they have not appealed for a written record of his wisdom 'with a view to arriving at faith through reason',[3] but in order that they might delight in a greater understanding of that which they believe and so that they might always 'be prepared to give a reason for the hope which is in them'.[4]

In the context of these assertions it seems that we ought to understand Christians as the intended audience.[5] Notwithstanding Anselm's remark that the questions surrounding the incarnation and atoning work of Christ are pondered by unbelievers, his covering letter to Pope Urban II commending the work to his scrutiny supports the suspicion that it is intended for believing eyes. Anselm claims that the combination of God's continued bestowal of knowledge and his promise that unless you believe you will not understand requires all Christians to explore the rationale of faith. He elaborates this principle by stating his conviction that understanding is that which 'stands midway between faith and revelation' and that the attainment of that revelation of glory 'for which we all pant in anticipation' is divinely directed.[6] Consequently, to assert the certain cynosure of the Father's frequent engagements with the 'logical principles' of the faith is, among other things, to affirm that believers will be nourished.

And yet, it is through this self-same process of expounding the reasonableness of the faith that foolishness is shattered and 'the rigid resistence of unbelievers'[7] is confuted. But notice how careful Anselm is to distinguish between those whose foolishness is shattered and those who believe. Anselm is under no illusion that mere intellectual persuasion is tantamount to a profession of faith. This is the same distinction we noticed in Chapter 4 of the *Proslogion*. There, after bringing the folly of the Fool to light, Anselm thanked God that in his case he had arrived at a greater understanding of that which he already believed, and, furthermore, that the extent of divine illumination was such that understanding is inevitable despite unbelief. In other words, it is possible for the unbeliever to understand certain principles of and reasons for Christian faith without trusting in them.

But does this not contradict the principle of the necessity of believing in order to understand? It would if our concept of understanding were one-dimensional. As noted in our discussion of the *Proslogion*, there is a clear difference between understanding and seeing. In the first four chapters of the *Proslogion* the Fool is brought to understanding (*intelligere*), but has not yet attained perception (*videre*). As Anselm moves through the rest of the *Proslogion* he begins to use the verb *videre* more frequently the more his discussion dons the garb of personal prayer and internal ruminations. In Chapter 14, the point at which Anselm turns from considering God's immanence to his transcendence, he mixes the two terms (*intelligere* and *videre*) in a way he had not before. In fact, he increases the poignancy of his distinction by introducing the verb *sentire*. While it is true that this verb can connote intellectual realization (in the sense of *intelligere*) or perception (in the sense of *videre*) the context of the chapter makes it clear that Anselm is distinguishing this verb from the other two. This leaves a third possibility: to experience. Thus, when Anselm claims that he has understood (*intelligere*) the preceding thirteen chapters with 'certain truth and true certainty', and has seen (*videre*) the illumination of 'light and truth' set before him, but has yet to experience (*sentire*) what he has perceived or understood, he is establishing a hierarchy of understanding. It is one thing for Anselm to understand the rudiments of truth, it is another for him to discern the light of God's nature in that truth; but it is still another matter to finally arrive at an experience of that self-same truth. To have accomplished understanding (*intelligere*) and sight (*videre*), but failed to attain *sentire* is to comprehend in part only and not to see God as he really is.[8]

This same sentiment is echoed in *On the Incarnation of the Word*. In the first section of that work Anselm takes a moment to make a 'prefatory comment'. This comment, it turns out, has once again to do with setting out the principles of proper method. In this case, the principles are directed towards Roscelin, but they are the same here as they are in the *Cur Deus Homo* and in the rest of Anselm's works. No Christian should decry the tenets of the faith despite their apparent difficulty; instead, such doctrines should be embraced and loved. For it is a certainty, says Anselm, that our finite minds will not be able to comprehend the magnitude of all divine truth.[9] But of greater interest to us at this juncture is Anselm's own summary of his prefatory comments: 'those who have not believed will not understand. For those who have not believed will not find by experience, and those who have not found by experience will not know.'[10] Once again, Anselm contends that belief and experience are necessary for genuine knowledge.

Armed with this fuller comprehension of Anselm's concept of understanding, we can now better appreciate his comments about the deleterious effects of unbelief on delineating the rational principles of faith. Unbelievers may wonder why God became a man or even if God exists, and to a certain extent they should be expected to gain an appreciable degree of understanding (*intelligere*) in such matters, but as is clear from 1 Peter 3:15 ('Always be prepared to give an answer to everyone who asks you to give the reason for the hope that you have') the Christian is called only to give a reason for the hope that is in them. Christians are not called to open the eyes of the (spiritually) blind or to raise from the dead the souls of the (spiritually) dead; rather, they are called simply to be able to explain why it is that they believe what they do. And since the writers of the New Testament continually demand progression and maturity, this passage in Peter's letter cannot be any less than a clarion call to an ever-deepening understanding of the substance of the faith professed.

What this means for the reader is that the *Cur Deus Homo* is thoroughly rooted in Christian presuppositions. Its arguments, its progression of thought, its content, are intended to be criticized and studied from within that same context.[11] Any attempt to shift the ground of examination, whether through anachronistic interpretation or modern philosophical speculation, will inevitably result in deracinating its constituent elements.

Now what we have said so far about the purpose of the *Cur Deus Homo* (to further Christians' understanding of the faith – in this case to address the doctrines of the incarnation and the atonement) and its intended audience comports well with the general methodology in the rest of the Anselmic corpus. But those familiar with this work will be aware that we have passed over one of its most troublesome aspects: the *remoto christo* principle. In the preface to the *Cur Deus Homo* Anselm makes a few remarks about the circumstances surrounding the work. He refers, for instance, to an unnamed heartache[12] and to overly eager scribes as two of the impetuses for writing. He gives a brief account for the title of the work, and, in the midst of describing its structure, casually informs us that the development of his argument supposes that Christ had never existed. How remarkable! After penning a letter to the Pope to ask him to inspect the work for error or misleading innovation, and after strenuously insisting upon the necessity of belief prior to understanding in the first chapter of the *Proslogion* and reiterating that conviction in the first chapter of the present work, how could Anselm make such a statement? Surely, to deny the existence of the subject of inquiry is either badly mistaken or not what it seems.

Then we read on and discover that the purpose for removing Christ from the investigation is to show that 'it is impossible that, without him, any member of the human race could be saved'.[13] What Anselm has done is to introduce a type of argumentation we might call the impossibility of the contrary. In other words, Anselm is seeking to show the necessity of the incarnation and atoning work of Christ by demonstrating the absolute necessity of those acts in the light of the remaining evidence. It is important here that we not fall into the trap of thinking that by eliminating Christ Anselm has eliminated all Christian doctrine. As will be evident in the rest of his book, the only way his argument can work is if he continues to rely on the tenets of the Christian faith. That he does so will become clear as we proceed.[14]

Apart from Christ or Apart from the Norm?

Before we can proceed, however, we must take a moment to address the difficulty of this position. In his study on the *Cur Deus Homo*, John McIntyre has argued that Anselm has not always been as scriptural as one is wont to believe. What McIntyre does is to draw distinctions between certain types of presuppositions which Anselm uses. The first group of presuppositions are those 'which his opponents are prepared to grant while they deny certain other articles of faith'.[15] In this case Anselm's task is to show how the existence of what is believed necessitates the existence of what is denied. The second group of presuppositions which McIntyre postulates on Anselm's behalf incorporate 'certain ideas commonly accepted in his time but not self-evident to any other age of human thought'.[16] He includes within this group the Platonic doctrine of Forms which have been infused, though transformed, into the *Monologion*. In addition, Anselm's formula 'that than which nothing greater can be thought' is an expression which could be filled by any deity, but he fills it with the God of the Bible. Similarly, in the *Cur Deus Homo*, the idea of satisfaction, though given Christian content, is an idea borrowed from feudal society.[17] McIntyre's claim is that these different presuppositions have prevented an appreciable number of 'sentences from Scriptures or Creeds'[18] from being incorporated.[19]

In all of this McIntyre is careful not to gainsay Anselm's approach. Nevertheless, he maintains that conceding to these presuppositions led Anselm away from relying on Scripture to substantiate the premises and sequences of his reasoning. Consequently, McIntyre proposes that Anselm reverted to using any combination of the above groups of presuppositions for two reasons. First, because his work has an apologetic edge to it, Anselm could not have expected to have made any connection with unbelievers unless he set aside any appeals to the authority of Scripture. Second, McIntyre intimates that although Christians would have appreciated appeals to the authority of Scripture, they required more than such simple appeals could provide.[20]

The converse of this proposition is, of course, most forcefully defended by Karl Barth. He avers that Anselm does proceed on the basis of explicitly scriptural principles.[21] Now let us be clear here, the contention is over 'Anselm's selection of his premises'.[22] Barth says they are scriptural,[23] McIntyre says cultural.[24] Let us begin our evaluation with McIntyre before attending to Barth's concerns.

Of the two main groups of presuppositions the first is the more intriguing. It is remarkable that McIntyre can simultaneously claim first, that 'the premises of St Anselm's arguments are not always entirely Scriptural';[25] second, that the *Cur Deus Homo* espouses theological presuppositions which are granted by Boso and the presumed reader;[26] and third, that the *Cur Deus Homo*, along with Anselm's other works, is, to some degree, an apologetic work which therefore cannot make any appeals to Scripture since the unbeliever would never countenance such assertions.[27] Do the first and third claims not contradict the second? Is it reasonable to postulate that Anselm would refrain from appealing to the authority of Scripture while, at the same time, assuming the validity of certain theological presuppositions? Is it likely that Anselm, who demonstrated the depth of his conviction about the blindness and lostness of unredeemed humanity in the *Monologion, Proslogion, De Incarnatione Verbi* and the three dialogues (not to mention his *Prayers and Meditations*) would have assumed that such people would grant him his theological presuppositions?

Another problem with McIntyre's approach here is that he equates a lack of explicit references to Scripture[28] with being unscriptural. Does the mind which has been saturated with the words of revelation need to continually provide direct quotations to an audience which is equally well steeped in the same body of knowledge? Consider Book 1, Chapter 3, for example. Boso offers the charges of unbelievers in a way that brings 1 Corinthians 1:23 ('but we preach Christ crucified: a stumbling block to Jews and foolishness to Gentiles') to mind when he says,

> Unbelievers, deriding us for our simplicity, object that we are inflicting injury and insult on God when we assert that he descended into a woman's womb; was born of a woman; grew up nurtured on milk and human food and – to say nothing of other things which do not seem suitable for God – was subject to weariness, hunger, thirst, scourging, crucifixion between thieves, and death.

Anselm's response resonates with passages which speak of restoration, such as Psalm 51 (a particular favourite of Anselm's). He then carries on to offer what amounts to a brief commentary on 1 Corinthians 15:21, 22. Paul wrote that 'since death came through a man, the resurrection of the dead comes also through a man. For as in Adam all die, so in Christ all will be made alive.' In a similar vein, Anselm wrote that 'it was appropriate that, just as death entered the human race through a man's disobedience, so life should be restored through a man's obedience.' Here we see the source of Anselm's aesthetic view of reality. He saw the beauty of God's truth and the fittingness of God's atonement in the master theologian of the New Testament. This is important because it shows us just how deeply the Bible influenced Anselm's thinking.

The second set of presuppositions Anselm is alleged to have adopted centred around ideas that were common currency during his lifetime; McIntyre offers three examples. He begins by charging Anselm with adopting the Platonic doctrine of Forms in the *Monologion*. This is certainly a common accusation and one we have already encountered and addressed in different contexts, but the constraints of the present inquiry demand that we take a moment here to consider its validity. An initial reading of the *Monologion* does appear to indicate a close affinity with much of Platonic philosophy. There is, for instance, the notion of the good as a kind of transcendent characteristic. On the other hand, Southern has noted that, in the *Monologion*, 'meditation turns from its purgative role to recognize in self-knowledge and in the mind's images of the external world the general essences in which all things have their being. In this process, the mind rises towards that contemplation of God, which can be approached but never achieved in this life.'[29]

In other words, the flow of thought in the *Monologion* seems to be from the material, present reality, up towards the perfect image of which all things on earth are but a mere shadow. In Chapter 1, Anselm clearly states that all goods which we know must be good through one supreme good.[30] Here we have Aristotelianism, not Platonism. Anselm has begun with diversity in this realm and reasoned to unity in the next.

Philosophical Traditions in Anselm

The difficulty with McIntyre's challenge is that it smacks of superficiality. To be sure, small portions of a number of Anselm's works could be construed in such a way as to build a case in favour of Platonic (or Aristotelian depending on where you are reading) persuasion, but in the light of his whole corpus and with respect to his monastic context, it becomes ever more difficult to sustain that case. We have shown, for example, that while some arguments could be advanced which propound the contradictions in Anselm's thought between the necessity of belief for understanding and the expectation of unbelievers understanding the rationality of the faith, they cannot be maintained under the collective weight of his whole corpus. In the same way, we must proceed cautiously when laying charges of Greek philosophical appropriation at the feet of any given work. Consequently, as to the upward motion of Anselm's thought, while it is true that he was engaging in lifting his thoughts heavenward, let us not forget that he could only do so because God had first imparted the content of those thoughts from above.[31]

This is what is distinctive about Christian thought in general, and Anselm's thought in particular: it begins with God reaching down to humanity and then humanity responding by reaching back to God.[32] The emphasis must, in the first instance, be placed on the initiating activity of God. So, while it is true that there is a resemblance between Plato's notion of the Forms being the perfected ideal of which this world is but a shadow, and the Bible's view that God is the creator of all things and has imprinted his image on humanity and his fingerprints, as it were, on the rest of creation,[33] we must guard against assuming that Anselm's ideas accrue blindly from Platonic or Aristotelian philosophy. In connection with this, Hans Urs von Balthasar has recognized that in the *Monologion* the

> ideas are deduced not primarily from below, from the contingence and the degrees of worldly qualities, which are ascending degrees of perfection, indeed of reality, and which persuade of the existence of something most perfect and most real in their sphere, but rather from above: from the free self-expression of God, who plans and imagines what he wills.[34]

My point here is not to suggest that Anselm was unaware of Plato or Aristotle, but to argue that their particular philosophies are incompatible with Anselm's portrayal of Christianity. What these philosophers do share with Anselm is a common belief that there is a unity throughout reality. The physical has contact with the metaphysical; the spiritual with the material. What McIntyre and so many others have identified is a component of Anselm's *weltbild* (world-view) which was common throughout the ancient and medieval world. The danger for us is that we too readily correlate similar concepts in different periods without respecting the attenuating beliefs in each period. Plato and Aristotle certainly believed in a coherent reality, but they could not affirm the kind of theological–aesthetic unity Anselm propounded.

The second charge from McIntyre against the essentially biblical nature of Anselm's propositions calls our attention to the formula in the *Proslogion*: 'that than which nothing greater can be conceived'. The trouble with McIntyre's suggestion that this formula could be applied to any deity is that it evinces a complete lack of conversance with the biblical witness, and the Psalms in particular. We have noticed elsewhere[35] that the opening chapter of the *Proslogion* is filled with scriptural quotations and allusions; many of which are taken from the Psalms. We have also observed that many of the Psalms Anselm chose (not to mention references from other places in the Bible) reflect the transcendent character of God and humanity's distance from him on account of our sin. We have, for instance, been 'banished far from your [God's] face' (Ps. 51:11) and we 'eat the bread of sorrows' (Ps. 127:2) because our sin has cast us away from God's presence. Overarching all of this is 1 Timothy 6:16, which is repeated a number of times throughout the *Proslogion*: 'you dwell in inaccessible light'. Anselm has not taken a philosophical construct and filled it with Christian content; instead, he has meditated on the Word of God and come to realize that the best description he can give of God is that he is 'that than which nothing greater can be thought'.

The third attempt McIntyre makes at discrediting Anselm's biblical approach centres around the word satisfaction (*satisfactio*). Is it not a feudal legal term? Has McIntyre not framed his theory of the atonement in feudal terminology?[36] Again, we must be careful not to misrepresent McIntyre. Southern has correctly written that McIntyre has successfully denied that the *Cur Deus Homo* is inextricably linked to feudal ideals.[37] McIntyre does believe, however, that Anselm has taken a contemporary construct and filled it with Christian meaning.[38] Thus, *satisfactio* is not a term Anselm has derived from revelation, but from society.[39] The bothersome aspect of this criticism is that it fuses the metaphoric use of a contemporary situation with the truth to which it is pointing.[40] Timothy Gorringe makes the same error in his treatment of Anselm's theory of the atonement in *God's Just Vengeance*. He argues that Anselm has defined sin as the failure to give someone his or her due, the extent of which is determined by that person's place in the social order.[41] Gorringe draws on *Cur Deus Homo* 1.11 where Anselm comments that just as a person is bound to recompense for injury or theft, so we, who have marred God's honour by our disobedience, are under obligation to repay to God the honour which we 'have violently taken from him'. This is our act of satisfaction 'which every sinner is obliged to give to God'.

Although neither Gorringe nor McIntyre refers to *Cur Deus Homo* 2.16, this is another passage in which Anselm seems to be deriving his under-standing of satisfaction from his socio-political context. In this instance he writes about a city whose citizens have sinned against the king. None of the citizens is able to make restitution for their wrongdoing, but, happily, it turns out that one of the citizens has not sinned against the king. This man, on account of his sinlessness, enjoys favour with the king and also loves the people. Between the two of them they devise a plan whereby the sinless man will provide the means of reconciliation through a service of some kind which will sufficiently please the king. The people need only express their solidarity with this man and his service in order for the king to ablate their guilt and grant pardon. This section combined with the general cultural outline provided by Gorringe certainly does give us something to think about. After all, feudalism was well ingrained in the psyche of medieval Europeans.[42]

The claim that Anselm has derived his metaphysical constructs from contemporary society and filled them with Christian meaning is, however, faulty on two counts. First, as mentioned above, the use of contemporary examples does not necessitate the conclusion that they were formative in Anselm's thinking. In other words, a metaphor is more often a reflection of an idea already formed, rather than the basis on which an idea is built. This is why, in *Cur Deus Homo* 2.16, after his elaborate story, he says, 'secundum hanc similitudinem' ('according to this parable'). The very nature of a parable is that it forges a point of contact between the speaker and his audience by employing current imagery which reflects the essence of a particular truth.[43] Applying truth to prevailing circumstances is insufficient reason to warrant the statement that the latter (prevailing circumstances) informed the former (truth).[44] This is especially so when, and here we see the second fault, the idea of satisfaction is 'woven into the fabric of both testaments [of the Bible]'.[45] A knowledge of the book of Leviticus alone would be enough to show that satisfaction weighs heavily in the Old Testament. Similarly, in the New Testament, Romans 3:21–6, 2 Corinthians 5:21, Galatians 3:13 to name but a few texts portray Christ as the one who took upon himself the wrath of God, and in so doing satisfied the requirements of the law so that those whom the Father has given him might be redeemed. Granted, the word 'satisfaction' is not used in these texts, but in the light of the flow of the biblical narrative from beginning to end, it cannot be denied that satisfaction is a strong theme.[46]

It would seem, then, that Barth was on the right track – at least with respect to the three main criticisms of Anselm's dearth of overt biblical references. We have overcome these hurdles of objection by demonstrating that an insufficient number of explicit biblical references (as judged by a modern interpreter) does not imply an absence of biblically derived authority. In fact, lest the aforementioned reasons be denied, we have the words of Anselm himself who proclaimed that the truth into which he and Boso have been looking is found in 'Holy Scripture'.[47] The language is very interesting here. Anselm has written that 'nos ubique sacra Scriptura docet, quae super solidam veritatem, quam adjuvante Deo aliquatenus perspeximus' ('it [the means of salvation achieved through the death of Christ] is taught to us everywhere in Holy Scripture, which is based upon the solid truth, which, by God's help, we have examined to some degree').

The first thing we notice is that Anselm completes his work by appealing to Scripture. This is entirely appropriate since it is from Scripture that he has learned what he has taught. Second, we notice the ubiquity of the plan of salvation in Scripture. Anselm was not a man given to commenting on small parts of small portions of small pericopes; he was a theologian who had grasped the flow of God's plan of redemption and had caught sight of the larger themes in the Word of God. Anselm was not inclined to focus narrowly on Scripture because he was addressing an audience which, to his mind, did not require it. Within the monastic community biblical exegesis could take a different form because its members were starting from a position of knowledge that later university and cathedral school theologians could never expect.[48]

Beyond Method and Logic

While I agree with Barth that Anselm was insisting on the necessity of the incarnation and atonement on the authority of Scripture and its doctrines, I am not interested in exculpating Anselm's work from the hands of natural theology. Instead, I want to argue that Anselm applied the *remoto christo* principle because he believed that the intrinsic beauty of God's truth is sufficiently apparent to persuade and to appeal to the 'spiritual aesthetic sense' in each person.[49]

In our present day this may not seem the most proficient way to set out an argument for any doctrinal truth, but the relationship between God and the world was much more intimate in the mind of the medieval monk than is typical for the modern Christian. One could argue that this may be because monks spent more time meditating on Scripture.[50] It seems more likely, however, that beauty was a concept derived from the writings of the Fathers and other theologians.[51] Pseudo-Dionysius, for example, believed that 'the material world is anagogically symbolic of the immaterial world, not just concerning the angels but also and especially concerning God'.[52] Now a statement like this does not tend to make one instantly mindful of beauty, but this is where medieval theologians began. While medieval theologians were keen to maintain a distinction between the creator and the creation, they were equally adamant that the creation was a reflection of the creator.[53] This is why Anselm writes in the *Monologion*, 'the supreme essence alone is that through which anything good is good, without which nothing is good, and out of, through and in which all things exist.'[54] And again in the *Proslogion* Anselm writes that God is, 'the supreme good needing no other and is [the one] whom all things have need of for their being and well-being'.[55] In addition, Anselm wrote that, 'it is therefore utterly evident, beyond a shadow of a doubt, that the supreme essence alone and through itself produced so much and so many things of such beauty – things so varied, yet ordered, so different, yet concordant – and produced them out of nothing.'[56]

Anselm's contention is that since all things emanate and have been produced from the supreme essence (that is, God), they necessarily have a correspondence to that divinity. Since God is beauty, we should expect to find that beauty reflected in the creation, and, no less, in his Word to us and in his interaction with us. This is why we ought to exercise caution when approaching medieval theology. What could be construed as natural theology is in fact theology thoroughly grounded in revelation to the extent that, like the apostle Paul, God's eternal and invisible attributes are seen in what has been created (Rom. 1:20).[57] We saw above how Pseudo-Dionysius was said to perceive the material world as 'anagogically symbolic' of the immaterial, but this does not impress as an entirely adequate interpretation. I believe Eco is correct to argue that,

> the passage from aesthetic pleasure to mystical joy is virtually instantaneous, more so than the term 'anagogical' suggests. Medieval taste, we may conclude, was concerned neither with the autonomy of art nor the autonomy of nature. It involved rather an apprehension of all of the relations, imaginative and supernatural, subsisting between the contemplated object and a cosmos which opened on to the transcendent. It meant discerning in the concrete object an ontological reflection of, and participation in, the being and the power of God.[58]

It is essential that we bear in mind those final words: 'discerning in the concrete object an ontological reflection of, and participation in, the being and the power of God'. To suggest that beauty is a transcendental characteristic[59] does not mean that beauty is somehow in competition with God. In the widely read book *The Consolation of Philosophy*, Boethius makes it clear through the lips of Dame Philosophy that to posit a characteristic as transcendental, and indeed supreme, is not to raise that characteristic to an equal, but autonomous level with God himself. After noting some of the more obvious faults with such an argument, Boethius concludes that the chief reason for denying any transcendental characteristic an ontological aspect apart from the nature of God is that two supremes are necessarily contradictory. That which is supreme is, by definition, over all things. The result is that the idea of supreme goodness is folded into the divine nature of God such that 'that which is the origin of all things is in its own substance supreme good.'[60] Thus, when a medieval theologian spoke about the supreme good or any other 'supreme' he was not so naïve as to miss the apparent contradiction between two supremes (the characteristic and the nature of God); rather, he considered that the characteristics of God were a part of the nature of God to the degree that each required the other and neither could be properly understood apart from the other. Compare Anselm's comments in the *Monologion* when he writes that all the characteristics of God, including beauty, 'indicate not a quality or quantity, but what the supreme nature is'.[61] For these reasons then (the intimacy between the creator and the creature, the communication of divine characteristics to the created order, the movement from above to below and then back again, and the ability in the medieval mind to balance supremacy of characteristics with the supremacy of the divine nature) the aesthetics of medieval theologians, 'like all their thinking, expressed an optimum synthesis. They see the world with the eyes of God.'[62] For this reason medieval theology can appeal to aesthetics as a standard by which to measure and judge their understanding of doctrines: it evinces 'a harmony of reason'.[63]

Furnished with this context we are now better able to appreciate Anselm's opening argument in the *Cur Deus Homo*. Towards the end of Chapter 3 Anselm responds to the purported objections of unbelievers by appealing to the intrinsic beauty of the incarnation and atonement. There he bids those who would mock and jeer at the Christian plan of salvation to consider just how fitting it really is:

> For when death had entered into the human race through man's disobedience, it was fitting that life should be restored through the obedience of a man. When the sin which was the cause of our condemnation had its beginning from a woman, it was fitting for the author of our justice and salvation to be born of a woman. Since the devil, when he tempted man, conquered him by the tasting of a tree, it was fitting for him to be conquered by man's bearing of suffering on a tree. And a good many other things, when we consider them carefully, show the inexpressible beauty of our redemption, thus accomplished.[64]

What is particularly notable about this statement is that, in the Latin, the first three sentences are actually a single sentence governed by the main verb (*oportet*) which stands at the beginning. The primal collocation of the verb in this sentence serves to emphasize its cardinal priority. The stress is on the 'fittingness' (*oportet*) of the plan of salvation and its relation to the beauty of redemption (a connection which we cannot afford to underestimate and will examine with some care in the following discussion).

Now it is this very concept (beauty), which many have ignored and some have dismissed. Timothy Gorringe, for example, has argued that according to *Cur Deus Homo* 1.3, 4 it is clear that aesthetic arguments simply will not suffice.[65] Gorringe carries on to say that Anselm has rejected intrinsic beauty as a category which is convincing for the doctrine of the atonement.[66] This contention seems to be based on two parts of the *Cur Deus Homo*. First, it finds its grounding at the beginning of Chapter 4 where Boso retorts that while the intrinsic beauty of the plan of redemption is clear to those who are already saved, it will appear to unbelievers like a painting on a cloud.[67] Second, in 1.13 Anselm makes it manifest that what really matters is that the universal order, especially as it pertains to God's justice and honour, is maintained.

In responding to the first point we must take care to consider the language Anselm employed. As a grammarian of the first degree Anselm gave careful attention to the construction of his works. Even Eadmer witnesses to Anselm's desire that his writings should not be copied for wider circulation until they have been scrutinized and approved by his most critical eye.[68] When we attempt to examine the *Cur Deus Homo* in a similar fashion we discover that Anselm relies heavily on the concept of fittingness. This word in its different forms occurs no less than seventy-six times. Clearly, the idea of the atonement and all that it entails (that is, incarnation, overcoming sin, and so on) is, in Anselm's mind, best described and discussed in categories that suggest an aesthetic perspective. The truth of this is best illustrated in 1.3 where Anselm offers his first line of defence against unbelief and ineluctably evinces the fittingness of the incarnation and atonement with the ineffable beauty of redemption. Now, as we shall see, the nature of this fittingness is quite particular, but we should never lose sight of the integral connection between the appropriateness and beauty of salvation.

Beauty and the Necessity of Fittingness

Anselm uses three words to convey the concept of that which is fitting or appropriate. The first is the set of words (by 'set' I mean the various verbal forms as well as the nouns) which derive from *convenio* (used approximately thirty-four times). When Anselm uses this word (or its opposite *inconvenio*) the implication is that something is in accord with right order.[69] The second word Anselm uses is the verb *decet* (used approximately seventeen times). When he uses this verb in any of its forms it tends to indicate that which is in character.[70] Third, Anselm uses the verb *oportet* (used approximately twenty-five times) to denote that which is morally necessary.[71]

What is interesting is that these terms seem to converge in 1.3 and 1.4. In 1.3 Anselm defends against unbelief by insisting that such a plan is in accord with right order (*convenientia*) since the nature of the Fall demands a response which reflects the moral necessity of those circumstances. If death entered the human race by the disobedience of a man then restoration can only be achieved through the obedience of a (God)-man. Similarly, if sin originated from a woman (argues Anselm) our redemption ought to originate from one who is born of a woman. The idea of the beautiful harmony of the creation and re-creation is set before us. Boso then interrupts Anselm and suggests that following a line of argument which offers notions which are 'appropriate'[72] (*convenientia*) will prove inadequate to the unbeliever. Boso then constrains Anselm to demonstrate 'the logical soundness of the truth, that is: a cogent reason which proves that God ought to have, or could have, humbled himself for the purposes which we proclaim'.[73]

Anselm answers, not as we might expect, by furthering his argument on the fittingness of God's activity. This time, however, Anselm says, 'it was not fitting (*decet*) that what God planned for mankind should be utterly nullified, and the plan in question could not be brought into effect unless the human race were set free by its creator in person.'[74] In other words, it would have been out of character to destroy the world at the Fall because that would mean that God would have to abandon what he began. For God to abandon what he started would be tantamount to admitting that his plans had been thwarted:[75] an unthinkable thought for a monk who believed that God was supreme goodness and beauty and was that than which nothing greater can be conceived. We must grant at this juncture, though, that the definitions of *decet* and *convenientia* do overlap. But we should expect this since acting in accord with right order is integrally related to the character of God.

The point of all this is that when Anselm is enjoined to leave aside beauty as the means for communicating the truth of the incarnation and atonement, he adeptly refuses to do so. What he has done is to move from commenting on the moral necessity of the atonement to addressing that which is in character both for humanity and for God. This is why the very next chapter considers 'that the redemption of mankind could not have been brought about by any other than a divine person'.[76] Even so, we soon discover that Anselm has, in his own mind, steadfastly refused to relinquish the persuasive power of the moral necessities lying behind the atonement. Yet Anselm does not return immediately to those thoughts. His first real foray into the discussion clears the ground by denouncing and firmly refuting the claim that God had to pay a ransom to the Devil. Indeed, of the three words available to him Anselm chooses to use only one of them in the following three chapters, and then only once. He remarks only on the appropriateness (*convenientia*) of humanity's punishment for their sin.

When, then, does Anselm return to the idea of *oportet*? He uses the term again in 1.19.[77] It is fascinating that Anselm should do this because Chapter 16 has just introduced the question of the fallen angels. Will, asks Boso, the number of the redeemed make up for the number of the fallen angels? In the ensuing discussion, which has been ignored altogether too much,[78] Anselm explains to Boso that the number of the redeemed will in fact make up the number of the fallen angels. This is a question which has been largely ignored by theologians and historians alike because it appears to bear no relation to the rest of the argument. Many commentators don't even mention the discussion, and some, like McIntyre, pass over it as medieval pedantry or, like Evans, suggest that it is a digression warranted only by the close friendship of Boso.[79] But are we justified in glibly passing over a part of the *Cur Deus Homo* which Anselm deemed worthy of inclusion, if not essential to the overall argument? I believe that we ought to reconsider this part of the work. We should make an attempt to understand its place in the context of the overall argument and in the broader cultural context we have already mentioned.

Fallen, But Still Fitting

The most likely context out of which the question of the angels and the redeemed arises is the writings of Augustine. In his *City of God* 22.1 Augustine writes that, 'He would by His grace collect, as now He does, a people so numerous, that He thus fills up and repairs the blank made by the fallen angels, and that thus that beloved and heavenly city is not defrauded of the full number of its citizens, but perhaps may even rejoice in a still more overflowing population.'[80] Also, in his *Enchiridion* Augustine writes:

> And so it pleased God, the Creator and Governor of the universe, that, since the whole body of the angels had not fallen into rebellion, the part of them which had fallen should remain in perdition eternally, and that the other part, which had in the rebellion remained steadfastly loyal, should rejoice in the sure and certain knowledge of their eternal happiness; but that, on the other hand, mankind, who constituted the remainder of the intelligent creation, having perished without exception under sin, both original and actual, and the consequent punishments, should be in part restored, and should fill up the gap which the rebellion and fall of the devils had left in the company of the angels. For this is the promise to the saints, that at the resurrection they shall be equal to the angels of God.[81]

I have quoted these two sections from Augustine because they summarize the content of Anselm's discussion,[82] and thus show a strong connection between the two. Just as Augustine believed that the number of the redeemed would make up the number of the fallen angels, so did Anselm. Just as Augustine saw the final goal of the completed number of the creation, so Anselm saw the future glory of such perfection as the goal of God's plan. And just as Augustine proposed the possibility of the number of the redeemed exceeding the number of the fallen angels, so Anselm argues strenuously that this must surely be the case. The reason he offers is that the number of the angels was never complete to begin with. This is a necessary supposition because unless it is true the creation of humanity becomes subordinate to the angels and then only exists for the purpose of filling. Furthermore, God did not create a completed universe. God created a universe which was made up of different parts that would, over time, develop and reach their own preordained number of completion.[83]

The significance of the balance and order in creation for Augustine is that it affirms that 'God created all things in the most correct way, in the best proportions and with the greatest beauty.'[84] For Anselm this means that each part of creation has its own perfection to attain to, but that each part also has a role to play in the final, glorious, consummation of perfection in the eschatological City of God.[85] It is for this reason that Anselm turns his discussion on the number of the angels into a discussion on the need for due recompense. He argues that humans living in the heavenly city ought (*oportet*) to be of the same character as those already there. Barring an act of divine activity on the part of humanity, however, this possibility can never reach actuality. The result is that Anselm concludes the *Cur Deus Homo* by summing up his final arguments which demonstrate the moral necessity of a God-Man to stand in the place of all humanity. For only a God-Man can offer the recompense which is 'proportional to the magnitude of the sin'.[86] Once again moral necessity (*oportet* is again used here) is placed before his readers. After explaining how it is that Jesus fulfils this need, Anselm concludes that anyone who 'does not repay God what he owes, will be incapable of being blessedly happy'.[87] This sentiment is again repeated later in the same chapter for emphasis.

What Anselm has done is to wed the notion of moral necessity (*oportet*) with the idea of the redeemed restoring the number of the fallen angels in order to convey the conviction that there is an aesthetic quality to the atonement. Frank Brown has rightly noted that 'what gives point and poignancy to Anselm's treatise is not its orthodoxy as such, however; it is rather the wonderful rigor with which Anselm presses traditional views into the aesthetic–moral dimension.'[88] The key to understanding Anselm's theory of the atonement lies not so much in its inherent logic or its progression from reasoned argument to reasoned argument, but in the broad picture he paints of the aesthetic nature of the plan and purposes of God as they are worked out in the history of humanity.[89]

If we may take another example, we discover in 2.8 that Anselm returns to the idea that it is fitting (*oportet*) that God 'should take the man who is the object of our quest from a woman without a man'. This is so because 'women might lose hope that they have a part in the destiny of the blessed ones, in view of the fact that such great evil proceeded from a woman: in order to prevent this, it is right that an equivalent great good should proceed from a woman, so as to rebuild their hope.'

Once again we see that God's activity responded to a moral dilemma. Despite the fact that we may find it strange that a woman should lose hope of salvation based exclusively on her gender relationship to Eve, in Anselm's mind the dictates of aesthetics required that God deal with the situation in a way consonant with its circumstances. Thus, what we have is a 'beautiful theological "painting" of the reasons for the God-man to be born of woman' which 'reflect the beauty of God's design for creation and redemption. And that design, as we have seen, exhibits God's evident love of balance and symmetry, accompanied by an unwillingness to leave any pattern imperfect or ultimately incomplete.'[90]

Where then does this leave the charge that Anselm has rejected aesthetic arguments on account of their insufficiency to convince? I believe the above reasons offer a significant rebuttal which clearly demonstrates that Anselm does not, in fact, abandon aesthetics as a category of consideration with respect to the doctrine of the atonement. Anselm began with aesthetics, and, after eliminating contending theories, reintroduced it into the main stream of his treatise. First he began by addressing the need for recompense based on who God is and what humanity had done (here *decet* becomes the pivotal term). After firmly establishing the requirements of God's character (*decet*) and the demands of right order (*convenientia*), Anselm moves on to consider the moral necessity (*oportet*) that remains and how it is fulfilled by the God-Man Jesus Christ. By this time Anselm has reached the end of Book 1, but he carries his argument continually forward in Book 2 where the conditions of the moral necessity of humanity are suitably fulfilled by the second member of the Trinity in the beauty and order of his person and activity.[91]

Perhaps the greatest obstacle to modern investigations of medieval texts is that they are motivated by the desire to uncover and scrutinize a work under the microscope of logic. Our indagations into the minutiae of argumentation have blinded us to the beauty of theology as it stands before us in its 'balance, shape and order'.[92] At the end of 2.8, after Anselm has delineated the necessity that the God-Man should be born of a woman, Boso replies that 'these pictures of yours are extremely beautiful and in accordance with logic.' Even though Boso began by denying the utility of aesthetics as 'sufficient grounds'[93] for providing reasons for the atonement, he has come to realize that Anselm's analogies, images and pictures, that is to say, his portrayal of the aesthetic appeal of the atonement, do not 'imply that they have any less force of conviction than logically watertight demonstrations would have'.[94] What remains for the modern interpreter is to come to that same appreciation. Drawing on a host of passages from Augustine's corpus, von Balthasar comments that 'the act of the mind again depends on the aesthetic capacity to perceive the quality of the eternal and divine in truth (something it can do only when it is collected and purified); otherwise, even if it draws the correct logical conclusions, it may miss the real experience of truth.'[95] Later on he adds that, 'in Augustine ... the certainty of the ultimate rightness of the *vera religio* does not rest in mere intuitions of heart and conscience or of faith, but resides in a seeing of the rightness which in the broad sense must be called an aesthetic vision and yet which stands up to rational examination and which can even be made visible to the person who purifies his mind's eye.'[96] These are the sorts of concepts on which Anselm was bred. These are the kinds of reflections which informed his perception of reality and revelation. Unless we too adopt such notions we cannot hope to properly understand the *Cur Deus Homo*.[97]

Justice and Honour in Harmony

Now, if we cast our minds back to the original doubts which set us on our investigation into the aesthetic nature of Anselm's theory of the atonement we will recall that there is yet another objection to this perspective. The objection was that 1.13 states plainly that what really matters in the atonement is that God's justice and honour are restored and satisfied.[98] When we read this part of the *Cur Deus Homo* we do indeed discover that 'there is nothing more intolerable in the universal order than that a creature should take away honour from the creator and not repay what he takes away.' But the reader will have noticed that there is more than just God's honour at stake here. Anselm does not merely say that it is intolerable that God's honour has been taken away. The context in which the honour of God has been violated and the justice of God requires satisfaction is the 'universal order'. The editors of the Oxford edition of Anselm's works in English have picked this up and taken the liberty of extending the importance of the 'universal order' to other statements in this chapter. They qualify Anselm's further clarification of his opening comment that there is nothing more unjust than to tolerate the 'most intolerable thing *in the universal order*' (my italics). The concluding words here are not in the original, but I agree with the implication that the injustice done to God is a matter of distorting the universal norm. I take this position because in the explanation Anselm offers he eventually gives us the principle which underlies his quandary. He says that when someone desires what is right,

> he is honouring God, not because he is bestowing anything upon God, but because he is voluntarily subordinating himself to his will and governance, maintaining his own proper station in life within the natural universe, and to the best of his ability, maintaining the beauty of the universe itself. But when a rational being does not wish for what is right, he dishonours God, with regard to himself, since he is not willingly subordinating himself to God's governance, and is disturbing, as far as he is able, the order and beauty of the universe.[99]

Sin is disobedience and, in particular, it is failing to subordinate one's will to the will of God.[100] For as God's creatures it is our place and station to will what he wills.[101] In this way we fulfil our purpose and 'maintain the beauty of the universe itself'. Once again Anselm has returned to the idea of beauty.[102] In light of this it is curious that Gorringe admits that 'honour in Anselm's theology, is a way of talking of the integrity of God's creation and of his purposes. To dishonour God is to disturb the order and beauty of the universe.'[103] Moreover, Gorringe also notes Anselm's words in 2.14 that the loveliness of the life of Christ is what outweighs our sin.[104] Consequently, Gorringe concludes that punishment restores the balance that a crime distorts, and 'Anselm's argument postulates this metaphysically. It has to, because the earthly is, after all, an analogue of the heavenly.'[105] Regardless of his reaction to Anselm's ideas on the atonement as 'rationalised vengeance',[106] surely it is obvious that Anselm has done anything but forfeited his claim to the intrinsic beauty of the satisfaction of the moral necessity of sin in the person of Jesus Christ.

Fitting Into the Flow: Anselm in History

To this point we have considered the *Cur Deus Homo* largely on its own terms, and rightly so. But where does Anselm fit in the history of the doctrine of the atonement? Was he really following the Fathers and the writings of the theologians of the early church? Or was Anselm striking out on his own? While it is difficult to believe that Anselm would have ventured to create a new theory of the atonement entirely of his own accord, scholars like L. Grensted[107] and G. Aulén have suggested that Anselm did step out from the accepted teaching and traditions of the church.[108]

Aulén, for example, has argued strenuously that the Fathers' 'classic' idea of the atonement was dominant in the early church precisely because it is the correct view of the atonement.[109] Beginning with Irenaeus, Aulén traces this doctrine through the writings of the Fathers. In *Against Heresies* 4.41.2 Irenaeus identifies the human race as children of the Devil; however, he does this cautiously. Irenaeus admits that while humanity is under the power of the Devil because of our disobedience, we are still children of God by virtue of the fact that we have been born (God is the creator of all things).[110] The reason for this caution is that Irenaeus does not want to give even the slightest hint that God is acting out of order. It would, after all, be unfitting for God to usurp the authority of the Devil in the way that the Devil did God's authority. What the Devil did was wrong. God, on the other hand, cannot act contrary to his character and therefore must deal with the Devil 'in an orderly way'.[111] In the end, argues Aulén, this means that Jesus' death on the cross was a ransom paid to the Devil.[112]

Plenty of other evidence from a number of other Church Fathers emanating from both the Greek and Latin churches is amassed into what looks to be formidable opposition against Anselm's theory (in spite of the admission that 'the idea of the transaction with the Devil met with strong criticism' and that a number of Fathers and prominent theologians before Anselm's day had rejected the idea).[113] From this vantage point Aulén feels justified in chiding Anselm for his theory, based as it is on the penitential system outlined in, primarily, Tertullian and Cyprian.[114] In addition, Aulén believes that, because of Anselm's view of sin, he accords too much dignity to humanity, thereby over-emphasizing Christ's humanity.[115]

Aulén's first criticism, that Anselm borrowed his ideas from the penitential system of Tertullian and Cyprian, is misguided. While it may or may not be true that these writers expressed their views of the atonement with respect to prevailing legal terminology, there is nothing to suggest that Anselm followed suit. In the first instance, there is no indication that Anselm read the works of Tertullian or, and especially, Cyprian. Second, Tertullian applied the idea of satisfaction to penitence, not to the atonement.[116] Granted, the concept of satisfaction developed over time and came to be applied to more than penitence, but, as I have already argued, Anselm's use of *satisfactio* carries a particularly aesthetic connotation; something no earlier writers had done. Consequently, it is inappropriate to suggest that Anselm used the term 'satisfaction' in the same way Tertullian did.

Aulén's second difficulty, that he believes Anselm overemphasizes the humanity of Christ, shows a poor understanding of Anselm's position. It is clear from the *Cur Deus Homo* that Anselm takes the power and presence of sin most seriously.[117] Indeed, he states that those who do not see the necessity for an atonement have not fully grappled with the severity and depth of sin. Moreover, in the *Proslogion*, Anselm makes no small comment on the devastating effects of sin on the intellect and understanding of humanity.[118] We can only see the light of God's truth in as far as he deals with the sin which impedes our vision. It is not that Anselm has neglected to consider the divinity of Christ; rather, his chief concern is to demonstrate the necessity for a God-*Man*. Since the power of sin is so great in the physical realm the only way God, a spirit, could adequately attend to our need for salvation from this sin-soaked condition would be through incarnation. We must bear in mind that much of what Anselm has to say is an attempt to reorientate his readers' minds to the deficiency within humanity that necessitates atonement through incarnation. Prior to Anselm, the reigning theory of the atonement was the ransom theory in which humanity, though important, occupied a subordinate position to the struggle between God and the Devil. By emphasizing the gravity of sin in the highest degree Anselm was aiming to redress this situation and re-establish the subordinate role of the Devil in light of the cardinal relationship between divinity and humanity. Although equal emphasis on the divinity and humanity of Christ is desirable, Anselm needed to frame his discussion in the way he did in order to counter the prevailing view effectively.

The simple answer to Aulén's complaint is, of course, found in the title: *Cur Deus Homo*, 'Why did God become a Man?' In a work with such a transparent title it is a wonder that Anselm should be charged with pressing the need for a God-*Man*. What else should we expect? In fact, I would add to this rebuttal that Anselm's treatment of the atonement gives us reason to establish the lost dignity of humanity.[119] This is what the incarnation and Christ's work achieve. That which was lost at the Fall has been and is continually being restored in the lives of Christians. This is another testament to the beauty and balance of God's plan of restoration.

Against all of this Aulén claims that 'God enters into this world of sin and death that he may overcome the enemies that hold mankind in bondage, and Himself accomplish the redemptive work, for which no power but the Divine is adequate. But for Anselm the central problem is: Where can a man be found, free from sin and guilt, and able to offer himself as an acceptable sacrifice to God?'[120] This is where Aulén has misrepresented Anselm. Anselm would never admit that the power of the atonement could come from humanity; instead, his point is the same as that made by John in Revelation when he reports an angel asking who is worthy to open the seals on the scroll and 'no one in heaven or on earth or under the earth could open the scroll or even look inside it' (Rev. 5:2). The point Anselm is striving to make is that only *God*, in the form of a man, could possibly achieve atonement between divinity and humanity. Let us be clear here, Anselm is neither denying God the freedom to act of his own accord, nor is he affirming any ability on the part of humanity to achieve salvation.

Granted, Anselm does say in 1.4 that 'it was not fitting that what God had planned for mankind should be utterly nullified, and the plan in question could not be brought into effect unless the human race were set free by its creator in person.' But we cannot mistake a statement like this to indicate that Anselm believed that God was somehow bound by his creation, as if subservient to it.[121] It is true that God's love is intricately tied to the plan of salvation (cf. Eph. 1:4), but to suggest that this is the only active characteristic in God's redemption would be to ignore, among many other things, his justice required by the enormity of our sin. If the apostle Paul was correct to say that sin required death (cf. Rom. 6:23) then, as Anselm cogently argues, the love of God alone is insufficient grounds for reconciliation.[122] Anselm is concerned that the totality of God's being be brought to bear on the question of the incarnation and atonement. The love of God is certainly integral, but it is not the only characteristic that comes into play. This is why Anselm wrote that 'it was not fitting [*decet*] that what God had planned' should be nullified by disobedience.[123] Anselm chose the word that, in the *Cur Deus Homo*, connotes that which is in accord with the character of God. It is, in the first place, fitting that God should save humanity because that redemption will *satisfy the very person of God* (his honour, his justice, his love, his mercy, his grace, and so on) which has been offended by disobedience. However, it is, in the second place, fitting that God should achieve this in a way which reflects the beauty of his person. The result is that God's creation is reconciled to himself in a way befitting his character and, most notably, his beauty. How ironic that the process of restoring God's honour, satisfying his justice, expressing his love, showing his mercy and extending his grace should be manifest in a way that overturns all the disobedience of humanity and rebellion of the Devil. The tools and means used to repudiate God were the tools and means used to reconcile humanity.[124]

Ultimately, Aulén's arguments rest on his conviction that for the Fathers, the necessity of the incarnation and atonement is the love of God and as such is not intended as a rational theory; whereas Anselm's treatment of the matter is preoccupied with 'rational demonstration' alone.[125] It is most unfortunate that Aulén should fall into the same frame of mind as so many others. He assumed that Anselm was using reason in the modern sense. He failed to consider that, for Anselm, reason did not mean some form of autonomous rationality or a system of logic based on a series of premises. Instead, Anselm's form of reasoning began in the revealed Word of God, was informed by the interpretations of the Fathers, and was continually nurtured in the fertile soil of monastic prayer and meditation. Anselm believed that what he was postulating stood firmly within the tradition of the church. Contrary to Aulén's main line of argument, this is particularly so in Anselm's rejection of the ransom theory of the atonement.

Anselm appropriated the principles and convictions that lay behind the thinking of preceding theologians and developed them in a different direction. When Irenaeus, for example, spoke about the rights of the Devil and the need for God to redeem people from under that oppressive regime, he did so with clear and unequivocal reference to God's fitting behaviour.[126] To be sure, Anselm denied the conclusion Irenaeus approved, but it ought to be clear by now that while Anselm failed to see any validity in a ransom paid to the Devil, he did pick up on the idea of God acting in a fitting manner. It is curious that Aulén did not recognize in Anselm the very axiom which was operative in Irenaeus. Had he done so he might have realized that Anselm applied the idea of fittingness in such a rigorous way that he could not conceive God acting in any way wherein the entirety of his being was not involved. This meant that a theory of the atonement which was mainly preoccupied with God's justice or righteousness was insufficient. In the end, this led Anselm not only to postulate a new theory of the atonement based on an aesthetic perspective, but also to reinterpret the concept of justice by applying that perspective.

Any study of the history of the doctrine of the atonement will show that no matter what one thought of the atonement (and there were differing ideas about this[127]) overall agreement lay in the notion that God must act with justice. For Irenaeus, as for Aulén's and many others' interpretation of the Fathers, this meant that God had to obey the laws of justice which he set out at the beginning of creation. This is, however, not the idea presented to us in the *Cur Deus Homo*. Anselm does not believe that God has to act justly with respect to the alleged rights of the Devil. Referring to Colossians 2:14 Anselm explains that the 'bond of the decree' which was set against humanity and was annulled by the death of Christ was not a bond made by the Devil but by God.[128] The bond or debt that was owed was not owed to the Devil, but to God. The sin of humanity which destroyed the harmony of the universal order necessarily put us in God's debt because it was his creation which was ruined. This position hints to us that, to Anselm's way of thinking, justice may not be subject to law. This position would be congruent with Anselm's other works where justice is believed to be part of God's nature.[129] Whereas law is never considered to be part of the transcendental nature of God, justice is. To suggest then that God must submit to that which is not part of his transcendental nature would be to posit a situation in which God was neither free nor, arguably, that than which nothing greater can be conceived. But is it the case that Anselm understood justice in this way?

McGrath has noticed that we find the seeds of Anselm's idea of God's justice in St Augustine. In *Contra Faustus* 12.27 Augustine defines the justice of God as that 'by which the natural order is preserved by the eternal law'.[130] Drawing on this and other evidence, McGrath argues that restoration of the relationship between God and man is not a matter of law so much as right order.[131] If we compare Augustine's *City of God* 19.20–21 we see again that unlike humanity God does not base his justice on law; rather, law is based on justice. The foremost priority in God's economy is justice, not law; and justice is a matter of right order. Consequently, the reason for rejecting any notion of the Devil's rights or the atonement as a ransom paid to the Devil lies in an Augustinian understanding of justice.[132] Thus, McGrath rightly notes that

> justice relates to the moral ordering of the universe, which the Devil clearly violated in his seduction of man. As the devil is part of the created order, he is subject to the same *iustitia* as that order. Himself a rational being, the Devil was under the same moral obligation to submit his will to God. Only if he were outside of God's creation, and could stand aloof from its moral ordering, could this theory of the 'Devil's rights' have any credibility.[133]

What this amounts to is yet another piece of evidence which helps us to clarify our understanding of Anselm as an aesthetic theologian. In refuting the accepted doctrine of the day, Anselm used the very term (justice) his opponents used, but reinterpreted it. Furthermore, he used the same basic premiss they did (fittingness), but applied it more rigorously. What strikes the reader at this point is how remarkably similar Anselm's method is to God's. God used the result of disobedience – death – to restore life. God used the originator of sin – woman – as the means by which to introduce the originator of sinlessness. God used the product of a tree – the cross – to counter the effects of the fruit by which the Devil introduced sin into humanity.[134] Similarly, Anselm used the cornerstone of the ransom theory of the atonement – justice – to defend its rejection. Anselm used the premiss of that theory – fittingness – as the basis for his new idea. Anselm took the perspective of the consummation of salvation – beauty – and applied it to the process leading to that end.

There can be no doubt that Anselm's thinking was infused with the necessity of an orderly universe. And this was so because to him the world is an expression of the nature of God. Indeed, as we saw at the beginning of this chapter, this was a world-view shared by Anselm's contemporaries. They were, as Eco puts it, 'disposed to conceive of beauty as a purely intelligible reality, as moral harmony or metaphysical splendor' and supremely as an attribute of God.[135] Beauty was what gave stability because beauty was evidence of an orderly mind at work. And in a world full of instability and uncertainty this belief was paramount in its import.

All of this is not to say, of course, that the *Cur Deus Homo* is without its shortcomings. Browning, for instance, believes that Anselm's theory does not address humanity's 'subjective experience of guilt'.[136] Root argues that there is no room for divine 'spontaneity and flexibility' in the *Cur Deus Homo*.[137] Hart criticizes Anselm for concentrating too heavily on what God saves us from to the exclusion of considerations on what God saves us to or for.[138] Turning to one of Anselm's near-contemporaries, Bernard of Clairvaux disliked Anselm's neglect of the life of Jesus.[139] The last two of these criticisms are, I think, more worthy than the former two. For Browning to complain that the *Cur Deus Homo* has not left room for the 'subjective experience of guilt' is, on the one hand, a poor attempt to judge a medieval work against modern psychotherapeutic standards and, on the other hand, to blatantly ignore Anselm's *Meditation on Human Redemption*. This meditation was written years after the *Cur Deus Homo* was completed[140] but was intended as a kind of summary of its contents. Part of that summary includes a summons to the Christian to consider the heaviness of death and the wretchedness of servitude in sin.[141] Browning is correct to note that there is not much in the way of explicit instruction to the reader about his or her guilt, but in a time when meditation was taken seriously, a few simple words would suffice. In fact, even if we set this meditation aside, it is surely one of the outcomes for readers that they feel the heaviness of their own sin in the face of the lengths to which God went to achieve their salvation.[142] Anselm tells us that those who do not accept the atonement have not considered the depth of their sin. The implication here is that any thinking Christian will, in the process of recognizing the need for atonement, be forced to reckon with their own 'subjective experience of guilt'.

The second criticism is equally disturbing. What sort of spontaneity or flexibility might Root desire? I suspect he finds Anselm's contention that God could not save humanity in any other way rather constricting. Be that as it may, if Anselm is going to remain faithful to the revealed Word of God what other choice does he have? Redemption and the necessity of the atonement are non-negotiable elements in the history of salvation. Based on the information Anselm had, his options for greater flexibility were severely limited.

But let us return to the *Meditation on Human Redemption*. For in it we see a number of things which aid and further our understanding of the discussion in the *Cur Deus Homo*. Recalling Hart's comment that Anselm neglected to elaborate on the end or purpose for which we are saved, we turn to the beginning of the meditation and discover that God has given the Christian life and freedom.[143] Further along we read that, concerning the salvation wrought for Christians, we ought to 'chew', 'bite' and 'suck' on that knowledge. We should let our 'heart swallow it' when we receive 'the body and blood of [our] Lord'.[144] We also find that anyone who understands the nature of their salvation will recognize the immense debt they owe to God: 'I owe you the whole of myself.'[145] In the present day, there is certainly much that is commendable in these exhortations and instructions, but they appear to us to be lacking in activity. In other words, while we want to affirm with Anselm that being precedes doing, we are unsatisfied with the activity of contemplation and meditation. This is because our context is so far removed from Anselm's. A medieval monk considered it the highest good to spend his days contemplating God's truth, meditating on the being of God and praying to him constantly. To be sure, they were not bereft of manual labour,[146] but their main goal was withdrawal from the cares and preoccupations of this world so that they could attend to the work of God. For the medieval monk the activity of meditation was an acceptable activity.

Now, having said that, we must be careful not to take Anselm's *Cur Deus Homo* or his *Meditation on Human Redemption* as the be-all and end-all on the atonement. I think we have in the meditation an inkling of a possible avenue of development. Anselm instructs his reader to 'look into your need and his goodness, and see what thanks you should render him, and how much love you owe him.'[147] If the Christian is called to determine the degree of need in their own life based on an introspective examination of the state of their soul and by comparing what is found with God's provision, it is no great stretch to suggest that the perceived need in the life of the Christian is also present in the life of other Christians as well as those who do not yet believe. Why should the Christian stop with himself? Having grasped something of the grandeur and splendour of the salvation accomplished for us, should that not provide us with sufficient motivation to expose the need in others and, once done, to apply the remedy of redemption? After all, the exegetical premise out of which the entire *Cur Deus Homo* grew was 1 Peter 3:15: let us be 'ready always to give satisfaction to all who ask the reason for the hope that is in us'.[148] Boso and his colleagues desired that Anselm should help them grow in their understanding of faith such that they would be better equipped to minister that grace to those around them.

The fourth criticism of the *Cur Deus Homo* is its lack of attention to the life of Jesus.[149] There is a great deal of emphasis placed on the death of Jesus and how that death affects life, but nowhere does Anselm offer us a sustained treatment of how the life of Christ contributed to the suitability of his death. This is an important aspect of New Testament theology (cf. Heb. 4:14ff and 5:8ff) and would, I believe, greatly enhance the argument of the *Cur Deus Homo*. What greater example do we have of the beauty of universal order than in the fulfilment of the law of God in the person of Jesus Christ? (Cf. Matt. 5:17.) Not only, then, do we see life in his death, but, in as far as we are enabled to follow his example we have life through his life. 'His life sets us an example for living.'[150]

In spite of these criticisms and suggestions for improvement we must not lose sight of the contribution the *Cur Deus Homo* makes to our theology. Anselm's appeals to fittingness (in all its various nuances), his understanding of justice, his perpetual accent on right order and his eye for balance and symmetry are what make his theory of the atonement lively and persuasive. And lest we detract from the centrality of Anselm's aesthetic perspective on the atonement let us consider that this was the only treatise for which he wrote a meditation. If the *Cur Deus Homo* was little more than a logical progression of a series of arguments guided by the cold hand of reason and logic, how could we explain the inspiration it gave to his third *Meditation*? How could we explain that even there Anselm is directing the reader's attention to more elements of beauty and symmetry in the person and work of his saviour? He writes, for example, that Christ hung on a cross but was still able to 'lift the load of eternal death from the human race'.[151] Someone who is hanging is, by definition, being lifted by something else, and yet here Anselm shows us that the one who was lifted was himself lifting. Furthermore, it was while Christ was on the cross, the instrument of torture and death, that he was engaged in removing the torture and death of sin in humanity. Anselm continues his observations and tells us that 'a man nailed to wood looses the bonds of everlasting death that hold fast the world.'[152] How interesting that the one who was held by something external to himself should be described as holding on to all that is external to himself – humanity. The beauty of Christ's salvation is further described: 'a man condemned with thieves saves men condemned with devils, a man stretched out on a gibbet draws all men to himself. O mysterious strength: one soul coming forth from torment draws countless souls with him out of hell, a man submits to the death of the body and destroys the death of souls.'[153]

Anselm carries on to speak of the incarnation and atonement of Jesus as a true revelation of God and a certain declaration of his true humanity. If we add to this Anselm's own summary of the *Cur Deus Homo* in his work on the Virgin conception and original sin we discover that the main thrust and intention of his 'book' is to show that, ultimately, 'nothing should be out of place in his [God's] kingdom.'[154] The beauty and order of the transcendental character of God is known in the immanency of his creation and redemption. Considering all these things together, then, it is no wonder that Eadmer wrote of the culmination of the *Cur Deus Homo* (the *Meditation on Human Redemption*) that it, 'found favour and gave joy to many'.[155]

Notes

1 This title comes from Christina Rossetti's poem *The Love of Christ which Passeth Knowledge* (London: Bloomsbury Poetry Classics, 1995). I have quoted from the last stanza which reads, 'Nailed to the racking cross, than bed of down / More dear, whereon to stretch myself and sleep: / So did I win a kingdom, – share a crown; / A harvest, – come and reap.' Here Christina Rossetti captures not the irony, but the fittingness of the establishment of the kingdom of God.

2 *Cur Deus Homo* 1.1 (S.2.47.5–7).

3 *Cur Deus Homo* 1.1 (S.2.47.8–11).

4 Cf. 1 Peter 3:15.

5 *Contra* Richard Campbell (1979), 'Anselm's Theological Method', in *Scottish Journal of Theology*, 6:541–62.

6 *Commendatio operis ad Urbanum Papam II* (S.2.40.10–12).

7 *Commendatio operis ad Urbanum Papam II* (S.2.39.3–4).

8 *Proslogion*, 14 (S.1.111.8ff); cf. 1 John 3:2 ('Dear friends, now we are children of God,

and what we will be has not yet been made known. But we know that when he appears, we shall be like him, for we shall see him as he is').

9   *De Incarnatione Verbi*, 1 (S.2.5.22ff).
10 *De Incarnatione Verbi*, 1 (S.2.9.5–8).
11 Cf. *Commendatio operis ad Urbanum Papam II* (S.2.41.1–5).
12 *Cur Deus Homo*, preface (S.2.42.6).
13 *Cur Deus Homo,* preface (S.2.42.13).
14 'St Anselm may forswear the authority of Scripture, but nevertheless it is clear that he moves within the limits which Scripture defines. To allow St Anselm freedom beyond these limits is to assign to him a freedom which he would himself be most unlikely to accept' (John McIntyre (1954), *St Anselm and his Critics: A Re-interpretation of the* Cur Deus Homo, Edinburgh: Oliver and Boyd, p. 17).
15 McIntyre, p. 47.
16 McIntyre, p. 47.
17 McIntyre, p. 46.
18 McIntyre, p. 38.
19 Although her study does not directly address this aspect of Anselm's writing, Mary Carruthers' *The Book of Memory: A Study of Memory in Medieval Culture* (Cambridge: Cambridge University Press, 1990) offers an interesting insight. She argues that the process of *cogitatio* is not so much a matter of 'reasoning out' or of logical progression of thought, but of 'mulling over' (p. 200). The process begins with a desire which inspires the memory, 'and through the memory's stored-up treasures the intellect is able to contemplate; the higher its understanding, the more desire flames in love as it both gets and gives more light' (p. 201). In short, the final product of *cogitatio* supersedes its constituent elements: the sum is greater than the parts. Eadmer's description of Anselm's thinking and writing process coalesces with Carruthers' contention well (cf. *VA*, pp. 29–30). Tallying the number of explicit references to Scripture hardly seems fitting, especially in the light of the importance of mediation and 'mulling over' in the medieval period.
20 McIntyre, p. 49.
21 Karl Barth (1958), *Anselm: Fides Quarens Intellectum*, London: SCM Press, p. 54.
22 McIntyre, p. 47.
23 The driving force behind Barth's contentions is that, by taking his principles from Scripture, Anselm's method militates against labelling him as a rationalist, and, still more important for Barth, denies Anselm the position of 'a patron saint of natural theology' (Karl Barth (1936–78), *Church Dogmatics*, vol. 2.1, ed. and trans. George Thomas Thomson & Harold Knight, Edinburgh: T&T Clark, p. 412).
24 Although McIntyre does not use this term, it does reflect his sentiments well since he clearly believes that Anselm's immediate social, intellectual and spiritual context, his culture, are the key factors effecting his theology.
25 McIntyre, p. 38.
26 McIntyre, p. 47.
27 McIntyre, p. 49.
28 McIntyre, p. 38.
29 Richard Southern (1995), *Saint Anselm: A Portrait in a Landscape*, Cambridge: Cambridge University Press, p. 121.
30 *Monologion*, 1 (S.1.14.5ff).
31 Von Balthasar comments that monastic contemplation was, above all, 'a praying reason which only hopes to find insight in dialogue with the eternal truth, and therefore ever again passes over from the form of meditation to that of prayer' (Hans Urs von Balthasar (1982), *The Glory of the Lord: A Theological Aesthetic*, vol. 1, trans. Erasmo Lasua-Merikakas, Edinburgh: T&T Clark, p. 212).
32 Cf. the overall force of the arguments in *Proslogion*, 1; *De Incarnatione Verbi*, 1; *Cur Deus Homo*, 1.1.

33 Cf. Romans 1:20, 'For since the creation of the world God's invisible qualities – his eternal power and divine nature – have been clearly seen, being understood from what has been made, so that men are without excuse.'

34 Von Balthasar, vol. 2, p. 229; cf. also *Monologion*, 1–6 and 31 (S.1.13–1.20; 1.48–50).

35 Cf. Chapter 3 on the *Proslogion*.

36 McIntyre, p. 85.

37 Southern, p. 221.

38 McIntyre, p. 46.

39 There is, of course, an immense amount of material that has been written on the occurrence and development of *satisfactio* from the time of Tertullian through to the Middle Ages when it became a much more important term. Tracing this development lies beyond the scope of this inquiry, not least because we do not know how well, if at all, Anselm was acquainted with Tertullian's writings or of anything written by subsequent authors who picked up on his idea of satisfaction. I suspect that, as in the case we have seen between Anselm and Irenaeus with respect to beauty and fittingness, while the links may not be direct, the conceptual similarity is such that, however convoluted the flow of information may be, there is sufficient correlation to warrant a case for continuity. For an introductory survey of this development see Jaroslav Pelikan (1971), *The Emergence of the Catholic Tradition (100–600)* and his (1978), *The Growth of Medieval Theology (600–1300)*, Chicago: University of Chicago Press.

40 G.R. Evans (1978), 'St Anselm and St Bruno of Segni: the common ground', *Journal of Ecclesiastical History*, 29:129–44 notes that seeking to illustrate ideas with examples drawn from common experience was also the practice of Bruno of Segni and likely the case with other contemporaries at the school of Laon. One wonders why the use of immediate circumstances should stir up such excitement and, as we shall see in the case of Timothy Gorringe, disapproval. Can the same truth not be effectively communicated through different cultural contexts without being expressly tied to or derived from them?

41 Timothy Gorringe (1996), *God's Just Vengeance*, Cambridge: Cambridge University Press, p. 93.

42 Space does not permit a discussion of her work here, but Susan Reynolds has argued well that feudalism was, perhaps, not as pervasive as we have come to believe. She does not deny that certain structures were in place which we have come to identify with feudalism, but, she contends, feudalism was not the all-important element of society that many modern scholars have advocated. Just as we are more apt to think in terms of a network of family and friends rather than of larger governmental structures (even at the municipal level), so medieval people were more inclined to think of their network of family and friends before their lords or kings, cf. Susan Reynolds (1994), *Fiefs and Vassals*, Oxford: Clarendon Press.

43 Cf. G.R. Evans (1976), 'St Anselm's Analogies', *Vivarium* 14, 2:81–93 where she posits that Anselm's analogies and parables are meant and formulated for rhetorical effect, as a kind of memory aid.

44 The charge that Anselm has been unduly influenced by his contemporary feudal context is a criticism that refuses to go away. Besides Gorringe and McIntyre, Marilyn McCord Adams also forwards a version of this argument in her article (1975), 'Hell and the God of Justice' in *Religious Studies* 11:433–47. While pages could be written to address this question and respond to each person I think it is instructive that the common thread to all of these complaints is that God is not permitted to be God, humanity is no longer in the dock, and sin is not taken seriously. This, it seems to me, is the essence of the feudal argument, and it would take more space than we have available to sort out the differing opinions on hamartiology, anthropology and soteriology.

45 B. Demarest (1988), 'Satisfaction' in *New Dictionary of Theology*, in Sinclair Ferguson and David Wright (eds), Leicester: InterVarsity Press.

46 Cf. Stanley G. Kane (1973), 'Fides Quaerens Intellectum in Anselm's Thought', *Scottish*

Journal of Theology, 26:40–62 where he comments that Anselm's treatises were 'problems prompted by the reading of Scripture', p. 54.

47 *Cur Deus Homo*, 2.19 (S.2.131.7–10).

48 It has long been argued that Anselm stands at the end of the monastic tradition which sought explicitly to tie the dictates of theology to references in the Bible and the Fathers, while at the same time standing at the threshold of a new era which relied more heavily on dialectic and reason. When making comparisons Anselm is invariably more readily connected to the later development (cf., for example, Eugene Fairweather (1970), *A Scholastic Miscellany*, Toronto: The Macmillan Company, p. 47). This is, I believe, a much mistaken view. As I have noted above, Anselm's theology was thoroughly steeped in Scripture despite the fact that he may not have conformed to modern preconceptions of appropriate exegetical method. Moreover, the claim that scholasticism (particularly during the late eleventh and early twelfth centuries) relied more heavily upon reason than revelation is a most contentious position (cf. Henri de Lubac (1998), *Medieval Exegesis*, trans. Marc Sebanc, Edinburgh: T&T Clark, p. 67). A more accurate description of where we might place Anselm in the larger scheme of theological tides comes from Robert Crouse who suggests that the interpretation of Augustine exercised an important influence on the direction of theological methodology (cf. Robert Crouse (1987), 'Anselm of Canterbury and Medieval Augustinians', *Toronto Journal of Theology*, 3:60–68). Consequently, we find that depending on how one interpreted Augustine's thoughts on the requirements of exegesis, their work would evince more or less detailed, verse-by-verse exposition.

49 G.R. Evans (1977), 'The *Cur Deus Homo*: The Nature of St Anselm's Appeal to Reason', *Studia Theologia*, 31:33–50, p. 41.

50 Beauty is particularly evident in the Old Testament: cf. Ps. 27:4, 96:6, 149:4; Is. 4:2, 28:5. Patrick Sherry also adds a number of references from Ps. 90:17, 145:5, 71:8, 46:6, 50:2; Prov. 3:17, 15:26, 16:24 and from Zech. 9:17 (as found in the MT) (Patrick Sherry (1992), *Spirit and Beauty*, Oxford: Clarendon Press, p. 63).

51 Although Augustine must be considered the primary source of Anselm's aesthetic approach to theology, we do not have the space to launch into a comparison of the two theologians. Needless to say, Sherry is very helpful in providing a starting point by directing our attention to, *Confessions* 3.6, 11.4, 10.27; Soliloquies 1.1, 1.3; *On True Religion* 40.74ff; *Ep.* 118; *Exposition on the Psalms* 79:14 and *On the Trinity* 6.10.11; cf. Sherry, p. 9.

52 Sherry, p. 48; cf. also Paul Rorem (1993), *Pseudo-Dionysius: A commentary on the texts and an introduction to their influence*, Oxford: Oxford University Press, p. 78. cf. also *The Divine Names* 4.7 and 4.10. Cf. also *The Celestial Hierarchy* 3.1, where Dionysius writes that the beauty of God is the 'source of perfection' which extends to 'grant every being according to merit, a share of light and then through a divine sacrament, in harmony and peace, it bestows on each of those being perfected its own form'.

53 *Proslogion*, 25 (S.1.118.20–1.119.19).

54 *Monologion*, 80 (S.1.87.5–7).

55 *Proslogion*, prologue (S.1.93.7–9).

56 *Monologion*, 7 (S.1.22.7–10).

57 The complexity of the relationship between revelation and creation in medieval epistemology is by no means easily extricated, but von Balthasar does an admirable job of describing the fine line that separates the two. He writes that, 'Anselm contemplates the highest rectitude of the divine revelation in creation and redemption; he discerns its truth from harmony, from the faultless proportions, from the way in which it must be so, something at once dependent on the utmost freedom and manifesting the utmost freedom, and this vision reveals to him absolute beauty: God's beauty in the freely fashioned form of the world', vol. 2, p. 211.

58 Umberto Eco (1986), *Art and Beauty in the Middle Ages*, trans. Hugh Bredin, London: Yale University Press, p. 15.

59 Umberto Eco (1997), *The Aesthetics of Thomas Aquinas*, Cambridge: Harvard University Press, p. 40.

60 Boethius (1969), *The Consolation of Philosophy*, London: Penguin Books, p. 101.

61 *Monologion*, 16 (S.1.31.1–2).

62 Eco, *Art*, p. 118.

63 Eco, *Art*, p. 119.

64 *Cur Deus Homo*, 1.3 (S.2.51.5–12).

65 Gorringe, p. 91.

66 Gorringe, p. 94.

67 *Cur Deus Homo*, 1.4 (S.2.51.16–21).

68 *VA*, pp. 30–31.

69 Take, for instance, *Cur Deus Homo* 1.10 (S.2.65.3–6), where Anselm refers to John 6:44 ('No one comes to me unless the Father has drawn him') and says, 'since everyone is drawn or impelled to something which he steadfastly desires, it is not inappropriate (*inconvenientia*) for it to be asserted of God that he draws or impels when he is the giver of such a desire.'

70 In *Cur Deus Homo* 1.12 (S.2.69.6ff), Anselm addresses the question whether it is fitting (*decet*) for God to forgive sin without restitution and determines that it would not be fitting (*decet*). This is the case because, notwithstanding Boso's complaints that God's freedom ought to allow such a contingency, freedom is only freedom when it conforms to that which is fitting. What is fitting with respect to God, continues Anselm, is that which is in accord with his nature. So, just as it is impossible that God should lie because his nature is contrary to it, so God cannot allow injustice without demanding restitution. The answer to the question lies in the nature of God.

71 *Cur Deus Homo* 2.11 (S.2.111.22–5) is an interesting example because when Boso begins to understand what sort of person is required (requirement with the force of moral necessity) to offer satisfaction to God for humanity's sins, he stops using *debeo* and begins using *oportet*.

72 *Cur Deus Homo*, 1.4 (S.2.51.21).

73 *Cur Deus Homo*, 1.4 (S.2.52.3–6).

74 *Cur Deus Homo*, 1.4 (S.2.52.9–11).

75 *Cur Deus Homo*, 1.18 (2.76.9ff).

76 *Cur Deus Homo*, 1.5 (S.2.52.13).

77 It is true that the word is used in 1.9 (S.2.61.17), 1.13 (S.2.71.20) and 1.18 (S.2.81.10) but while those occasions refer to moral necessity they are not connected to either the incarnation or the atonement.

78 McIntyre, p. 82.

79 Evans, '... Appeal to Reason', p. 47.

80 As found in *Nicene and Post-Nicene Fathers*, series 1, vol. 2.

81 Augustine, *Enchiridion*, 29 in *Nicene and Post-Nicene Fathers*, series 1, vol. 3.

82 *Cur Deus Homo*, 1.16–18 (S.2.74–2.84).

83 *Cur Deus Homo*, 1.18 (S.2.77.16–2.78.9).

84 Augustine, *De Quantitate Animae* 80 as cited in von Balthasar, p. 100.

85 Cf. *Cur Deus Homo*, 2.19 (S.2.77.16–2.78.9).

86 *Cur Deus Homo*, 1.20 (S.2.86.19–20).

87 *Cur Deus Homo*, 1.24 (S.2.93.11).

88 Frank Burch Brown (1993), 'The Beauty of Hell: Anselm on God's Eternal Design', *Journal of Religion* 73:329–56, p. 348.

89 For these reasons and those yet to be explored, it seems to me that when we read of *satisfactio* in the *Cur Deus Homo* we should read its aesthetic overtones. This is not to deny that *satisfactio* connotes moral necessity, but it is to suggest that our ideas of moral necessity or reparation should be located within an aesthetic framework.

90 Brown, p. 335.

91 Note that *oportet* predominates in the second book; cf. 2.3 (S.2.98.19, 21), 2.8

(S.2.103.20, 2.104.11, 20), 2.9 (S.2.107.7), 2.10 (S.2.108.27), 2.11 (S.2.110.30, 2.111.20, 22), 2.12 (S.2.112.8), 2.16 (S.2.118.2, 5), 2.19 (S.2.131.7).

92   Brown, p. 333.
93   *Cur Deus Homo*, 1.4 (S.2.51.16ff).
94   Evans, '... Appeal to Reason', p. 42.
95   Von Balthasar, p. 111.
96   Von Balthasar, p. 139.
97   The force of this necessity is made particularly cogent in light of Sherry's comment that since some theologians write of sanctification as a restoration of beauty, perhaps 'both sanctification and aesthetic beauty might be subsumed under a wider concept of beauty.'
98   Gorringe, p. 94.
99   *Cur Deus Homo*, 1.15 (S.2.73.3–9).
100 Cf. also *Cur Deus Homo*, 1.11 (S.2.68.12).
101 This is a concept which most likely came to Anselm through Boethius who wrote that 'a thing exists when it keeps its proper place and preserves its own nature. Anything which departs from this ceases to exist, because its existence depends on the preservation of its nature' (Boethius, 4.2). However, it must be admitted that this concept was widely accepted in the Middle Ages (growing, as it did, from the works of seminal authors such as Boethius and Augustine) and need not necessarily be attributed to Boethius.
102 We also discover, somewhat unsurprisingly, that this is accompanied by the use of *oportet*, though in a less straightforward manner. In Chapter 13, Anselm says that 'There is nothing, therefore, which God preserves more justly than the honour of his dignity.' Boso replies, 'I concede this to be so (*oportet*).' What Anselm has done is to put into Boso's mouth the verb he uses to signify moral necessity. This has the effect of adding further emphasis to Anselm's point, and justifies his desire to move on to consider the nature of God's honour and thus, the degree of restitution required by sinners. It is this discussion which allows Anselm to ruminate on the nature of sin and, especially, the way in which it is possible that God's honour should be violated. It is certainly a circuitous route which links *oportet* with beauty and order in the universe, and a point that would be insufficient on its own to prove a link between the two; however, on the basis of the foregoing discussion, this is a small but important part of the case which demonstrates the convergence of the needs of humanity and the requirements of God in an aesthetic solution.
103 Gorringe, p. 95.
104 Gorringe, p. 96.
105 Gorringe, p. 97.
106 Gorringe, p. 100.
107 L.W. Grensted (1962), *A Short History of the Doctrine of the Atonement*, Manchester: Manchester University Press.
108 Gustav Aulén (1978), *Christus Victor*, London: SPCK, p. 15.
109 Aulén, p. 6; *contra* J. Rivière (1934), *Le Dogma de la Rédemption*, Paris: Libraire Philosophique J. Vrin, where he argues that the medieval view of the atonement aligns with the ancient.
110 Irenaeus, *Against Heresies*, 4.41.2 in *Ante-Nicene Fathers*, vol. 1.
111 Aulén, p. 28.
112 It is not my intention to critique Aulén's argument as such, simply to interact with certain aspects of it. I cannot, however, pass over this particular part of Aulén's thesis without comment. While it is true that Irenaeus does speak of humanity as children of the Devil in a certain sense, he does not in that context draw the conclusion that Jesus' death was a ransom paid to the Devil.
113 Aulén, p. 50.
114 Aulén, p. 86.
115 Aulén, p. 87.
116 Cf. Pelikan's discussion in Jaroslav Pelikan (1971), *The Emergence of the Catholic*

Tradition, vol. 1, Chicago: University of Chicago Press, p. 147ff; cf. also Tertullian's *On Repentance*, in *Ante-Nicene Fathers*, vol. 3. This is not to suggest, though, that the penitential discipline was unimportant to Anselm.

117 Cf. *Cur Deus Homo*, 1.11 (S.2.68.14ff); cf. also *De Concordia* 3.7 (S.2.273.20–25). The obvious evidence of Anselm's view on sin and its effects is his *On the Virgin Conception and Original Sin*. This is a relatively minor work in Anselm's corpus that he wrote at the urging of his friend Boso. In it, he agrees to answer how it is possible that Jesus could have been born without sin if he was born with a human nature. In order to answer this question Anselm takes a considerable amount of time addressing the nature of sin and how it is imputed to members of the human race. It is, however, a curious work. It does not bear the marks of Anselm's usual care and caution. In fact, it reads more like one of his letters than a treatise. At the end, for instance, instead of claiming that what he has written conforms with the Fathers and the Scriptures, he tells Boso that the foregoing is a summary of his thoughts and is 'more conjecture than assertion'. Essentially, then, what we are left with is a work that was not likely intended to bear the scrutiny of scholarly indagation. Rather, it was a work written to a colleague in payment of a debt of friendship. Perhaps this is why it received such scant attention from Eadmer in his biography (little more than acknowledgment in Chapter 44) and why Southern seems nonplussed and even a little suspicious (Southern, p. 411).

118 *Proslogion*, 1 (S.1.98.16).

119 *Meditation on Human Redemption*, lns. 129–30 (S.3.87.102–103).

120 Aulén, p. 87.

121 Cf. *Meditation on Human Redemption*, lns. 138–43 (S.3.88.109–13).

122 Cf. *Cur Deus Homo*, 1.12 (S.2.69.27–30).

123 *Cur Deus Homo*, 1.4 (S.2.52.9).

124 Cf. *Cur Deus Homo*, 1.3 (S.2.50.29–2.51.12).

125 Aulén, p. 45.

126 Cf. Aulén, p. 28; cf. also the more likely source in Augustine's *De Trinitate* 13.10.

127 Aulén, p. 37.

128 *Cur Deus Homo*, 1.7 (S.2.58.1).

129 *Proslogion*, 9 (S.1.108.7) and 11 (S.1.109.24).

130 Cited in Alister McGrath (1981), 'Rectitude: the moral foundation of Anselm of Canterbury's soteriology', *Downside Review*, 99:204–13, p. 206.

131 McGrath, p. 206.

132 Cf. Robert Crouse (1987), 'Anselm of Canterbury and Medieval Augustinians', *Toronto Journal of Theology*, 3:60–68, p. 65 where he states that Anselm was largely ignored in the later twelfth century because his interpretation of Augustine was not of the same vein as his younger contemporaries and later theologians. This would help to explain why Anselm's theory of the atonement was not more widely accepted in the decades following his death, cf. also Brian Leftow (1995), 'Anselm and the Necessity of the Incarnation', *Religious Studies*, 31:167–85, p. 167.

133 McGrath, p. 210.

134 *Cur Deus Homo*, 1.3 (S.2.50.29–2.51.12).

135 Eco, *Thomas Aquinas*, p. 6.

136 Don S. Browning (1964), *Atonement and Psychotherapy*, Philadelphia: The Westminster Press, p. 249.

137 Michael Root (1987), 'Necessity and Unfittingness in Anselm's *Cur Deus Homo*', *Scottish Journal of Theology*, 40:211–30, p. 230.

138 Trevor Hart (1990), 'Anselm of Canterbury and John McLeod Campbell: Where Opposites Meet?', *The Evangelical Quarterly*, 62:311–33, p. 333.

139 G.R. Evans (1982), '*Cur Deus Homo*: St Bernard's theology of redemption: a contribution to the contemporary debate', *Studia Theologica*, 1:27–36, p. 28.

140 *VA*, p. 122.

141 *Meditation on Human Redemption*, lns 1–2 (S.3.84.3–4).

142   *Cur Deus Homo*, 1.21 (S.2.88.18).
143   *Meditation on Human Redemption*, lns 14 and 16 (S.3.84.13–14).
144   *Meditation on Human Redemption*, lns 167–9 (S.3.89.132–4); cf. also George H. Williams (1957), 'The Sacramental Presuppositions of Anselm's *Cur Deus Homo*', *Church History*, 26:245–74, which attempts to draw comparisons between the *Cur Deus Homo* and Anselm's sacramental presuppositions.
145   *Meditation on Human Redemption*, lns 247 (S.3.91.192–3).
146   Cf. St Benedict (1998), *Rule*, Timothy Fry (ed.), New York: Vintage Books, Chap. 47.
147   *Meditation on Human Redemption*, lns 191–3 (S.3.98.151–2).
148   *Cur Deus Homo*, 1.1 (S.2.47.10–11).
149   Evans, 'St Bernard', p. 28.
150   Evans, 'St Bernard', p. 27. While this statement is true, we should note that the emphasis for Anselm lies more on Christ's work on the cross, than his life as a whole.
151   *Meditation on Human Redemption*, lns 26 (S.3.84.23).
152   *Meditation on Human Redemption*, lns 27 (S.3.85.26–7).
153   *Meditation on Human Redemption*, lns 29–33 (S.3.85.27–9).
154   *De Conceptu Virginali*, 6 (S.2.147.12–22, esp. lns 18–19).
155   *VA*, p. 122.

Chapter 7

Conclusion

This exposition of Anselm's works has sought to highlight the pleasure that can come from reading through Anselm's works. Reading through Anselm's works closely and in concert with one another has, I hope, provided a renewed appreciation for the place of beauty and fittingness as foundational for much of what he wrote. His prayers, his arguments and his explorations all evince a model of reality, a *weltbild* which puts a premium on unity, harmony and fittingness; all of which express the relatedness of particularity in the singularity of divinity.

None of this is intended to deny the place or usefulness of propositional rationality; instead, Anselm's method of expatiating on all manner of topics reminds us that logic is not the only way of understanding God or his relation to humanity. What logical reason could there be, inquired Boso of Anselm, for an almighty, transcendent God to humiliate himself by taking the form of a human, suffering in his body and dying on a cross? None, says Anselm. The activity of God is sometimes best explained with reference to the person of God alone. God acts because it is fitting that he should; it is right that he should; it is in accord with the truth and justice which are a part of, but in no way separate from, God's being.

In short, God acts truly and freely. In the three dialogues (*De Veritate*, *De Libertate Arbitrii* and *De Casu Diaboli*), Anselm explained that just as God's actions are true and free because they are in harmony with who he is, so our actions can be true and free when they are in harmony with God's. Such a conclusion does not comport well with many notions of freedom and truth, but then, how many notions of freedom and truth appeal to unity and harmony with the divine as transcendent standards which permit us to measure the creation by the creator? Whether or not such categories are a better way or the only way to judge truth and freedom, Anselm is asking his audience to at least consider that these categories deserve a place in our world-view precisely because they are present in God and reflected in reality.

Similarly, the question facing modern readers of the *Proslogion* is: what *weltbild*, which world-view is best adapted to discerning the divine nature? Is reality sufficiently coherent that the words we speak and the thoughts we think correlate with what they signify? When we say that God is that than which nothing greater can be thought and is also greater than that which can be thought, are we genuinely describing the immanence and transcendence of God?

In the *Proslogion* as in the *Monologion* and the *De Grammatico* Anselm's answer is a resounding yes! Reality is a coherent whole, resonating with the communicable attributes of God. We see goodness because God is goodness; we see truth because God is truth; we see unity because God is unity. Our thinking begins with the mundane and the created, but creation bears the fingerprints of God which give us the opportunity to raise our sights to the heights of the divine.

And raise our sights to the divine is exactly what Anselm did in his *Prayers and Meditations*. There we saw how Anselm endeavoured to reflect the beauty of divine truth in the *usus loquendi* of created language. The re-creation effected by God in the hearts and minds of humanity is there mirrored by the transformation of ordinary words to portray the order and balance of redemption achieved through the fitting activity of God. In Anselm's *Prayers* as in his treatises the desire to attain to the beatific vision is ubiquitous. He has tasted God's truth and found that the Lord is good. He has heard the divine Word and listened to his order. He has smelled the incense emanating from the prayers of the faithful and found it pleasing. He has been touched by God who has opened his eyes to see the glorious harmony of salvation. Everywhere Anselm turns he sees the *Imago Dei* in his *Imago Mundi*.

Bibliography

Abulafia, Anna Sapir (1990), 'St Anselm and those outside the church', in *Faith and Identity*, Oxford: Basil Blackwell, pp. 11–37.

Adams, Marilyn M. (1975), 'Hell and the God of Justice', *Religious Studies*, 11: 433–47.

Anselm (1998), *Anselm of Canterbury: The Major Works*, eds Brian Davies and G.R. Evans, Oxford: Oxford University Press.

Anselm (1990), *The Letters of Saint Anselm of Canterbury*, 3 vols, ed. and trans. Walter Fröhlich, Kalamazoo, MI: Cistercian Publications.

Anselm (1946–61), *Sancti Anselmi Opera Omnia*, 6 vols, ed. F.S. Schmitt, Edinburgh: Thomas Nelson and Sons.

Ansley, C.R.P. (1961), 'St Anselm de-mythologized: creation in *Cur Deus Homo*', *Theology*, 64: 17–23.

Aquinas, Thomas (1924), *The Summa Contra Gentiles*, ed. and trans. the English Dominican Fathers, London: Burns Oates and Washbourne.

Aristotle (1941), 'Categoriae', in McKeon, Richard (ed. and trans.), *The Basic Works of Aristotle*, New York: Random House.

Aristotle (1941), 'De Interpretatione', in McKeon, Richard (ed. and trans.), *The Basic Works of Aristotle*, New York: Random House.

Artz, Frederick B. (1958), *The Mind of the Middle Ages: 200–1500*, New York: Alfred A. Knopf.

Augustine (1992), 'Concerning the Teacher', in Oates, Whitney J. (ed.), *Basic Writings of Saint Augustine*, Grand Rapids, MI: Baker Book House, vol. 1.

Augustine (1994), 'On Christian Doctrine', in Schaff, Philip (ed.), *A Select library of The Nicene and Post-Nicene Fathers*, Edinburgh: T&T Clark, series 1, vol. 2.

Augustine (1994), 'On the Trinity', in Schaff, Philip (ed.), *A Select library of The Nicene and Post-Nicene Fathers*, Edinburgh: T&T Clark, series 1, vol. 3.

Aulén, Gustaf (1978), *Christus Victor*, trans. A.G. Hebert, London: SPCK.

Baldwin, John W. (1971), *The Scholastic Culture of the Middle Ages*, Lexington, KY: D.C. Heath and Company.

Barlow, Frank (1983), *William Rufus*, London: Methuen.

Barraclough, G. (1968), *The Medieval Papacy*, London: Thames & Hudson.

Barral, Mary R. (1975), 'Anselm and contemporary man', in *Analecta Anselmiana*, Band 4/2, Frankfurt am Main: Minerva, pp. 197–207.

Barral, Mary R. (1984), 'Truth and justice in the mind of Anselm', in *Les Mutations socio-culturelles au tournant des XIe–XIIe siècles*, Paris: Centre National de la Recherche Scientifique.

Barth, Karl (1958), *Anselm: Fides Quaerens Intellectum*, London: SCM Press.

Barth, Karl (1936–78), *Church Dogmatics*, eds and trans. George Thomas Thomson and Harold Knight, Edinburgh: T&T Clark.

Bauerschmidt, F. (1999), *Julian of Norwich and the Mystical Body Politic of Christ*, Notre Dame, IN: University of Notre Dame Press.

Benedict (1998), *The Rule of St Benedict*, ed. and trans. Timothy Fry, New York: Vintage Books.

Beneivenga, Ermanna (1993), *Logic and other Nonsense*, Princeton, NJ: Princeton University Press.

Benson, R.L. and Giles Constable (eds) (1982), *Renaissance and Renewal in the Twelfth Century*, Cambridge, MA: Harvard University Press.

Bestul, Thomas H. (1983), 'St Anselm, the Monastic Community at Canterbury, and Devotional Writing in Late Anglo-Saxon England', in Evans, G.R. (ed.), *Anselm Studies: An Occasional Journal*, New York: Kraus International Publications, pp. 185–98.

Bestul, Thomas H. (1988), 'St Augustine and the *Orationes sive Meditationes* of St Anselm', in Schnaubelt, J.C. et al. (eds), *Anselm Studies: An Occasional Journal*, vol. 2, New York: Kraus International Publications, pp. 597–606.

Boethius (1969), *The Consolation of Philosophy*, trans. V.E. Watts, London: Penguin Books.

Bosanquet, Bernard (1949), *A History of Aesthetic*, London: George Allen & Unwin Ltd.

Bouwsma, O.K. (1970), 'Anselm's Argument', in Bobik, Joseph (ed.), *The Nature of Philosophical Inquiry*, Notre Dame, IN: University of Notre Dame Press.

Bowen, J. (1975), *A History of Western Education*, vol. II, *Civilization of Europe, Sixth to Sixteenth Centuries*, London: Methuen & Co. Ltd.

Brecher, Robert (1985), *Anselm's Argument: The logic of divine existence*, Aldershot: Gower.

Brett, Martin (1975), *The English Church under Henry I*, Oxford: Oxford University Press.

Brooke, R.B. and C.N.L. Brooke (1984), *Popular Religion in the Middle Ages: Western Europe 1000–1300*, London: Thames & Hudson.

Brooke, Z.N. (1931), *The English Church and the Papacy from the Conquest to the Reign of John*, Cambridge: Cambridge University Press.

Brown, Frank Burch (1993), 'The Beauty of Hell: Anselm on God's Eternal Design', *Journal of Religion*, 73: 329–56.

Brown, Michelle (1996), *The Book of Cerne*, Toronto: University of Toronto Press.

Brown, Peter (1981), *The Cult of the Saints*, Chicago: University of Chicago Press.

Brown, Peter (1985), *Society and the Holy in Late Antiquity*, London: Faber & Faber Ltd.

Brown, Robert (1988), 'Some Problems with Anselm's View of Human Will', in Schnaubelt, J.C. et al. (eds), *Anselm Studies: An Occasional Journal*, vol. 2, New York: Kraus International Publications, pp. 333–42.

Browning, Don S. (1964), *Atonement and Psychotherapy*, Philadelphia, PA: The Westminster Press.

Bullough, D.A. (1991), *Carolingian Renewal*, Manchester: Manchester University Press.

Butler, C. (1961), *Benedictine Monachism*, Cambridge: Speculum Historiale.

Butler, C. (1922), *Western Mysticism: The Teaching of SS. Augustine, Gregory and Bernard on Contemplation and the Contemplative Life*, London: Constable.

Butterworth, E.J. (1990), *The Identity of Anselm's Proslogion Argument for the Existence of God with the Via Quarta of Thomas Aquinas*, Queenston, Ontario, Canada: Edwin Mellon Press.

Campbell, Richard (1980), 'Anselm's Background Metaphysics', *Scottish Journal of Theology*, 33: 317–43.

Campbell, Richard (1979), 'Anselm's Theological Method', *Scottish Journal of Theology*, 6: 541–62.

Campbell, Richard (1988), 'Freedom as Keeping Truth: The Anselmian Tradition', in Schnaubelt, J.C. et al. (eds), *Anselm Studies: An Occasional Journal*, vol. 2, New York: Kraus International Publications, pp. 297–318.

Campbell, Richard (1976), *From Belief to Understanding*, Canberra: Australian National University.

Cantor, Norman F. (1958), *Church, Kingship and Lay Investiture in England: 1089–1135*, Princeton, NJ: Princeton University Press.

Carruthers, Mary (1990), *The Book of Memory: A Study of Memory in Medieval Culture*, Cambridge: Cambridge University Press.

Carruthers, Mary (1998), *The Craft of Thought: Meditation, rhetoric, and the making of images*, Cambridge: Cambridge University Press.

Chandler, Hugh (1993), 'Some Ontological Arguments', *Faith and Philosophy*, 10: 18–32.

Chenu, Marie-Dominique (1968), *Nature, Man, Society in the Twelfth Century: Essays on New Theological Perspectives in the Latin West*, ed. and trans. Jerome Taylor and Lester K. Little, Chicago, IL: University of Chicago Press.

Clanchy, M.T. (1990), 'Abelard's mockery of St. Anselm', *Journal of Ecclesiastical History*, 41: 1–23.

Clayton, Mary (1990), *The Cult of the Virgin Mary in Anglo-Saxon England*, Cambridge: Cambridge University Press.

Colish, Marcia L. (1983), 'St Anselm's Philosophy of Language Reconsidered', in Evans, G.R. (ed.), *Anselm Studies: An Occasional Journal*, vol. 1, New York: Kraus International Publications, pp. 113–23.

Croix La, Richard R. (1972), *Proslogion II and III: A Third Interpretation of Anselm's Argument*, Leiden: E.J. Brill.

Crouse, Robert D. (1987), 'Anselm of Canterbury and Medieval Augustinians', *Toronto Journal of Theology*, 3: 60–68.

Dales, Richard (1992), *The Intellectual Life of Europe in the Middle Ages*, London: Brill.

Dalmais, Irenee, Pierre Jounel and Aime Martimort (1983), *The Church at Prayer: The Liturgy and Time*, vol. 4, ed. Aime Martimort, trans. Matthew J. O'Connell, London: Geoffrey Chapman.

Davie, Ian (1994), 'Anselm's Argument Re-assessed', *Downside Review*, 112: 103–20.

Davies, Brian and G.R. Evans (1998), *Anselm of Canterbury: The Major Works*, Oxford: Oxford University Press.

de Bruyne, Edgar (1947), *L'Esthétique du Moyen Age*, Louvain: Editions de L'Institute Supérieur de Philosophie.

de Bruyne, Edgar (1946), *Etudes d'esthetique medievale*, 3 vols, Bruges: Tempelhof.

de Lubac, Henri (1960), *The Discovery of God*, trans. Alexander Dru, Grand Rapids, MI: William B. Eerdmans.

de Lubac, Henri (1998), *Medieval Exegesis: The Four Senses of Scripture*, trans. Mark Sebanc, Edinburgh: T&T Clark.

Decorte, Jos (1989), 'Saint Anselm of Canterbury on ultimate reality and meaning', *Ultimate Reality and Meaning*, 12: 177–91.

Delooz, Pierre (1983), 'Towards a sociological study of canonized sainthood', in Watson, Stephen (ed.), *Saints and their Cults*, Cambridge: Cambridge University Press.

DePaul, Michael (1981), 'The Rationality of Belief in God', *Religious Studies*, 17: 343–56.

Dicker, Georges (1988), 'A Refutation of Rowe's Critique of Anselm's Ontological Argument', *Faith and Philosophy*, 5: 193–206.

Dillistone, F.W. (1990), 'Liturgical Forms in Word and Act', in Jasper, David and R.C.D. Jasper (eds), *Language and the Worship of the Church*, London: Macmillan.

Downey, James Patrick (1986), 'A primordial reply to modern Gaunilos', *Religious Studies*, 22: 41–9.

Drury, John (1975), 'God, Ugliness and Beauty', *Theology*, 76: 531–5.

Eadmer (1964), *History of Recent Events in England*, trans. Geoffrey Bosanquet, London: The Cresset Press.

Eadmer (1972), *Vita Anselmi*, ed. and trans. R.W. Southern, Oxford: Clarendon Press.

Eco, Umberto (1997), *The Aesthetics of Thomas Aquinas*, trans. Hugh Bredin, Cambridge: Harvard University Press.

Eco, Umberto (1986), *Art and Beauty in the Middle Ages*, trans. Hugh Bredin, New Haven, CT: Yale University Press.

Englebretsen, George (1984), 'Anselm's Second Argument', *Sophia*, 23: 34–7.

Evans, G.R. (1989), *Anselm*, London: Geoffrey Chapman.

Evans, G.R. (1980), *Anselm and a New Generation*, Oxford: Clarendon Press.

Evans, G.R. (1978), *Anselm and Talking About God*, Oxford: Clarendon Press.

Evans, G.R. (1982), *Augustine on Evil*, Cambridge, Cambridge University Press.

Evans, G.R. (1977), 'The *Cur Deus Homo*: The Nature of St. Anselm's Appeal to Reason', *Studia Theologica*, 31: 33–50.

Evans, G.R. (1982), '*Cur Deus Homo*: St Bernard's theology of redemption: a contribution to the contemporary debate', *Studia Theologica*, 1:27–36.

Evans, G.R. (1991), *The Language and Logic of the Bible*, Cambridge: Cambridge University Press.

Evans, G.R. (1991 and 1992), 'Making the theory fit the practice: Augustine and Anselm on prayer', 2 parts, *Epworth Review*, 18: 78–81; 19: 57–68.

Evans, G.R. (1993), *Philosophy and Theology in the Middle Ages*, London, Routledge.

Evans, G.R. (1983), 'Similitudes and signification-theory in the 12th century', *Downside Review*, 101: 306–11.

Evans, G.R. (1976), 'St Anselm's Analogies', *Vivarium*, 14: 81–93.

Evans, G.R. (1977), 'St Anselm and Knowing God', *Journal of Theological Studies*, 28: 430–44.

Evans, G.R. (1981), 'St Anselm and sacred history', in *The Writing of History in the Middle Ages*, Oxford: Clarendon Press.

Evans, G.R. (Ap 1978), 'St. Anselm and St. Bruno of Segni: the common ground', *Journal of Ecclesiastical History*, 29: 129–44.

Evans, G.R. (1976), 'St Anselm's images of trinity', *Journal of Theological Studies*, 27: 46–57.

Evans, G.R. (1978), 'Why the Fall of Satan?', *Recherches de Théologie ancienne et médiévale*, 45: 130–46.

Fleteren, F. von and Joseph C. Schnaubelt (1996), *Twenty-four Years (1969–94) of Anselm Studies*, vol. 3, Lewiston, NY: Edwin Mellon Press.

Franklin, Melissa (1993), 'The Indispensability of the Single-Divine-Attribute Doctrine', *Religious Studies*, 29: 433–42.

Fröhlich, Walter (1984), 'Anselm and the bishops of the Province of Canterbury', in *Les Mutations socio-culturelles au tournant des XIe–XIIe siècles*, Paris: Centre National de la Recherche Scientifique.

Fröhlich, Walter (1988), 'Anselm's *Weltbild* as Conveyed in His Letters', in Schnaubelt, J.C. et al. (eds), *Anselm Studies: An Occasional Journal*, vol. 2, New York: Kraus International Publications, pp. 483–525.

Fröhlich, Walter (1984), 'The genius of Anselm's collection of letters', *American Benedictine Review*, 35: 249–66.

Frölich, Walter (1990), *The Letters of Saint Anselm of Canterbury*, Kalamazoo, MI: Cistercian Publications.

Gale, Richard M. (1988), 'Freedom versus unsurpassable greatness', *International Journal for Philosophy of Religion*, 23: 65–75.

Garsh, Stephen (1988), 'Anselm of Canterbury', in Dronke, P. (ed.), *A*

History of Twelfth Century Western Philosophy, Cambridge: Cambridge University Press.

Geary, Patrick (1994), *Living with the Dead in the Middle Ages*, London: Cornell University Press.

Geisler, Norman L. (1973), 'Missing premise in the ontological argument', *Religious Studies*, 9: 289–96.

Gibson, Margaret (1978), *Lanfranc of Bec*, Oxford: Clarendon Press.

Gilbert, Katherine Everett and Helmut Kuhn (1956), *A History of Esthetics*, London: Thames & Hudson.

Gilson, Etienne (1955), *History of Christian Philosophy in the Middle Ages*, London: Stead & Ward.

Gollnick, James T. (1976), 'The monastic–devotional context of Anselm of Canterbury's theology', in *Monastic Studies*, 12, Pine City, NY: Mount Saviour Monastery, pp. 239–48.

Gorringe, T. (1996), *God's Just Vengeance*, Cambridge: Cambridge University Press.

Grant, Colin (1989), 'Anselm's argument today', *Journal of the American Academy of Religion*, 57: 791–806.

Gray, Christopher B. (1976), 'Freedom and necessity in St Anselm's Cur Deus Homo', *Franciscan Studies*, 14: 177–91.

Grensted, L.W. (1962), *A Short History of the Doctrine of the Atonement*, Manchester: Manchester University Press.

Grim, Patrick (1982), 'In Behalf of "In Behalf of the Fool"', *International Journal of Philosophy and Religion*, 13: 33–42.

Gunton, Colin E. (1993), *The One, the Three and the Many*, Cambridge: Cambridge University Press.

Harper, John (1991), *The Forms and Orders of Western Liturgy*, Oxford: Clarendon Press.

Harrison, Carol (1992), *Beauty and Revelation in the Thought of Saint Augustine*, Oxford: Clarendon Press.

Hart, Trevor A. (1990), 'Anselm of Canterbury and John McLeod Campbell: where opposites meet?', *Evangelical Quarterly*, 62: 311–33.

Harthan, John (1977), *Books of Hours*, London: Thames & Hudson.

Hartshorne, Charles (1983), 'Anselm and Aristotle's First Law of Modality', in Schnaubelt, J.C. et al. (eds), *Anselm Studies: An Occasional Journal*, vol. 1, London: Kraus International Publications.

Hartshorne, Charles (1965), *Anselm's Discovery: A Re-examination of the Ontological Proof for God's Existence*, La Salle, WI: Open Court.

Hartshorne, Charles (1985), 'Our Knowledge of God', in Rouner, L. (ed.), *Knowing Religiously*, Notre Dame, IN: University of Notre Dame Press.

Hasker, William (1968), 'Is there a second ontological argument?', *International Journal for Philosophy of Religion*, 13: 93–101.

Hayen, Andre (1968), 'The Role of the Fool in St. Anselm and the Necessarily Apostolic Character of True Christian Reflection', in Hick, J. and Arthur McGill (eds), *The Many-Faced Argument*, London: Macmillan.

Henle, Paul (1961), 'Uses of the Ontological Argument', *Philosophical Review*, 70: 102–109.

Henry, D.P. (1974), *Commentary on the* De Grammatico, Boston, MA: D. Reidel Co.

Henry, D.P. (1964), *The* De Grammatico *of St Anselm*, Notre Dame, IN: University of Notre Dame Press.

Henry, D.P. (1993), *The Logic of St Anselm*, Aldershot: Gregg Revivals.

Henry, D.P. (1988), 'St Anselm and the linguistic disciplines', in Schnaubelt, J.C. et al. (eds), *Anselm Studies: An Occasional Journal*, vol. 2, New York: Kraus International Publications.

Herbert, A.G. (1936), *Liturgy and Society*, London: Faber & Faber Ltd.

Heron, Alasdair (1983), 'Anselm and the *Filioque*: A Responsio pro Graecis', in Evans, G.R., *Anselm Studies: An Occasional Journal*, New York: Kraus International Publications.

Hestevold, H. Scott (1993), 'The Anselmian "single-divine-attribute doctrine"', *Religious Studies*, 29: 63–77.

Hick, J. and A. McGill (eds) (1968), *The Many-Faced Argument*, London: Macmillan.

Hollister, C. Warren (1993), 'William II, Henry I and the Church', in Meyer, Marc (ed.), *The Culture of Christendom*, London: The Hambledon Press.

Hope, D.M. (1978), 'The Liturgical Books', in Jones, Cheslyn et al. (eds), *The Study of Liturgy*, London: SPCK.

Hope, D.M. (1978), 'The Medieval Western Rites', in Jones et al., *The Study of Liturgy*.

Hopkins, Jasper and Herbert Richardson (eds and trans.) (1976), *Anselm of Canterbury*, 4 vols, Toronto: Edwin Mellon Press.

Howe, Leroy T. (1968), 'Existence as a perfection: a reconsideration of the ontological argument', *Religious Studies*, 4: 78–101.

Irenaeus (1996), *Against Heresies*, in Roberts, Alexander and James Donaldson (eds), *The Ante-Nicene Fathers: translations of the writings of the Fathers down to A.D. 325*, vol. 1, Edinburgh: T&T Clark.

Johnson, Oliver (1965), 'God and St Anselm', *Journal of Religion*, 45: 326–34.

Jones, Richard (1981–82), 'The Religious Irrelevance of the Ontological Argument', *Union Seminary Quarterly Review*, 37: 143–57.

Kane, Stanley G. (1973), 'Anselm's definition of freedom', *Religious Studies*, 9: 297–306.

Kane, Stanley G. (1981), *Anselm's Doctrine of Freedom and the Will*, Toronto: Edwin Mellon Press.

Kane, Stanley G. (1973), 'Fides Quaerens Intellectum in Anselm's Thought', *Scottish Journal of Theology*, 26: 40–62.

Kant, Immanuel (1965 [1929]), *Critique of Pure Reason*, trans. Norman Kemp Smith, New York: St Martin's Press.

Kant, Immanuel (1978 [1790]), *Critique of Judgement*, trans. James Creed Meredith, Oxford: Clarendon Press.

King-Farlow, John (1982), 'Nothing Greater can be conceived', *Sophia*, 21: 19–23.

Knowles, M.D. (1963), *The Monastic Order in England: A History of its Development from the times of St. Dunstan to the Fourth Lateran Council*, Cambridge: Cambridge University Press.

Knowles, M.D. (1948), *The Religious Orders in England*, Cambridge: Cambridge University Press.

Kuhn, H. and Gilbert Kuhn (1956), *A History of Esthetics*, 2nd edn, London: Thames & Hudson.

Landou, Iddo (1992), 'An Answer on behalf of Gaunilo', *Philosophy and Theology*, 7: 81–96.

Law, Vivien (1993), 'The Historiography of Grammar', in Law, Vivien (ed.), *History of Linguistic Thought in the Early Middle Ages*, Amsterdam: John Benjamin Publishing Company.

Law, Vivien (ed.) (1994), *History of Linguistic Thought in the Early Middle Ages*, Amsterdam: John Benjamin Publishing Company.

Law, Vivien (1982), *The Insular Latin Grammarians*, Woodbridge: The Boydell Press.

Law, Vivien (1994), 'The Study of Grammar', in McKitterick, R. (ed.), *Carolingian Culture: Emulation and Innovation*, Cambridge: Cambridge University Press.

Lawrence, C.H. (1989), *Medieval Monasticism*, London: Longman.

Leclercq, J. (1986), 'Prayer and Contemplation: Western', in McGinn, Bernard and John Meyendorff (eds), *Christian Spirituality: Origins to the Twelfth Century*, London: Routledge and Kegan Publishers.

Leclercq, J. (1974), *The Love of Learning and the Desire for God*, London: SPCK.

Leclercq, John (1991), 'The Renewal of Theology', in Benson, R.L. et al. (eds), *Renaissance and Renewal in the Twelfth Century*, Toronto: University of Toronto Press.

Leclercq, J. and J.P. Bonnes (1946), *Un Maître de la vie spirituelle au xi siècle: Jean de Fecamp*, Paris: J. Vrin.

Leclercq, J., Francois Vandenbrooke and Louis Boyer (1968), *The Spirituality of the Middle Ages*, London: Burns & Oates.

Leff, Gordon (1980), *Medieval Thought*, London: Marlin Press.

Leftow, Brian (1995), 'Anselm and the Necessity of the Incarnation', *Religious Studies*, 31: 167–85.

Leftow, Brian (1988), 'Anselmian polytheism', *International Journal for Philosophy of Religion*, 23: 77–104.

Leftow, B. (1990), 'Individual and Attribute in the Ontological Argument', *Faith and Philosophy*, 7: 235–42.

Leftow, B. (1989), 'Perfection and Necessity', *Sophia*, 28: 13–20.

Le Goff, Jaques (1993), *Intellectuals in the Middle Ages*, Oxford: Blackwell.

Lewis, C.S. (1964), *The Discarded Image*, Cambridge: Cambridge University Press.

Lochhead, David M. (1966), 'Is existence a predicate in Anselm's argument?', *Religious Studies*, 2: 121–7.

Losconcy, Thomas (1996), 'The Anselm–Gaunilo Dispute about Man's knowledge of God's Existence: An Examination', in von Fleteren, F. and Joseph C. Schnaubelt (eds), *Twenty-four Years (1969–1994) of Anselm Studies*, vol. 3, Lewiston, NY: Edwin Mellon Press.

Losconcy, Thomas A. (1984), 'Will in St Anselm: an examination of his biblical and Augustinian origins', in *Les Mutations socio-culturelles au tournant des XIe–XIIe siècles*, Paris: Centre National de la Recherche Scientifique.

Luhtala, Anneli (1993), 'Syntax and Dialectic in Carolingian Commentaries on Priscians's *Institutiones Grammaticae*', in Law, Vivien (ed.), *History of Linguistic Thought in the Early Middle Ages*, Amsterdam: John Benjamins Publishing Company.

Luscombe, D.E. (1996), *Anselm: Aosta, Bec, Canterbury*, Sheffield: Sheffield Academic Press.

Luscombe, David (1997), *Medieval Thought*, Oxford: Oxford University Press.

Luscombe, D.E. (1983), 'St. Anselm and Abelard', in Evans, G.R. (ed.), *Anselm Studies: An Occasional Journal*, vol. 1, New York: Kraus International Publications.

MacDonald, A.F. (1926), *Lanfranc: A Study of his life, work & writing*, London: Humphrey Milford.

Macintyre, Alasdair (1990), *Three Rival Versions of Moral Enquiry*, London: Duckworth.

Malcolm, Norman (1960), 'Anselm's Ontological Arguments', *Philosophical Review*, 69: 42–62.

Maloney, J. Christopher (1981), 'God is a term than which none greater can be used', *International Journal of Philosophy and Religion*, 12: 3–15.

Marenbon, John (1983), *Early Medieval Philosophy*, London: Routledge & Kegan Paul.

Marenbon, J. (1981), *From the Circle of Alcuin to the School of Auxerre: Logic, Theology and Philosophy in the Early Middle Ages*, Cambridge: Cambridge University Press.

Martin, James A. (1990), *Beauty and Holiness: The Dialogue Between Aesthetics and Religion*, Princeton, NJ: Princeton University Press.

Martinich, Aloysius P. (1977), 'Scotus and Anselm on the existence of God', *Franciscan Studies*, 15: 139–52.

Mason, Perry C. (1978), 'Devil and St Anselm', *International Journal for Philosophy of Religion*, 9: 1–15.

Maurer, A. (1982), *Medieval Philosophy*, Toronto: Pontifical Institute of Medieval Studies.

McGill, Arthur C. (1968), 'Recent Discussions of Anselm's Argument', in Hick, John and Arthur C. McGill (eds), *The Many-Faced Argument*, London: Macmillan.

McGrath, Alister E. (1985), 'The Moral Theory of the Atonement: an Historical and Theological Critique', *Scottish Journal of Theology*, 38: 205–20.

McGrath, Alister E. (1981), 'Rectitude: the moral foundation of Anselm of Canterbury's soteriology', *Downside Review*, 99: 204–13.

McGrath, P.J. (1994), 'Does the Ontological Argument Beg the Question?', *Religious Studies*, 30: 305–10.

McIntyre, John (1954), *St Anselm and his Critics: A Re-interpretation of the Cur Deus Homo*, Edinburgh: Oliver and Boyd.

McKitterick, Rosamond (1977), *The Frankish Church and the Carolingian Reforms: 784–895*, London: Royal Historical Society.

McNeill, J.T. and Helena M. Gamer (1990), *Medieval Handbooks of Penance*, New York: Columbia University Press.

Morreall, John (1984), 'The aseity of God in St. Anselm', *Sophia*, 23: 35–44.

Morris, Thomas V. (1988), 'Dependence and divine simplicity', *International Journal for Philosophy of Religion*, 23: 161–74.

Nichols, Aiden (1985), 'Anselm of Canterbury and the Language of Perfection', *Downside Review*, 103: 204–17.

Nortier, Geneviève (1971), *Les Bibliothèques Médiévales des Abbayes Benedictines de Normandie*, Paris: P. Lethiesseux in the series, *Bibliothèque d'Histoire et d'Archéologie Chrétiennes*.

O'Connor, M.J.A. (1968), 'New aspects of omnipotence and necessity in Anselm', *Religious Studies*, 4: 133–46.

Paulsen, David L. (1984), 'The logically possible, the ontologically possible and ontological proofs of God's existence', *International Journal for Philosophy of Religion*, 16: 41–9.

Pearl, Leon (1986), 'The misuse of Anselm's formula for God's perfection', *Religious Studies*, 22: 355–65.

Pelikan, Jaroslav (1971), *The Emergence of the Catholic Tradition (100–600)*, Chicago: University of Chicago Press.

Pelikan, Jaroslav (1979), 'A first-generation Anselmian, Guibert of Nogent', in *Continuity and discontinuity in church history*, Leiden: E.J. Brill.

Pelikan, Jaroslav (1978), *The Growth of Medieval Theology (600–1300)*, Chicago: University of Chicago Press.

Plantinga, A. (1975), 'Aquinas on Anselm', in Orlebeke, Clifton and Lewis Smedes (eds), *God and the Good: Essays in honor of Henry Stob*, Grand Rapids, MI: Eerdmans.

Plantinga, A. (1967), *God and Other Minds*, London: Cornell University Press.

Plantinga, A. (1974), *God, Freedom and Evil*, New York: Harper and Row.

Pseudo-Dionysius (1987), *The Divine Names* in *The Complete Works*, trans. Luibheid, London: SPCK.

Richmond, James (1975), 'The Absurdity of God's Non-Existence: St. Anselm and the Study of Religion', in Preston, R.H. (ed.), *Theology and Change*, London: SCM Press Ltd.

Rivière, Jean (1934), *Le Dogme de la Rédemption au début du Moyen Age, Bibliothèque Thomiste*, Paris: J. Vrin.

Robinson, W.S. (1984), 'The Ontological Argument', *International Journal for Philosophy of Religion*, 1: 51–9.

Rogers, Katherin (1993), 'Anselm on praising a necessarily perfect being', *International Journal for Philosophy of Religion*, 34: 41–52.

Rogers, Katherin (1988), 'Can Christianity be Proven?: St. Anselm of Canterbury on Faith and Reason', in Schnaubelt, J.C. et al. (eds), *Anselm Studies: An Occasional Journal*, vol. 2, New York: Kraus International Publications.

Rogers, Katherin (1996), 'The Traditional Doctrine of Divine Simplicity', *Religious Studies*, 32: 165–86.

Rohatyn, Dennis (1982), 'Anselm's Inconceivability Argument', *Sophia*, 21: 57–63.

Root, Michael (1987), 'Necessity and Unfittingness in Anselm's *Cur Deus Homo*', *Scottish Journal of Theology*, 40: 211–30.

Rorem, Paul (1993), *Pseudo-Dionysius: A commentary on the texts and an introduction to their influence*, Oxford: Oxford University Press.

Russell, B. (Ap 1985), 'The Ontological Argument', *Sophia*, 24: 38–47.

Sagal, Paul T. (1973), 'Anselm's refutation of Anselm's ontological argument', *Franciscan Studies*, 33: 285–91.

Schlesinger, George N. (1985), 'Divine perfection', *Religious Studies*, 21: 147–58.

Schmiechen, Peter M. (1973), 'Anselm and the faithfulness of God', *Scottish Journal of Theology*, 26: 151–68.

Schnaubelt, J.C. et al. (eds) (1988), *Anselm Studies: An Occasional Journal*, 2 vols, New York: Kraus International Publications.

Shepherd, Anne (1987), *Aesthetics: An Introduction to the Philosophy of Art*, Oxford: Oxford University Press.

Sherry, Patrick (1992), *Spirit and Beauty*, Oxford: Clarendon Press.

Smalley, Beryl (1941), *The Study of the Bible in the Middle Ages*, Oxford: Clarendon Press.

Sontag, Frederick E. (1982), 'Anselm and the concept of God', *Scottish Journal of Theology*, 35: 213–18.

Southern, R.W. (1953), *The Making of the Middle Ages*, London: Hutchinson.

Southern, R.W. (1988), 'Sally Vaughn's Anselm: An examination of the Foundations', *Albion*, 20: 181–204.

Southern, R.W. (1963), *St Anselm and his Biographer*, Cambridge: Cambridge University Press.

Southern, R.W. (1995), *St. Anselm: A Portrait in a Landscape*, Cambridge: Cambridge University Press.

Southern, R.W. (1990), *Western Society and the Church in the Middle Ages*, London: Penguin.

Southern, R.W. and F.S. Schmitt (eds) (1969), *Memorials of St. Anselm*, London: Oxford University Press.

Staunton, Michael (1997), 'Eadmer's *Vita Anselmi:* a reinterpretation', *Journal of Medieval History*, 23: 1–14.

Stolz, Anselm (1968), 'Anselm's Theology in the *Proslogion*', in Hick, John and Arthur C. McGill (eds), *The Many-Faced Argument*, London: Macmillan Press.

Synan, Edward A. (1988), 'Truth: Augustine to Anselm', in Schnaubelt, J.C. et al. (eds), *Anselm Studies: An Occasional Journal*, vol. 2, New York: Kraus International Publications.

Tellenbach, Gerd (1993), *The Church in Western Europe from the 10th to the early 12th Century*, Cambridge: Cambridge University Press.

Tellenbach, Gerd (1940), *Church, State and Christian Society at the Time of the Investiture Contest*, trans. R.F. Bennett, Oxford: Blackwell.

Torrance, T.F. (1968), 'Ethical Implications of Anselm's *De Veritate*', *Theologische Zeitschrift*, 24: 309–19.

Vallicella, William F. (1993), 'Has the Ontological Argument been Refuted?', *Religious Studies*, 29: 97–110.

van Buren, Paul M. (1973), 'Anselm's Formula and the Logic of "God"', *Religious Studies*, 9: 279–88.

van Fleteren, Frederick and Joseph C. Schnaubelt (eds) (1996), *Twenty-five years (1969–1994) of Anselm studies*, Lewiston, NY: Edwin Mellon Press.

Vaughn, Sally N. (1987), *Anselm of Bec and Robert of Meulan, the Innocence of the Dove and the Wisdom of the Serpent*, Los Angeles: University of California Press.

Vaughn, Sally N. (1988), 'Anselm: saint and statesman', *Albion*, 20: 205–20.

Vaughn, Sally (1993), 'Lanfranc, Anselm & the School of Bec', in Meyer, Marc (ed.), *The Culture of Christendom*, London: The Hambledon Press.

Vaughn, Sally N. (2002), *St Anselm and the Handmaidens of God*, Turnhout: Brepols Publishers.

Vigneux, P. (1980), 'Necessity and Reason in the *Monologion*', *Revue des Sciences Philosophiques et Théologiques*, 64: 3–25.

von Balthasar, Hans Urs (1982), *The Glory of the Lord: A Theological Aesthetic*, vol. 2, trans. Andrew Louth, Francis McDonaugh and Brian McNeil, ed. John Riches, Edinburgh: T&T Clark.

Walker, C.R. (1952), 'St Anselm: a revaluation', *Scottish Journal of Theology*, 5: 362–73.

Ward, Benedicta (1986), 'Anselm of Canterbury and his Influence', in McGinn, Bernard and John Meyendorff (eds), *Christian Spirituality: Origins to the Twelfth Century*, London: Routledge & Kegan Publishers.

Ward, Benedicta (1977), *Anselm of Canterbury: A Monastic Scholar*, Oxford: SLG Press.

Ward, Benedicta (1973), *The Prayers and Meditations of St Anselm*, London: Penguin Books.

Watson, Gordon (1989), 'A study in St Anselm's soteriology and Karl Barth's theological method', *Scottish Journal of Theology*, 42: 493–512.

Watson, Gordon (1977), 'Karl Barth and St Anselm's theological programme', *Scottish Journal of Theology*, 30: 31–45.

Weeks, Ian (1990), 'A Disproof of the Existence of God', *Sophia*, 29: 21–8.

Welch, Adam C. (1957), *Anselm and his work*, Edinburgh: T&T Clark.

Williams, George Hunston (1957), 'The Sacramental Presuppositions of Anselm's *Cur Deus Homo*', *Church History*, 26: 245–74.

Williams, Thomas (1995), *Anselm: Monologion and Proslogion with the Replies of Gaunilo and Anselm*, Cambridge: Hackett Publishing Company, Inc.

Wilmart, A. (1932), *Auteurs spirituels et textes dévotes du moyen age latin*, Paris: Études Augustiniennes.

Wilmart, A. (ed.) (1917–24), *Bobbio Missal*, London: Henry Bradshaw Society.

Woolf, Rosemary (1986), *Art and Doctrine: Essays in Medieval Literature*, London: The Hambledon Press.

Yamazaki, Hiroko (1988), 'Anselm and the Problem of Evil', in Schnaubelt, J.C. et al. (eds), *Anselm Studies: An Occasional Journal*, vol. 2, New York: Kraus International Publications, pp. 343–50.

Index